HOMOSEXUAL

HOMOSEXUAL

Oppression and Liberation

Dennis Altman

*with a new Introduction by Jeffrey Weeks
and a new Afterword by the author*

New York University Press

NEW YORK AND LONDON

NEW YORK UNIVERSITY PRESS
New York and London

Library of Congress Cataloging-in-Publication Data
Altman, Dennis.
Homosexual : oppression and liberation / Dennis Altman ; with a
new introduction by Jeffrey Weeks ; and a new afterword by the
author.
p. cm.
Includes bibliographical references and index.
ISBN 0-8147-0623-1 (cloth). — ISBN 0-8147-0624-X (pbk.)
1. Homosexuality. 2. Gay liberation movement—History.
I. Title.
HQ76.A585 1993
305.9'0664—dc20   93-18284
                         CIP

New York University Press books are printed on acid-free paper
and their binding materials are chosen for strength and durability.

Manufactured in the United States of America

10   9   8   7   6   5   4   3   2   1

This book is dedicated to
Reinhard Hassert
and the women and men
of Gay Liberation.

Contents

Acknowledgments

Many people have contributed to the making of this book, preeminently of course the people about whom I have written. My life has been greatly enriched by the warmth with which I was greeted by men and women from gay liberation in various cities of America, and I hope that this book will in some small way reflect my feeling for them.

Equally, I have been greatly helped by large numbers of colleagues, both faculty and student, at the University of Sydney. Their encouragement and interest was often what I needed to force myself back to the typewriter.

It is invidious to single out individuals for special thanks, but I do want to mention in New York Harris Dienstfrey, Paul Goodman, La Mont Mitchell, Lillian Roxon, Phillip Spitzer, Marvin Surkin, and John Ware; in Boston Rick and Leonie Gordon; in Los Angeles Christopher Isherwood; in London Jim Anderson and David Fernbach; and in Sydney Terry Irving, Judy Keene, Sylvia Krietsch, and Henry Mayer.

This book is dedicated to Reinhard Hassert; it is sufficient to say that without him it would probably never have been written.

Introduction to the 1993 Printing

JEFFREY WEEKS

Most books lag behind change, describing to their readers a world they already know. Some fortunate books anticipate change, capturing a moment and pushing it forward into a hitherto unimagined future. Dennis Altman's *Homosexual: Oppression and Liberation* is one of these lucky books, and over twenty years after its first publication in 1971, and perhaps fifteen years since I last read it in full, I can pick it up now and marvel at its success at distilling a unique historical moment, and in anticipating key features of a future we now live.

The book is, of course, preeminently a product of its time—its assumptions, hopes, fears, style, and language (do radicals anywhere still have "rap-sessions?") It could not be anything else, and that is part of its attraction to a new generation of readers. But what is striking is how many of the ideas in this book, despite an infinitely less generous cultural climate, and in the shadow of a devastating epidemic that no one could have foreseen, are still relevant, indeed being acted out in a new wave of lesbian and gay activism, and refined and developed in what is increasingly being termed *queer theory.* Here, of course, the cheeky ironies of history tweak Dennis Altman's tail: one of the tasks of the book was to refuse the opprobrious label of *queer.* He quotes a phrase of the early 1970s: "chick equals nigger equals queer." For Altman's generation, which is also mine, it was essential to reject a language (*queer, fag,* and so forth) which execrated and marginalized us. The book is, in part, about forging a new language of homosexual politics; the language shaped then in the context of a new movement is now being reconstructed to meet new demands. But the constant need to do so is again part of the message of this book. The terrain of sexual politics, like all politics, constantly shifts, demanding new definitions and redefinitions. But in doing that necessary work we should not forget the context in which the terms of the debate were set. The republication of this book, then, is more than a pious homage to a pioneer; it is an essential part of understanding the history we are living and making.

The fundamental context of *Homosexual: Oppression and Liberation* was the emergence of the gay liberation movement in the United States in 1969. Although the movement itself is not discussed explicitly until chapter 4 of the book, it is the founding experience that gives the book meaning. As Dennis Altman remarks in the Introduction to the book, "the best social analysis grows out of personal experience," and it was the living of the experience of the new movement that shaped his arguments. The title, though chosen by the publishers rather than the author, sums up rather well the trajectory of the book. *Homosexual* harks back to the traditional, clinical description. It is a come-on to an audience unfamiliar with the new arguments, new language. But the second terms, *Oppression* and *Liberation,* point forward to a new world of politics. The idea that homosexual people were opressed, not only individually but as a group or category of human beings, was new to the vast majority of us in the 1960s, though anticipated in some earlier, European as well as American literature and sexual politics. The idea that homosexuals, acting collectively, could transform the conditions of their individual and social lives, that we could be "liberated," was transformative; in the language of the time, "revolutionary."

Unless you lived through the experience, it is difficult now to recapture fully the impact of those heady early days of gay liberation. Edmund White, in his novel, *The Beautiful Room Is Empty,* has his characters describe the Stonewall riots of June 1969, the symbolic beginning of gay liberation, as "our Bastille Day...the turning point of our lives"; and although few experienced those riots, many thousands were indelibly affected by their aftermath, in all their confused glory. I have decribed some of that confusion and glory in my own first solo book, *Coming Out: Homosexual Politics in Britain from the Nineteenth Century to the Present* (1977/1990).

I have to say that as a student in Britain at the time, just about to start my first job as a teacher, I was completely ignorant of the riots. So were the vast majority of American people. As White's narrator says, "we couldn't find a single mention in the press" of this turning point. I was skeptical of the garbled reports of the new movement carried in the British media over the next year. I remember a jokey item on the BBC's premier radio news program about a gay march, and shuddered with horror. That could never happen here, thank God! It was not until the London Gay Liberation Front was started in October 1970, at the London School of Economics where I was then working, that I felt any real interest. I went along to a meeting nervously, especially as I was on home ground. I was ready to leave at the first opportunity, but stayed, went back the next week, and the next, and the rest, if not history, is certainly my history. My politics, my personal relationships, my living arrangements, my personal appearance, even my career: all were challenged and transformed by those early days, and their impact and influence are still with me as I write. Many of my current intellectual and political preoccupations, like a background radiation, can be traced back to those early moments, a sort of "big bang" of my adult life, and though many of my ideas have changed, my basic commitments have not.

But what someone like myself, a young academic, trained as a historian of ideas, lacked was precisely a systematic presentation of the ideas of gay liberation. I needed a map. My own attitude toward my gayness had been formed from a rag-bag of sources in the 1960s: a barely articulated resistance to the psychologizing of the standard textbooks of the period; reading between the lines of writers like Christopher Isherwood and Angus Wilson; and the essays (especially *The Fire Next Time*) and novels of James Baldwin. Baldwin was probably the single most important influence on me prior to gay liberation. I read *Giovanni's Room* while going for a university interview in 1964, my first time away from home on my own; I devoured *Another Country* when I came to London as a student later that year. I recognized myself in these books, and excitedly wrote about it to a school friend, quoting chunks of *Another Country*. For his reply I received the burned remains of my letter, with the scribbled comment that he never wanted to read such disgusting things again; this from the instigator of my earliest, confused sexual experimentations. I had no language to take the argument further, except that of an individualist appeal to the truth of my own needs and desires.

The rhetoric of gay liberation began to provide me with a wider rationale for "coming out," a heady brew of liberationist aspirations, and a new affirmation of collective belonging. The leaflets and early journals of gay liberation began to seep through to London from the United States, passed from hand to hand or occasionally obtainable in the more radical bookshops. The new feminist texts, most famously from Kate Millett, Shulamith Firestone, and Germaine Greer, began to fill my bookshelves, though few mentioned homosexuality except in passing. A framework for a new sexual politics was emerging, through practical experience in demonstrations, zaps, consciousness-raising groups, "functional groups," as we called them, such as the Counter-Psychiatry Group, and in informal networks for discussion, and gradually, for writing: articles, manifestos, pamphlets. But what we needed was a framework that would pull all these experiences together, giving them a theoretical structure and some sense of history, which in turn could feed back into practice.

Dennis's Altman's book was the first full-scale work to try to do that. It must have been mid-1972 before I heard of it (unusually for me, I did not write the date in the copy I bought then and have before me now), and eagerly sought out a copy, a photographic reproduction of the first American edition, with an Author's Note on the inside cover pointing out a few minor typographical errors. I can't say it changed my life in the way reading Baldwin or going to my first GLF meeting did. It did something rather different, and of lasting importance: it helped make sense of the helter-skelter experiences and readings of the previous, hectic eighteen months. It helped give shape to a host of inchoate ideas. It started many intellectual hares running, some in quite different directions from those the author at that stage might have intended. I read it at precisely the moment that I was preparing myself to write about sexuality: I published my first effort on the theme later that year, an article entitled "Ideas of Gay Liberation." The book provided a good part of the map I needed. I have not taken all the pathways it indicated, and I have tried to construct maps of my own since. But this book helped point me in a direction from which I have not fundamentally erred ever since.

I refer to my own experiences here not because they were special but because they were, I believe, representative. Relatively few of us probably read the book when it first appeared. Most people picked up the ideas it synthesized and circulated more informally. But the point that needs underlining is that I, and many others, were picking up these ideas in Britain, in continental Europe, in Australasia, as well as in North America. Gay liberation may have taken on many different national guises, but several of its key elements have had an international significance. Here was an Australian political scientist writing about what seemed a quintessentially American phenomenon, and soon finding that its impact was also back at home, and throughout the developed world. Dennis Altman has proved since then that he is an ideal interpreter and translator, equally at home intellectually in Australia, North America, Europe, and most recently in Southeast Asia. The internationalism of his commitments and activities is perhaps the most impressive thing about his career as a whole, and it is already latent in this book.

I want now to pick out three strands in *Homosexual: Oppression and Liberation* which seem to me to be of enduring importance: the emphasis on identity; the relationship between community and social movement; and Altman's still controversial looking forward to the "end of the homosexual."

The book's central concern, Altman writes in his Introduction, is the "question of identity." It has also been the central concern of all subsequent lesbian and gay literature and politics. Coming out, the public assertion and affirmation of one's homosexuality, of identity, was at once the most simple and the most fundamental activity of the new sexual politics of the 1970s. Of course, there were many "known" homosexuals before 1969, and many of them had made brave political and personal statements. But think of some of the consequences, just for some of the homosexual writers Altman respects and refers to in the book. Gore Vidal's first novel, explicit for the time (the late 1940s), had all but ruined his career before it had barely begun; Christopher Isherwood had gone into exile, and literary silence for a while, rather than endure the hypocrisies of England; James Baldwin had to endure the vituperations of his fellow blacks, convinced he had sold out to white faggotry. But for Altman's generation, writing as a gay person became for the first time not merely desirable, but a necessity, even if coming out was, as he says, a "long and painful process."

A new emphasis had entered the discourse of identity: an awareness of the historical and social factors that had shaped attitudes toward and inhibited the expression of homosexuality. "To be a homosexual in our society," writes Altman, echoing Erving Goffman's discussion of "spoiled identities," "is to be constantly aware that one bears a stigma." The task of the new identity-politics (though that term was only to be fully articulated a decade after this book first appeared) was to understand why homosexuals were stigmatized, or to put it in another, more political, way, why homosexuals were oppressed; and how to fight that oppression.

Oppression, the "denial of identity," could take three forms: persecution, discrimination, or tolerance. Of these, in the ostensibly permissive climate of the early 1970s, the most common was liberal tolerance, "annihilation by blandness" in Christopher Isherwood's phrase. Here we can see the influence of another of Altman's mentors, Herbert Marcuse, whose emphasis on "repressive desublimation," the controlled deregulation of sexuality in order to bind individuals ever more tightly to the system with chains of gold, had a powerful, if in retrospect, short-lived influence on 1960s radicals. In a cultural climate like that of the 1980s and early 1990s, tolerance does not, perhaps, seem such a bad thing as it might have done earlier. But the real point that Altman was making still rings true: there is a form of toleration which lives with difference without fully validating it; the sort of tolerance which says "what a pity you are homosexual, but we still love you." Altman's case was that this form of liberal pity was as unacceptable, and as damaging to self-pride, as the more overt forms of hatred of homosexuality. It fell far short of full acceptance.

Altman's arguments, then, asserted the validity of homosexuality in its own terms, and in particular its importance for a resolute and affirmative sense of self and of belonging, that is for identity. This offered a major break with traditional writings about homosexuality, which in effect had seen it as a symptom of failed identification, that is failure to be a normal, heterosexual person. Instead, Altman was asserting, on the contrary, that in a world of diverse sexualities, there was no intrinsic difference between heterosexuality and homosexuality. The imperative toward heterosexuality was a cultural, not an essential or inherent, phenomenon, and homosexual identities had been formed in part through resistance to that imperative.

Here Altman was broaching, though not yet explicitly developing, what was to become the central theoretical issue in lesbian and gay politics: were homosexuals a distinct minority, characterized by a more or less inherent attraction to their own sex, or was the category of homosexual a historical and social invention, formed in specific historical conditions, and likely to disappear as conditions changed. As the book unfolds, it is the latter position which is developed, and here it looks forward to the most creative historical, sociological, and literary work of the next twenty years. The reference points are clearly there. In particular, there are the references to Mary McIntosh's ground-breaking article of 1968, "The Homosexual Role," which argued that what was required was not an explanation of the homosexual condition, but an understanding of how homosexuality came to be seen as a defining condition of some people and not others in the first place. This opened up immensely creative paths of historical investigation, to be followed through in the next few years by writers such as Michel Foucault, Jonathan Katz, John D'Emilio, Randolph Trumbach, Carroll Smith-Rosenberg, Lillian Faderman, and many others, including myself. But Altman uses other sources as well, especially those from the Freudian Left, such as Marcuse, who questioned the fixity of the heterosexual norm.

I'll take up some of the implications of the constructionist position below. The important issue to note here is that the stress on a positive gay identity in Altman's usage becomes more than an assertion of self; it is also, and crucially, a political stance. It both questions the naturalness and fixity of the heterosexual norm, and affirms the positive value of homosexuality as a way of life. Within that framework, there are limitations. The emphasis is overwhelmingly on male gayness; lesbianism is apologetically minimized. The

different meanings of identity for lesbians, which later lesbian scholars such as Lillian Faderman, Carroll Smith-Rosenberg, and Martha
Vicinus were to clarify, are missed, as Altman has acknowledged
in subsequent writings. Other controversial topics, such as the s/m
culture that was already developing, are mentioned as transient
products of a hostile environment. The main comparison is not
with the feminist movement, which seems most obvious now, but
with the black movement, and not the civil rights movement but
new militants such as the Black Panthers.

From the perspective of twenty years' later this may seem a little
strange, but it does reflect very accurately the mood of the early
1970s, when the political identification of the new gay movement
was less with its own homophile predecessors (who were often
reviled for their "liberalism"), but with that amorphous, and as it
turned out, ephemeral, thing called "the movement," the would-
be revolutionary mobilization which had arisen in America in the
wake of opposition to the Vietnam War and the rise of black militancy. For Altman's generation of activists, the oppression of homosexuality could not be seen as an isolated remnant of old
prejudices. "The oppression of homosexuals," he writes, "is part
of the general repression of sexuality, and our liberation can only
come as part of a total revolution in social attitudes."

This brings me to the second significant strand in Altman's book,
the emphasis on a gay *movement* and on its complex relationship
to the idea of "community." A movement committed to radical
political militancy was the indispensable prerequisite for achieving
lesbian and gay liberation, and in the developing divide between
the different strands of the gay movement represented by the Gay
Liberation Front and the Gay Activists' Alliance, Altman's instincts
are with the former. Again, this is a distinction which history has
overtaken. The cutting edge of gay radicalism in the early 1970s
critically challenged the existing "gayworld" for its "ghetto men-
tality," its emphasis on sexuality to the exclusion of wider cultural
issues, its erection of a "pseudo community" which refused the

implications of a wider sexual and social oppression, and hence the meaning of true community. Gay liberation, Altman argues, stands for the realization of such a true community, based on the "eroticization of everyday life."

Subsequent writings by gay scholars, including Altman himself, as well as historic experience, have put this argument into a different light. Writers such as John D'Emilio, in *Sexual Politics, Sexual Communities,* and Alan Berube, in *Coming Out Under Fire,* have shown that the emergence of a strong sense of gay community over the previous generation had itself been the necessary precondition for the emergence of gay liberation. Moreover, the main impact of the new gay sense of purpose and militancy over the two decades after 1969 was not the revolutionary transformation of society but a vast expansion of the lesbian and gay world. Altman himself was to anatomize that transformation in his book *The Homosexualization of America, the Americanization of the Homosexual* (1982). In turn, that expansion, with its ease of sexual interaction, was to make possible both the tragically rapid spread of HIV and AIDS in the male gay community after 1980, *and* the extraordinary gay response toward it, with its massive mobilization of activism, care, fund raising and creativity, particularly through the invention and widespread adoption of safer sex. Again, Altman was at hand to document the response in his 1986 book *AIDS in the Mind of America* (published outside the U.S.A. as *AIDS and the New Puritanism*).

In the past twenty years, then, the relationship between "movement" and "community" has shifted. No longer is it possible or desirable to counterpose one to the other. On the contrary, a sense of community is what makes possible a movement or movements, though each is necessarily challenged and changed by the other. But community does more than simply affirm a collective existence, crucial as that is. It also makes possible a greater sense of individuality. It is no longer possible to believe, as Altman suggests in *Homosexual: Oppression and Liberation,* that "the ultimate extension of gay community is the gay commune." On the contrary, the past two decades have shown that a sense of community and belonging, and the openness about our sexualities that it makes possible, have give rise to a vast variety of possible life-styles and patterns of relationships. In retrospect, we can see that the emergence of gay liberation was a dramatic, but not isolated, moment in the long-term breakdown of fixed patterns of domestic and sexual life. Gay liberation heralded the public presence and celebration of sexual diversity. The political and ethical implications of that are still being forged in a climate where, as Altman writes elsewhere, sex has become a new front line of politics. But whatever the efforts of moral conservatives and sexual fundamentalists of left and right to the contrary, it seems clear to me that there is no going back to the idea of a single sexual morality or way of life. Diversity and difference are the new watchwords of sexual politics.

This does pose challenging problems for contemporary lesbian and gay politics. On the one hand, developments over the past twenty years have established a strong sense of gay identity and community, giving rise to what has been described as a sort of gay ethnicity, especially in cities such as San Francisco and New York where there is often a strong sense of geographical as well as social rootedness. This has been a vital development in affirming a sense of pride in self and social belonging. But on the other hand, it tends to reaffirm the sense of the separateness and unity of the category of "the homosexual" which gay liberation sought to challenge, and which the realities of contemporary sexualities make untenable. As Altman recognizes, the new movement of the early 1970s was already straining against the challenge of difference: between men and women, between different racial and ethnic groups, between people with different desires, life-styles, class positions, or political or religious affiliations. The politics of difference has tended to accentuate these divisions over subsequent years, and the recent development of a "queer politics" has underlined the dilemmas. For here we have simultaneously the idea of a radical "queer nation" and a challenge to the patterns of lesbian and gay life as they have developed during the 1970s and 1980s.

The spirit of some of the radical queer politics is, in fact, remarkably close to that of early gay liberation, as expressed in Altman's book. For here community and movement are in the end seen not as a confirmation of but as a radical challenge to the idea of a fixed and separate homosexual category. For Altman, the aim of gay politics is ultimately to make the terms *homosexuality* and *heterosexuality* meaningless, to bring about the "end of the homosexual," and of "the heterosexual." It is a political movement whose aim is its own demise: "gay liberation will have achieved its full potential when it is no longer needed." And it will no longer be needed when the categorical differences between the "normal" and the "abnormal" disappear.

This is the third theme I want to look at, and as I have already suggested it is still the most contested. Sexual liberation, for Altman, involved (as the title of chapter 3 suggests), a move toward "the polymorphous whole." Altman's discussion of this concept is, I think, particularly illuminating; note for instance his analysis of the repressed homosexuality underlying the hypermasculinity of a writer like Norman Mailer, where denial of homosexuality is the very definition of what it is to be a true man. In the discussion of the fear and loathing that an antihomosexual culture generates, Altman is clearly looking forward to the concept of *homophobia* that George Weinberg was to elaborate in *Society and the Healthy Homosexual* (1972), and which has since become a key analytical term in lesbian and gay studies (for example, in the work of Eve Kosovsky Sedgwick).

Altman owes some intellectual debt here to Marcuse, and to Norman O. Brown, whose writings have gone out of fashion but to whom Altman is clearly indebted. The Freudianism of Altman's work was itself unfashionable at the time the book was written both among gay liberationists (many of whom saw psychoanalysis, at least in the form common in the U.S.A., as repressively normative and antihomosexual) and feminists. Later feminist psychoanalysis, notably at first the work of Juliet Mitchell, owing much to the recovery of Freud attempted by the French analyst Jacques Lacan, was to open up new perspectives on the Freudian tradition, though little attention was paid in this new critical psychoanalysis to homosexuality. An exception, that again Altman anticipates, though coming from a quite different intellectual tradition, is Guy Hocquenghem, whose *Homosexual Desire* puts forward a fuller theory of the impact of antihomosexual paranoia: "The problem is not so much homosexual desire as the fear of homosexuality."

The key lesson of the radical psychoanalytic tradition is that it fundamentally questions the fixity of sexual identities. For Freud at his most radical, gender and sexual identities are only ever precarious achievements, all the time destabilized and undermined by unconscious desires. The basic bisexual and polymorphously perverse nature of the human animal is constrained and limited by cultural imperatives and norms, but the desires that nature gives rise to are never obliterated; they lurk dangerously in each individual unconscious.

But if identity, and sexual difference, are precarious at the level of the unconscious, they are also in large part a fiction at the level of social and cultural life. This is, I know, a controversial statement, and one that many lesbian and gay activists would bitterly challenge. The search for a gay gene, or special type of homosexual brain, or whatever, which is frequently welcomed by self-appointed gay spokespeople, attests to a constant wish to find an explanation rooted in nature for homosexual difference. As I have already indicated, Altman rejects such fantasies, and anticipating Foucault and other writers argues for the historical shaping of the homo-hetero distinction. This is not to deny the value of constructing lesbian and gay identities as an essential way of combating discrimination, and of negotiating the hazards of everyday life. Such identities are, in words I have used elsewhere, necessary fictions. But fictions they are, nonetheless.

If this is true, if sexual difference is hardened into sexual division because of cultural norms based on a fear of sexual variety, then it follows that in a culture which is more at ease with sexual diversity and plural value systems, and where by implication the dominance of heterosexual and traditional family value systems is questioned, the rationale for rigid distinctions between people begins to disappear; and the end of both the "homosexual" and the "heterosexual," in the common usage of those terms, looms.

We seem quite a long way from that situation today. And yet there are signs in contemporary culture of a new willingness and ability to play with identity, to see it as akin to a staged event. Altman's emphasis on the homosexual role becomes in recent writing a stress on identity as a performance, or rather a series of performances (see Judith Butler's book, *Gender Trouble*). In both, however, we can see the dual emphasis: lesbian and gay identities are constructed, but apparently essential; they play with the inherited structures of power, challenging and undermining them; but at the same time they are deadly serious.

Identity, community, challenging the inevitability of the heterosexual/homosexual distinction: I have suggested that these are the dominating themes of the book. They are not separate themes, because they are intimately connected to the new politics of homosexuality that Altman is simultaneously describing, analyzing, and helping to create. Underlying all is the conviction that sexuality should not be easily divided into neat categories in a hierarchical relationship where homosexuality is inevitably marginalized where it is not execrated. On the contrary, "homosexuals are a minority quite unlike any other, for we are a part of all humans. . . . Everyone is gay, everyone is straight. That is why the homosexual has been so severely oppressed."

The publication of Altman's book in the early 1970s was a key moment in the popularization and dissemination of the radical sexual agenda that this quotation illustrates. The achievements, disappointments, political setbacks, and personal and community tragedies of the past decades have dimmed some of the utopian hopes, transformed the language of radical politics, and set new and often difficult dilemmas. But Altman's book speaks to us still because its agenda has not yet run its course. Gay liberation, he writes, is a "process by which we develop a theory and practice out of our experience, living, as it were, our liberation." Few have argued this case with greater élan and vivacity. It is a pleasure to introduce it to a new generation of readers.

Introduction to
the 1971 Printing

DENNIS ALTMAN

In the great flood of material written about homosexuality over the past few decades there have been two markedly separate approaches. The first, found mainly in novels and "confessionals" (of which Donald Cory's *The Homosexual in America,* written in 1951, was probably the most influential), has been almost exclusively personal and biographic, describing from the inside how it feels to be homosexual. The second, largely the product of social scientists aiming for academic respectability or journalists aiming for a fast buck, has been descriptive and analytic, viewing homosexuality from the point of view of an outsider. Some homosexuals have written the latter kind of book, and a few authors, Thomas Mann in *Death in Venice* for example, have sought to write the former without being themselves homosexual. It is my hope to combine the two approaches, believing as I do that the best social analysis grows out of personal experience, and that experience without analysis is insufficient for understanding why homosexuals are stigmatized by society.

Until very recently homosexuals wrote about themselves in only very personal terms, usually in heavy tones of guilt and self-hatred. The homosexual in literature has generally been a tragic figure, doomed to a bitter, unhappy, and lonely life. At the same time, most attempts to see homosexuality in a broader context have tended to reinforce social opprobrium and homosexual misery through a moralistic approach often cloaked in pseudo-scientific terminology. With the recent growth in homosexual self-affirmation, the time for such books has passed, and we homosexuals are beginning to examine ourselves not as lonesome deviants from the good society but rather as the oppressed victims of a society that is itself in need of basic change. The heterosexual writer who ostentatiously kisses his wife and children good-bye in the first chapter before embarking on his voyeuristic tour of the homosexual world is today likely to find the doors to that world slammed in his face—and that, on the whole, seems a healthy development.

Nor is the psychiatric approach immune from this way of seeing the homosexual, for psychiatry almost always begins with the assumption that homosexuality is a deviance to be explored (though as Mary McIntosh, an English sociologist, has pointed out, "the conception of homosexuality as a condition is, in itself, a possible object of study"). Psychiatrists speak of a homosexual problem; they do not speak of a heterosexual problem. To that extent they too are participating in a system of social control.

One of the concerns of this book is to show the varied and deep-seated ways in which homosexuals are oppressed. For too long homosexuals have allowed themselves to be defined by a heterosexual world which at worst persecutes and at best tolerates them. Society's attitude is expressed in the hundreds of subtle ways in which it determines what is "normal" and what "deviant"; what is allowed, and what should be censured. Today, homosexuality, once largely ignored, can be loudly discussed in the media, but even so there has been no fundamental change in the underlying hostility toward it. The essence of current permissiveness seems to be the merciless exposure of everything that differs from the statistical norm, not necessarily the acceptance of these differences. To speak thus of homosexual oppression will likely lead to my being attacked as paranoid, hysterical, chauvinist, etc. So too are blacks or women attacked, if in talking of oppression they appear obsessed with their "stigma," but discovering the extent of one's stigma makes it difficult not to be obsessed by it.

This book is only partly concerned with homosexual oppression. With the emergence of the gay liberation movement, homosexuals have, for the first time in modern societies "come out" in large numbers and asserted rather than apologized for themselves. "Gay is angry, gay is proud," and the origins and significance of this new attitude are also among my main concerns.

Perhaps I should indicate how this book came to be written. In the summer of 1970 I went to the United States to spend a period on leave from my post as teacher of (American) politics at Sydney University. This was my third visit to the United States; I had previously spent two years at Cornell University and revisited the country in the winter of 1968–69. This last visit coincided with the growth of the gay liberation movement, and first in San Francisco and later in New York I became deeply involved in that movement.

As I worked on the book, first in New York and California, and then back in Australia, two aspects of the subject came to seem particularly worth exploration. The first was the experience of personal liberation through self-affirmation as a homosexual and the possibilities of and limitations upon individual, as distinct from social, liberation through such affirmation. The second was the need to evaluate certain contemporary writers from a homosexual standpoint, rather as Kate Millett has sought to evaluate them from the perspective of a woman seeking liberation.

It is not necessary to accept the thesis that *all* American literature is preoccupied with homosexuality—"Leslie Fiedler," wrote the literary critic Joseph Epstein, "has instructed us that the great American novelists form one long daisy-chain of failed queers . . . "—to recognize how substantial a preoccupation this is. In American literature there is the continuing theme of men, often of different races, retreating together into the wilderness, beyond society, in an implicitly homosexual relationship; this is very different from English novels, where the concern, even when homosexuality is involved, is much more with complex interactions within society. Even in postwar writing the difference persists: the homosexual in the American novel, as in Burroughs, Rechy, or even Baldwin and Vidal, is far more likely to appear an outsider than, as in the novels of Iris Murdoch or Angus Wilson, a participant in a world of social relationships.

It seems a reflection of the nature of America's preoccupation with sex that homosexuality is a far more central literary theme on that side of the Atlantic. It is as impossible to talk of current American culture without talking of homosexuality as to talk of it without discussing Jews or blacks: the self-affirmation of minorities. Because I am concerned with the changing mores of our time I have concentrated on contemporary and American writers; because I am writing as a homosexual, my view is probably somewhat different from that of received wisdom.

Gay liberation, of course, is no longer confined to the United States, and since I began this book similar movements have emerged in most Western countries, including Australia and Britain. Where it seems appropriate I have sought to include references to other countries, though I have not attempted to provide an exhaustive history of the movements outside the United States.

This is neither a book about homosexuality per se nor a history of the homosexual movement. Rather its central concern is the question of identity, of why and how a movement for gay liberation has emerged at this particular point in history. The question touches us all, for human liberation rests on our ability to liberate that part of ourselves, homosexual or heterosexual, that we have repressed. We all need to come out of our particular closets.

1. *Coming Out: The Search for Identity*

To be a homosexual in our society is to be constantly aware that one bears a stigma. Despite the recent upsurge in open discussion—"the love that dare not speak its name," said one observer, "has become the neurosis that doesn't know when to shut up"—there is still little genuine acceptance of homosexuality as a valid sexual and social life-style. As a homosexual I am constantly made aware of this, in the jokes and caricatures of stage and films, in the pain of my parents, in my own uncertainties as to how I may be affected by a book like this, written under my own name.

Over the past few years I have come to realize that my homosexuality is an integral part of my self-identity, and that to hide it can only make my life, if less precarious, more difficult and unsatisfying. Yet I have not totally escaped the necessity to live a double life, at least in certain situations, nor rid myself of the tenseness that results from being constantly with people who assume everyone is straight and are incapable of the imagination or empathy necessary to transcend this attitude. Like most gay people, I know myself to be part of a minority feared, disliked, and persecuted by the majority and this gives my life a complexity and an extra dimension unknown to straights.

Our society, of course, stigmatizes other groups: nonwhites most obviously, and women, at least in some circumstances. Even worse perhaps are the stigmas borne by the old, the invalid, the crippled, the ugly. Yet the stigma of the homosexual is unique in one central sense. Our gayness is not something, like skin color, or sex, or infirmity, immediately apparent to both us and others. We have to discover our homosexuality, and having discovered it, we have a wide range of options, hardly available to others who are stigmatized, as to how far we should reveal our stigma.

I shall in later chapters seek to develop some theories that explain just why homosexuals are so stigmatized, and what changes would be necessary to remove that stigma. For the moment I am concerned with the experience of being-a-homosexual in contemporary Western society. For, let there be no confusion: the very concept of homosexuality is a social one, and one cannot understand the homosexual experience without recognizing the extent to which we have developed a certain identity and behavior derived from social norms.

The conventional definition of homosexuality has always been a behavioral one: a homosexual is anyone who engages in sexual acts with another of his or her sex (homosexual is a generic term, including both men and women). If he or she has sex with both men and women, then he or she is bisexual. What could be simpler?

Yet a moment's thought will show the inadequacy of the purely behavioral approach. Human beings are distinguished by a capacity for experience as well as by their behavior, and homosexuality is as much a matter of emotion as of genital manipulation. Celibacy, for example, is not an unknown state (we are all celibate for a time, and some manage life-long celibacy, either through determination or bad luck), yet are we to deny a celibate any sexual definition at all? Homosexuals often discover their homosexuality before any overt sexual experience, yet they are no less homosexual for that. Equally, many men or women have engaged in homosexual acts without being in any experiential sense homosexuals, for example in prison, at school, as prostitutes. As we each examine our own sense of identity we realize how much more complex is the question of homosexuality than a mere Kinsey-like computation of orgasms.

Three cases:

I am sitting on some steps in the East Village in New York City with a very attractive kid called Robbie. We rap about being gay. He is not, he claims, but he has many gay friends. Moreover he is going to a gay dance that night; perhaps he will see me there? I hope so, I say. I want to ask him home with me, but am a little scared.

After a ten-year-old marriage a well-known journalist announces he is divorced. The children stay with him, in their suburban home, and his male secretary moves in to help keep house. It appears they have been sleeping together for six years.

In the Tombs, Manhattan's House of Detention for Men, a friend of mine spent three weeks. While there he was raped, frequently, brutally, and with much-resulting physical and mental pain. The rapists included wardens and fellow prisoners. All considered themselves straight, bragged of their adventures with women, and vehemently denounced "faggots."

Gore Vidal has claimed that "homosexual" should be used only as an adjective to describe a sexual activity, not as a noun to describe a recognized type, for we are all basically bisexual (more of that later). In an ideal society this would undoubtedly be true, and one might expect that if, as most writers in the field suggest, there is a continuum between homo- and heterosexuality, sexual behaviour would reflect this. Yet most people seem to regard the two as mutually exclusive categories and there is considerable emphasis on the need to identify as either straight or gay. Thus the expression "coming out," common among homosexuals, implies much more than a first sexual act with another man or woman. Rather it is bound up with the whole process whereby persons come to identify themselves as homosexual, and recognize thereby their position as part of a stigmatized and half-hidden minority. For the moment I shall consider bisexuals as part of this minority, although their case is somewhat different. Nonetheless, author Kate Millett has had reason to note that it is her homo- rather than her heterosexuality with which she is branded.

The development of a homosexual identity is a long process that usually begins during adolescence, though sometimes considerably later. Because of the fears and ignorance that surround our views of sex, children discover sexual feelings and behavior incompletely, and often with great pangs of guilt. This is true even for the heterosexual, as a whole literary tradition, whose recent variations include Philip Roth's *Portnoy's Complaint* and Dan Wakefield's *Going All the Way,* makes clear. How much greater, then, is the guilt of the teenager who discovers himself attracted to others of his or her own sex? Dave McReynolds, the pacifist and political activist who first wrote openly of his homosexuality in 1969, has described how he waited for each birthday hoping he would become "normal" and his guilt on realizing he was irredeemably "queer." Others, like myself, manage to enter into our twenties without a full realization that we are not like others—that we are, in fact, one of *them.*

The actual origins of homosexuality remain a mystery, despite a profusion of psychoanalytic theories. We know that much of what is considered natural sexual behavior is, in fact, learned, and that somewhere along the way homosexuals diverge from the more common path and develop a different pattern of sexual response. To many this is proof of a pathology, and men like Dr. Irving Bieber and Dr. Charles Socraides, both well-known exponents of "curing" homosexuals, have made their name by so branding homosexuals. "We consider," writes Bieber in his book *Homosexuality: A Psychoanalytic Study of Male Homosexuals* "homosexuality to be a pathologic biosocial, psychosexual adaptation consequent to pervasive fears surrounding the expression of heterosexual impulses." Of course his study is based exclusively on men sufficiently disturbed to be undergoing treatment.

Most psychiatrists tend to locate the origin of homosexuality in "maladjusted" family life, yet such an explanation is not altogether convincing. Too many homosexuals have strong and loving fathers, too many heterosexuals have dominant mothers for any very obvious connection to be seen. It is probably true that in modern Western societies *most* mothers overdominate their sons, and this fact is often disregarded by those concerned to discover the etiology of homosexuality. What Americans call "momism" is a general feature of our culture, reflected both in homosexual sons (e.g. Sebastian in Tennessee Williams' *Suddenly Last Summer*) or heterosexual (e.g., Portnoy). Which is not to deny that there may be some relationship, only to point out that it is more complex than popularized versions of Freudian psychiatry would suggest. Those particularly influenced by Freud see homosexuality as determined in very early childhood, and there is a strong emphasis on childhood experiences in novels such as Radclyffe Hall's *Well of Loneliness* or Sanford Friedman's *Totempole*. Others have sought to demonstrate some genetic origin, on the whole not very convincingly, although recent research does suggest there may be some correlation between homosexual behavior and chemical balance in certain hormones. A correlation however is far from being a cause.

Too often speculation on homosexuality tends to confuse it with effeminacy in boys or butchness in girls. Thus one comes across statements such as that by Robert Stoller, a Los Angeles professor of psychiatry, in his book *Sex and Gender* that "masculine homosexual men are an exception I cannot discuss since I do not yet understand them." Most studies of homosexuality, however, and certainly my own experience, tend to suggest that the majority are in fact masculine or feminine as we measure these things in our society. Most homosexuals do not have doubts about their own masculinity or femininity, nor do they wish to be taken for or in fact become the opposite sex: many transvestites and transexuals consider themselves determinedly heterosexual. As Simone de Beauvoir wrote in *The Second Sex,* "homosexuality can be for a woman a mode of flight from her situation or a way of accepting it."

This confusion of sex roles with sexual preference continues to influence the public imagination and even the psychiatric. There is a connection, but it is far more complicated than the assumption that homosexuality involves wanting-to-be-the-other-sex. Norman Mailer, whom I shall have frequent reason to quote, refers for example to "queers" as "humans-with-phalluses who choose to be female." Which is nonsense: most homosexuals choose no such thing, they choose rather to love/sleep with others of their own sex which is a completely different phenomenon.

Mailer uses the word "choose" which would be rejected by both biological and psychiatric determinists, and indeed probably by most homosexuals. "I can't help what I am" is a frequent comment in homosexual conversation. I suspect this is less true than the orthodox wisdom suggests, and that there is at least sometimes an element of deliberate choice in the adoption of homosexuality. Robert Lindner in his book *Must You Conform?* refers to homosexuality as "a form of rebellion" and the homosexual as a "non-conformist' and there is some truth in this. To become a homosexual, particularly for women, is to reject the program for marriage, family, and home that our society holds up as normal.

I must admit to considerable confusion in my own mind as to the way in which we develop our various patterns of sexual response. The interaction of biological urges and social pressures is a process that is little understood. Homosexuality, as we now know, exists in some form in virtually all human societies, and is associated with very different personality types and adjustment to sex roles. Thus some people can simultaneously assert that *most* fashion models and *most* masculine women are lesbians. Perhaps the most sensible conclusion is that there are many reasons which may account for an individual's homosexuality, that this becomes part of her or his total concept of identity, and that it is almost impossible to eradicate it without doing damage to the whole personality. (It may, of course, be possible to frighten a "patient" out of overt sexual acts, an approach which underlies so-called aversion therapy.)

The "problem" of the genesis of homosexuality ceases to be of great concern once one is prepared to accept homosexuality as neither a sin nor a pathology but rather as one way of ordering one's sexual drive, intrinsically no better nor worse than the heterosexual and with the same potential for love and hate, fulfillment or disappointment. In Iris Murdoch's novel *A Fairly Honourable Defeat,* remarkable among books that touch on the gay experience because the homosexuals end more happily than the heterosexuals, one of the protagonists, Axel, sees his homosexuality as "a fundamental and completely ordinary way of being a human being." Such is my own perspective.

Discovering the Gayworld

For the moment I am concerned with the whole experience of coming out, the discovery that one is predominantly attracted to others of the same sex and the development of a way of dealing with this. Of course many homosexuals never do come out, but rather spend miserable and lonely lives, unable to function fully as straights and equally unable to accept their essential gayness. Perhaps the most pitiful victims of our stigma are the men and women who have been frightened away from full acceptance of themselves. Gene Damon, editor of the lesbian magazine the *Ladder,* has written of "the women who make up our vast sea of lifelong spinsters, whose outward mannerisms and behaviour quite rightly lead to the erroneous assumptions that they are sexless beings."

Yet most of us have struggled, for a time at least, against the realization of our gayness, and coming out is therefore a long and painful process. I fought my homosexuality for a long time, aided for a while by my ignorance: the very concept was so alien that I barely recognized my desires for what they were. At the age of fifteen I had a long and pretentious relationship with a girl: we read second-hand psychology and listened to Tchaikovsky together, I wrote her long and romantic letters and was scared of any real physical contact; at sixteen I had a dogged and unrewarding in-fatuation for the headmaster's daughter; at seventeen I returned to the first girl and had my first fuck, in the front seat of a car (why the *front* I cannot now remember), both her legs in plaster from an accident and I disgracing myself by almost total inadequacy.

That to me was what sex was all about, and I barely related this to my fantasies about large, muscular men or my desire to use the public showers at the beach. At university I dated widely and with-out much satisfaction; others were making girls, I couldn't. I saw myself as unattractive and physically inept, not realizing that it was my own lack of interest, or perhaps my fears, that were holding me back. Even after I had entered homosexual life I continued to force myself into pseudo-heterosexual affairs, trying to convince myself that I was essentially bisexual, or even that my homosex-uality was just a stage I would grow out of. These affairs were very anxious and difficult for both myself and my girlfriends. There was great relief in stopping the whole pretense, and accepting that I was only fooling myself, if not always others, in imitating the straight world. Entry into the homosexual world was in some ways a great relief, for I discovered that I could attract others sexually and came to understand how far sexual attraction is a matter of a person's ability to accept and project his or her own sexuality.

Over the years I have watched others come out, and seen the same patterns repeating themselves: the desperate, yet at the same time furtive search for other gay people, the miserable attempts to make it as a straight, the fear of revealing oneself. After all, to come out means defying the most basic and deep-seated norms of a society that sees itself as based exclusively on the heterosexual family struc-ture. The wonder is not how many homosexuals are neurotic but how many manage to develop happy and productive lives in the face of their repudiation of social norms.

As a homosexual comes out he or she is likely to move into contact with other homosexuals, and hence develop a concept of his or her identity based on the fact that our society defines "homosexual" in a certain way. This, after all, is the essence of Vidal's point; for having chosen to define homosexuality as a significant and exclusive sort of identity, society can hardly be surprised that homosexuals accept this and develop their own mannerisms and behavior. The rigid either/or dichotomy of hetero- and homosexuality has produced in turn the gayworld, a phrase borrowed from Martin Hoffman, whose book with this title strikes me as one of the best on the subject. In writing of the gayworld I am forced to write almost exclusively of the male homosexual world, for contact between gay men and women has usually been slight, and almost always of a private nature. I have never been to a lesbian bar, nor would I be particularly welcome in one, and the great bulk of writing about homosexuals has been male-oriented. Lionel Tiger in *Men in Groups* has gone so far, in fact, as to claim that "there may be analytic and practical profit in seeing male homosexuality as a specific feature of the more general phenomenon of male bonding," implying that female homosexuality has other sources. While this line of thought suggests a greater separation between the experiences of male and female homosexuals than I can accept—this problem will be explored in a later chapter—it is nonetheless true that there are major differences between the male and female gayworlds, and the latter has been largely neglected in both literature and social science. The one exception seems to be in film, where apparently female homosexuality is more acceptable than male— especially when, as in *The Fox* or *Therese and Isabelle,* a straight man triumphs in the end. That what all lesbians need is a good stud is one of the more persistent heterosexual myths.

Basically the male gayworld is a highly complex series of places, either wholly or partly designed for making sexual contacts. Most large Western cities contain a number of bars, bathhouses, clubs, parks, beaches, streets, and public toilets where homosexuals can make contact and, in some cases, have sex; even small towns are likely to have a park area or public toilet known to homosexuals, and probably to the police, as a meeting place. This sort of phenomenon is far less common in the case of women. Only very large cities have bars catering specifically for them; more often they will be a minority in male-oriented bars. Far more than men, female homosexuals are dependent upon social networks of friends, parties, and more recently, clubs and dances often run by gay organisations. The need for somewhere to meet was an important impetus in the formation of groups like America's Daughters of Bilitis, the Australian Lesbian Movement, and Kenric in London.

Once one has discovered this world, it seems remarkable that anyone could be unaware of its existence. Yet even in cities like New York and San Francisco, generally considered the two most blatantly gay of American cities and, with Amsterdam and Copenhagen, international "gay meccas," much of this gayworld is apparently almost totally hidden from straight society. We, on the other hand, know better what the straight world is like, for those who are oppressed always know more of what is above them than vice versa. (As Lorraine Hansberry once observed, blacks have been washing whites' laundry for the past three hundred years; they ought to know them.) This double vision of the oppressed is one that underlies much of the work of Jean Genet, most obviously his plays *The Maids* and *The Balcony*, and is closely related to his own homosexuality.

Apart from a couple of preliminary, and very frightened, encounters on a vaguely gay section of beach, my first real introduction to homosexual life was in the bathhouses. These resemble nothing so much as giant steaming whorehouses in which everyone is a customer; clad only in white towels men prowl the hallways, groping each other in furtive search for instant sex, making it in small, dark cubicles on low, hard, come-stained beds.[1] Disgusting?—yes, perhaps. Yet lasting friendships are quite commonly begun in bathhouses, and to this extent the whorehouse analogy is not fully accurate. It is a feature of male homosexual life that sex usually precedes intimacy to a much greater extent than among heterosexuals.

Gradually I discovered the rest of the gayworld. The bars, for example, with their lonely crowds of drinkers, men too uptight and scared of losing their "macho" image to make a move toward friendship. (From what I gather, women's bars share this same tense, vaguely hostile atmosphere. Gay bars, whatever else they may be, are not gay.) As social barriers have relaxed and more places allow dancing between homosexuals, some of the tenseness has broken down, though the unfriendliness remains. Even in their own habitat, homosexuals are often remarkably tense and scared of contact.

Yet, as always, to generalize is to lose the texture of reality. Take for example two bars, both American, yet each with their counterpart in most large Western cities:

The first, in New York's Lower East Side, two blocks east of the theater playing *Oh! Calcutta!*, and in an area referred to in the dissenting report to the President's Commission on Obscenity and Pornography as "sleazy and disreputable". A small bar area in the front; a dance floor behind. Juke-box and colored lights, with a platform for occasional amateur drag shows and films. The clientele mixed, but preponderantly young, long-haired with clothes running to leather fringes and psychedelic colors. A number of blacks, Harlem-slick and in Afros. Some of the men here have the sleek hair and turtleneck look of the too-elegant fag, but most are casual,

---

1. In New York, at least, bathhouses have now become radical chic, with large areas devoted to the cabaret-type entertainment patronized by heterosexuals wishing to be "with it." See the cover story on Bette Midler in *Rolling Stone* (15 February, 1973).

untidy, not immediately recognizable as gay. There is a slight hint of marijuana in the air and some of those dancing are obviously high. A couple of women dance, hugging in the middle of the floor. The jukebox features hard rock, soul, some lollipop pop.

The other bar lies in the armpit of one of Los Angeles' freeway intersections. It is small and crowded by a large pool table set right of the bar. Photos and posters of excessively muscled young men around the walls; a motor bike in pride of place above the bar. The men here—no women—are somewhat older, with a carefully studied toughness. Macho jeans, boots, jackets; one guy wears what resembles a leather rubber suit with an opening through which one sees his buttocks in tight, white jeans. This is a leather bar, and many of the men here are into sadomasochism. But how, I ask my companion, does one know which ones? It has something to do, he claims, with the way one wears one's keys on the belt. The jukebox plays country and western, pop rock, including one patriotic song that starts: "We don't smoke marijuana . . . "

This contrast by no means exhausts the range of gay bars. There are bars that cater largely to transvestites, and bars patronized by the rich and elegant, including, sometimes, expensive hustlers (male prostitutes). There are bars with dark back rooms and known, with no sense of hyperbole, as "orgy bars"; there are others, and in the same city, which cater to a gay clientele while desperately maintaining a straight ambiance, firing employees who seem in any way gay. There are gay restaurants and clubs, often featuring drag shows, plus drag shows that cater to a straight audience; in England, in particular, drag shows are popular forms of working-class entertainment, and have become "in" places for tourists, listed in guides to nightlife in the cities. There are bars for gay women, bars (rare) catering equally for men and women, bars where straight women, known colloquially as "fag hags," come with their gay boyfriends.

For many homosexuals, however, contacts are made more furtively than at baths or bars. All cities have their "beats," areas of streets, beaches, parks where men "cruise"; sometimes, as in Sydney's Kings Cross, there appears to be competition between female prostitutes and men looking for free sex. More often there is a scary tenseness about the whole thing, a tenseness that, for many, adds to the excitement.

Least attractive are the public toilets, where men make contact and, quite frequently, fellate each other. For those interested there is an ingenious sociological study of the phenomenon by Laud Humphreys with the delightful title of *Tearoom Trade* (though on the whole the book strikes me as a prime example of the dominant tendency in sociology to engage in intellectual voyeurism). Men who frequent what Americans call "tearooms" (or, in England, "cottages") expose themselves to fairly constant danger, danger of being arrested or maybe beaten, yet it seems that it is often the danger itself that attracts them. I have heard homosexuals admit that they frequented toilets or parks in the full knowledge that the police were likely to appear. It is well known that Central Park in New York is dangerous after dark, yet it is thick with homosexuals, quite aware of the danger of being robbed or mugged. Anyone who has cruised in such areas knows the heightened apprehension and self-awareness that danger produces, and the sexual excitement that such danger enhances. For many, one suspects, it is this, rather than the sexual act itself, that is the real purpose of the game.

Less dangerous are the run-down movie theaters that exist in many large cities, where men make contact and masturbate or fellate each other in the cinema-dark, as a surprisingly explicit scene in the movie *Midnight Cowboy* made clear. (Tennessee Williams in a story called *Hard Candy* described the death of an old man in such a theater.) With the virtual end of restrictions on pornography in America, and their easing elsewhere, there are, of course, cinemas that show homosexual films exclusively; like other pornographic movie houses they are characterized by high prices, a humorless clientele, and movies featuring plastic bodies which—for it is impossible to conceive of them as fully human—simulate sex as if it were a fairly boring form of calisthenics. Yet such movies draw large numbers of men, able silently to enact their fantasies for a short time and perhaps to make sexual contacts.

Once individuals have discovered their homosexual desires and the existence of a world in which these can be satisfied, the question of how they will deal with them, integrate them into their total life, becomes a major preoccupation. In this sense being homosexual *is* different from being heterosexual, for it involves a whole set of decisions rarely faced by most "normal" people about how to manage one's sexuality. The range of possibilities is enormous, for with sufficient effort a homosexual can disguise his being, and there are many marriages in our society which are unhappy because of this. Not all such marriages are of course disastrous, as is true of the situation described in Angus Wilson's *Hemlock and After*. The theme is in fact a common one in recent writings, appearing in Simon Gray's play *Butley* and Christopher Isherwood's *A Meeting by the River,* although there the man returns to his wife. A large proportion of the men who frequent baths, toilets, and cinemas have wives and children; many lesbians are, or have been, married.

It would be possible to graph homosexuals according to the extent that they are prepared to come out openly. At one extreme are those who seek to maintain a self-image of heterosexuality, engaging in homosexual sex furtively, with hostility, and often when drunk; at the other are those honest to both themselves and others about their homosexuality. Many of the former are married and fall into the group Humphreys categorizes as "trade." Sometimes, however, such men will themselves patronize hustlers, seeking deliberately to reduce the act of sex to as impersonal and physical a level as possible. They avoid, above all, any lasting or nonphysical contact with other homosexuals: bathhouses or toilets, with their clinical or dirty atmosphere, their provision of instant sex and easy exit, are tailor-made for such men. Often they will come together in a sexual coupling without exchanging a word; after orgasm, and in a resurgence of guilt and often anger, they will part quickly and thereafter avoid acknowledging each other. I am not sure whether there are equivalents among lesbians; certainly women do not have access to such places of instant sex.

A strange variant of this extreme, which is basically one that seeks to divorce homosexuality from the rest of one's life, is found among some hustlers. On one level a hustler lives entirely in a gayworld; visibility is, after all, necessary if he is going to succeed. But among hustlers there is a common pattern, caught perfectly in Andy Warhol's movie *My Hustler,* of denying any homosexual impulses, of justifying what they do as only a means to make money, and of sleeping with women to prove the point. Many hustlers will express great contempt for fags, perhaps not surprising considering the men who use them. I once spent a night in New Orleans with a hustler, a boy from Savannah, Georgia, who was lonely and vulnerable, and we went together around the bars, drinking and playing the jukeboxes, enjoying the transitory warmth of each other's company. But he made it quite clear that while he would like to sleep with me, it had to be for money.

The hustler is in a somewhat different position to the female prostitute, for he engages primarily in homosexual sex, and is thus twice stigmatized, while the prostitute sells herself mainly to heterosexuals. That prostitution leads to lesbianism—or vice versa—is one of the favorite generalizations about female homosexuality, and like most generalizations more honored in the breach than in the observance. In any case, selling oneself as a means of coming to terms with stigmatized homosexual desires has few counterparts among women.

The way in which hustling becomes a means of denying one's homosexual impulses is the underlying theme of John Rechy's two books, *City of Night* and *Numbers,* which for a time enjoyed a vogue among the American avant-garde. It is fashionable to denigrate Rechy as a writer: "City of Dreadful Night" was the heading of one review. Probably much of what is said about him is true, in particular his maudlin invocations of early childhood experiences

to "explain" his homosexuality. Yet his books, for all their awk-
wardness and sentimentality, do convey some part of the pain of
being homosexual in our society, a point often missed by straight
reviewers. Richard Gilman, who attacked Rechy in the prestigious
journal the *New Republic,* was later to argue that he could not
really criticize Eldridge Cleaver, for Cleaver took his blackness as
"absolute theme and necessity," and hence must be judged by other
blacks. I find this a dubious judgment, for it is surely precisely the
role of literature to communicate across divisions of this kind. Yet
it is interesting that Gilman felt no such hesitation in approaching
Rechy, and it seems to me that those who write about books in
which homosexuality is a central concern need at least to explain
their own attitudes toward sexuality, and avoid judging these books
from a exclusively heterosexual viewpoint which is often unrecognized just because it is so all-pervasive.

In both books, Rechy's protagonist is groping for the capacity
to overcome the guilt and self-denial which his homosexuality creates, and which lead him into compulsive hustling. In *City of Night*
the protagonist resolutely resists any attempt to establish other than
a cash relationship with his bed-partners; in *Numbers* there is the
same compulsive search for sex-without-commitment, without even
the excuse of seeking money. Admittedly much of *Numbers* is not
very good pornography of the 42nd Street variety. At the same
time, there is a sense that pervades the book of much of the gay
life of Los Angeles (automobilized, like everything else in Southern
California), and the guilt or self-hatred that prevents any integration
of sexuality into one's total life. As in *City of Night,* the hero flees
from any emotional involvement as a homosexual, seeking merely
to amass sexual contacts, frightened, as he wrote in the earlier book,
to seek "the undiscovered country which may not even exist" of
reciprocal feeling.

For those who are willing and able to be more honest with
themselves, the gayworld offers a more meaningful source of identity and community than Rechy's characters find in cruising Times

Square or Griffith Park. In some ways, indeed, it can be an attractive life, offering considerable variety, social diversity, and much sexual opportunity. The sheer opportunities, at least while young, for homosexual sex are so great that there is always the danger of pretty much neglecting everything else. Very often, and most particularly on hot, restless summer nights, I have forgone a movie I wanted to see, or friends I should have visited, to go to a bar or stroll along a certain beach. The use of sex as a means of escape is not of course confined to homosexuals, though one would hardly guess this from the put-downs of promiscuity that accompany most discussions of homosexuality. Promiscuity seems to me often a matter of habit as much as anything else; many homosexuals, like some heterosexuals, learn early that sex is an easily available palliative for boredom or self-doubt and hence resort to it.

Many male homosexuals who live in large cities will move almost exclusively in gay social circles which offer a continual round of bars, dancing, theatre-going, and, always present, the opportunity for sexual encounter. "Below my window as I type," wrote Dave McReynolds with some longing in his "Notes for a More Coherent Article," "is a very attractive kid of nineteen wearing an army jacket and smoking a cigar." Ah yes. This is the gayworld that is pictured in Mart Crowley's *Boys in the Band,* and undoubtedly much of its brittleness and hostility is caught in that play. Yet there is more strength to that world than Crowley's portrait of unredeemed misery seems to suggest, just as a black ghetto has its supportive elements unsuspected by a sociology that moralizes in the name of value-free science. Not all gay parties or dances or, especially, relationships are corrupted by self-hate.

Especially relationships. Yet in the great outpourings of literature—fictional, scholarly, sensational—about homosexuals, lasting relationships are barely explored. It is so much easier, as I have discovered, to write about the transient nature of much of the gayworld, which is more exotic, more colorful than the ups and downs of long-lived relationships. Yet these exist, and are subject to the same stresses as heterosexual relationships, with the great distinction that society far from reinforcing them places impediments in their way.

Many homosexuals—more women, it is generally believed, than men—will be involved in long-lasting relationships during their lives. Sometimes these will be remarkably close imitations of traditional marriage, with each partner playing out the role of husband or wife. More likely they will be less well defined, and, in conventional eyes at least, sometimes scandalously promiscuous. (Donald Cory has suggested that more homosexuals should understand Ernest Dowson's line: 'I have been faithful to thee, Cynara! in my fashion.') While it is impossible to generalize about homosexual relationships, it is necessary to stress that they exist, and in greater number than most straights suspect. They are not, of course, sanctified by any religious or legal contract, nor are there similar obstacles to their dissolution; in a society where concealment of one's homosexuality can be important it is far easier to manage a series of "one-night stands" than a lasting relationship. (Try telling your boss you can't move to a new job because of your lover.) They are not held together by children, and the partners are less likely to be financially dependent upon each other than in a heterosexual relationship. Yet they survive, and perhaps the very obstacles to such partnerships can become strengths, for homosexual relationships are an existential assertion less easily corrupted by convenience and conformity than straight ones. Which is not to deny, of course, that corrupted relationships do exist.

Even long-standing homosexual couples will move in the gayworld, for it is here that their relationship is most openly accepted. In Australia, and to a lesser extent Britain, that world is known as *camp*, and though that word has taken on a special precocity ever since Susan Sontag discovered it languishing in a little-known Isherwood novel *(The World in the Evening)* and launched it with a somewhat altered meaning on its successful career, it is peculiarly descriptive of much of the social gayworlds. The play acting, the exaggeration, the carefully cultivated vulgarity of camp: where are they more obvious than in the salons and receptions of gay society. There are many entertainers, usually aging movie queens—Judy Garland, Bette Davis, Joan Crawford, Mae West—whose continued success is based largely on the camp sensibility of a certain section of gay society. There is too a whole cult of transvestism and exaggerated sexual role playing that is intimately connected with the gayworld, yet has also had, via the influence of Andy Warhol and his large group of camp followers, a major effect on our social and artistic mores. More than the self-hatred of *Boys in the Band* is involved in all this.

Camp carries with it certain suggestions of effeminacy and in this sense to "camp it up" becomes a form of assertion of identity common in homosexual gatherings. Part of coming out is the adoption of the characteristics seen as belonging to homosexuals, so that men will sometimes seem effeminate or women over-aggressive; often this is a pose that is soon relinquished. There is also the sense, touched on in Sontag's notes, in which camp is used by homosexuals seeking to integrate their lives into the wider society. "The Jews," writes Sontag, "pinned their hopes for integrating into modern society on promoting the moral sense. Homosexuals have pinned their integration into society on promoting the aesthetic sense. Camp is a solvent of morality. It neutralizes moral indignation, sponsors playfulness."

Sontag's comment about camp neutralizing moral indignation is perhaps borne out in the frenetic quality that underlies much of the glitter of gay life. Often highly intelligent and sensitive homosexuals will seem crude and uncaring in a gay environment, as if here they wish only to satisfy their sexual or sensual emotions, and there is something vulgar and pathetic in a group of middle-aged homosexuals, freed momentarily from the need for concealment, "shrieking" together. Laud Humphreys has suggested that the more an individual seeks to hide or reject his homosexuality, the more repressed, uptight, and illiberal his other attitudes will be. Or, as Gore

Vidal put it in *Myra Breckinridge,* "all the hustlers voted for Gold-water in '64." It is a strange paradox that homosexuals, who suffer from the opprobrium of respectable society, are often its most stalwart defenders. I well remember the scorn for demonstrators shown by homosexual friends after I took part in one of the early anti-Vietnam marches; and the gay liberationists, of whom I shall write later, are feared and disliked by many fellow homosexuals. In many ways this conservatism seems a process of overcompensation, similar to that of those blacks who, having succeeded in the white world denounce bitterly any black who questions the worth of this achievement. I suspect, however, that there are more complicated reasons, and that the very marginality of the homosexuals' position tends to make them particularly cautious of anything that might upset the precarious way in which they have arranged their lives. Insecurity produces conservatism as much as it does radicalism.

Again, however, nothing and everything is typical. Many homosexuals live neither in the constant whirl of the fashionable queen, nor in the pinched desperation of "making it" in dark places. There are many homosexuals who avoid almost entirely the public places of the gayworld. There are those who have found for themselves a group of predominantly heterosexual friends or colleagues among whom they move freely, completely accepted by them. In at least certain segments of our society, in the universities, the theater, etc. homosexuals move in a milieu that knows and accepts them. But here one too easily stereotypes, and the most closeted homosexuals are often found in those places where one might expect the most acceptance. Most importantly, as I shall argue later, an increasing number of younger homosexuals have adopted the mores and values of the counterculture, hostile to both the respectability of straight society and the pseudo-respectability of camp. With all the common elements that I inevitably stress, there is as much variety in the gayworld as in the straight. The "typical homosexual" is about as real as the "typical black" and the fact that either can be talked about suggests only the social need for stereotypes.

What is probably true is that most of us have moved in a broader range of behavior and social levels than is true of straights; our homosexuality, like all stigmas, makes us in part *déclassé*. This is one of the advantages that the writer Paul Goodman has claimed for his homosexual experiences, and it is true that homosexuals tend to know a greater range of persons in terms of usual social categories than do most heterosexuals, even if their knowing is largely of a passing nature.

In a confessional article first published in 1970 the novelist Merle Miller, avowing his homosexuality, tells of growing up in Marshalltown, Iowa, where his friends were all in some way or another fellow aliens. Yet ultimately our emotions are of course human emotions, neither bigger nor smaller, more or less grandiose. The homosexual who recognizes this, and who understands that his emotional as well as his sexual needs lie, at least in part, with his own kind, is well on the way to fully coming out. "You first *know* you are a homosexual," Christopher Isherwood has said, "when you discover you can fall in love with another man." The real tragedy of the baths-bars-beats scene is not their sordidness—we all have a sneaking fondness for the sordid, and nothing is lost in giving in to it at times—it is rather that so many of those involved refuse to accept their homosexuality as anything other than a genital urge.

Mimicry and the Outsider. In certain fundamental ways the homosexual world mimics the straight, often exaggerating, indeed perfecting its flaws. Despite speculation to the contrary, Edward Albee's *Who's Afraid of Virginia Woolf?* is not really a play about homosexuals—"If I had wanted to write a play about four homosexuals I would have done so," Albee has said—but this doesn't much matter; the very speculation suggests that many critics recognize the extent to which gays and straights mirror-image each other. It is perhaps not accidental that homosexuals have often been associated with the theater—there are, it is claimed, astrological links—

for our life is bound up with pretense and reflection, with being-what-we-are-not. Our social experience helps make us mimics.

It is the mimicry of the straight world by the gay that seems to be what Kate Millett is getting at when she talks of Genet understanding women in a way straight men can't. Indeed the most perfect image of what society has defined as a woman is the drag queen, and transvestite models have been remarkably successful. I should admit that I do not fully understand the motivation of transvestites, and have considerable reservations about their mimicry of the ultrafeminine at a time when more women are moving beyond the feminine stereotype. Moreover most transvestites are, at least overtly, heterosexual, although drag queens are part of the gayworld in a way they are not of the straight. Yet the transvestite more than anyone else in our society knows the way in which we are trapped by the conventional blue/pink dichotomies of man and woman. Gore Vidal perceived something very significant in the person of Myra Breckinridge, which is that we have given our genitals an importance which above all else defines what we are. It is worth noting that queens can be more feminine than most women, and not many men are more butch than the homosexual stud. And, further, most homosexuals fall somewhere in between.

(One aside: the popularity of female impersonators may be a socially approved way of mocking the myth of pedestal-femininity without confronting it in any fundamental way; both men and women can laugh at drag queens without recognizing that it is they themselves who are, in the end, being laughed at, that Genet's Divine and Rechy's Miss Thing are in fact ridiculing our whole assumptions about sex roles.)

It is in the playing of social roles that the gayworld seems best to mirror the straight. Because there is, as yet, no genuine homosexual community, homosexuals take their cues from the straight world, and, as is often true of out-groups (who, in America, is more waspish in behavior than the middle-class Negro?) end up *plus royaliste que le roi.*

Compare, for example, class and homosexual society in three Anglo-Saxon societies. In Britain one is immediately struck by the extent to which the gayworld is stratified by class. In his posthumously published novel,' *Maurice,* E. M. Forster has one of his characters suggest that "feeling that can impel a gentleman towards a person of lower class stands self-condemned." Oscar Wilde was guilty as much for associating socially with the lower classes as for sleeping with them; he, like Edward Fitzgerald, translator of the *Omar Khayyam,* or J. R. Ackerley, editor of the *Listener* and author of the autobiographical *My Father and Myself,* was obsessed with sexual attraction to the "lower orders." Ackerley relates how he constantly sought a "special friend," and how this search was restricted to working-class boys who were, of course, neither his social nor his intellectual equals.

Now such an attitude, it could be argued, reveals only Ackerley's guilt about homosexuality: did homosexuality matter less when performed with someone from a lower class, which has always been the excuse for English upper-class promiscuity? A woman might argue that he sought a partner who would play out the female role of subordination and that among men this required someone from a lower class. Either explanation may be true, or both. The fact remains that gay life in Britain reflects, indeed exaggerates, the national preoccupation with class. Just because the gayworld does in fact lead to some movement between classes—not only women use their bodies for social mobility—that world is even more aware of class assumptions than the straight.

A kind of class reflection can also be seen in Australia, where a sense of class is still strong (private schools and the right suburb are very important), coexisting uneasily with the egalitarianism that affronted Lawrence. (Read the first chapter of *Kangaroo.*) Compared to the American gayworld, the Australian one seems to produce a larger number of queens, obviously effeminate men and often fond of drag. Such men tend to be working class in origin, and it is as if they are seeking to reject their class background by mimicking a lower-middle-class image of femininity, the only alternative model they have to the tough booziness of their fathers. There are few more assiduous followers of the fashion dictates of the *Women's Weekly* than Australian queens.

Something of this sort seems true also in America, although American homosexuals share some of the illusions of classlessness of the straight world, and there the forbidden sexual object tends to be defined by race rather than class, a matter to be discussed in later chapters. Yet the extreme male homosexual role-player in America, whether he be super-fem or super-stud, is most likely to come from a poor background. Whether something similar applies to women I am not sure. Certainly it is generally lower-class occupations that provide the most opportunity for women to act out a butch role: bus conductress, truck or taxi driver, factory worker etc. Middle-class occupations such as teaching or librarianship tend to impose conventional images of femininity more stringently. But again the available literature provides little guidance, although Maureen Duffy's novel *The Microcosm* suggests that class permeates the British female gayworld as well as the male.

Beyond class there are other critical characterizations of gay life that seem to epitomize and often exaggerate the larger society. It has been a common observation about homosexual life that it is marked by loneliness, by compulsive "scoring," by dread of aging. I would not dispute this as a generalization, although a recent study by the sociologist Martin Weinberg entitled "The Male Homosexual" throws doubt on at least the last of these points. Hoffman in *The Gay World,* on the other hand, sees in these characteristics the most distinguishing features of homosexual life. Yet one wonders whether these are not in fact general characteristics of contemporary urban society, highlighted, yes, within the gayworld, but essentially shared with the rest of society. The singles bars on New York's East Side where Dustin Hoffman and Mia Farrow meet each other

in the film *John and Mary* or the funny-pathetic sex ads that fill
the back pages of the underground press resemble very closely the
less attractive aspects of gay life.

Just as class in Britain can be understood by watching the way
it is played out within the homosexual world, so the whole set of
fears about loneliness and old age that social commentators such
as Philip Slater *(The Pursuit of Loneliness)* or Andrew Hacker *(The
End of the American Era)* have identified as central to contemporary
America find their reflection among homosexuals. They are enormously highlighted and exacerbated by our stigma, as will be discussed later on. But they are not the mark, exclusively, of the
homosexual. Western society places great premium on youth, on
beauty, on constant gregariousness. Is it surprising that all these
should be characteristic of the gayworld? In the next chapter I shall
stress how our stigma has led to certain peculiar social and psychological pressures. For the moment I wonder whether the aging
or the ugly or the lonely homosexual is basically any worse off than
the aging or the ugly or the lonely heterosexual.

Yet if the homosexual mimics straight society he stands outside
it as well; the actor is ever conscious of the proscenium arch, even
if he persuades the audience to forget it. Much of the tension of
gay life results from the knowledge that we are continually acting,
that we are not as we appear. In a sympathetic essay entitled "But
He's a Homosexual," Benjamin de Mott discusses the significance
of homosexual writing in these terms: "A tide of suspicion flows
towards [the homosexual], perpetually demanding that he justify
his difference; relaxation into unthinking self-acceptance in the
presence of other eyes is prohibited." From this self-consciousness,
de Mott argues, stems the fact that "the most intense accounts of
domestic life and problems in recent years, as well as the few unem-
barrassedly passionate love poems, have been the work of writers
who are not heterosexual," citing as examples Albee, Williams,
Genet, and Auden.

The tension is greater the more one fears disclosure, and beyond a certain point, I suspect, becomes so crippling that it constricts rather than enlarges the imagination. Even when one is fairly open about one's homosexuality, it becomes a constant burden. In one of his early short stories, "Previous Condition," James Baldwin writes of the sheer weariness of continually bearing a stigma. There are times when I myself don't disclose my homosexuality—a choice denied others stigmatized—because I am tired of being viewed, however sympathetically, as an outsider.

But, of course, the internal knowledge of outsideness is always there, and this can produce both heightened sensitivity and considerable neurosis. I am somewhat suspicious of those who would glorify the outsider. Sartre, who has written copiously about outsiders and in particular about that best-known of all contemporary outsiders, Jean Genet, seems to me a prime example of someone who would atone for his (as he sees it) regrettable bourgeoisness through obsession with whatever scapegoat (Jew; homosexual; Algerian) is to hand. Yet it is true that one does see certain things more clearly from outside. Homosexuals have been important in American literature for much the same reason as Jews and Southern women.

In whatever way one's homosexuality is resolved, there is always this knowledge that one is, in some ways, separate from one's straight peers. Such knowledge often comes early; precedes, in fact, a conscious awareness of one's gayness. Most homosexuals I know had unhappy adolescences, though who can say if their homosexuality produced the unhappiness or the unhappiness their homosexuality. In my case I was aware of not belonging, of being excluded through some perception by my peers that I was apart from them. I had no idea why exactly that was; I put it down, as do others in similar situations, to excessive bookishness or timidity or artistic bent, anything other than the real cause.

In *The Well of Loneliness,* a book that suggests there is a closeness as well as a separation between the experiences of the male and female homosexual, the heroine, Stephen, feels that same separateness from her peers: "While despising these girls, she yet longed to be like them—yes, indeed, at such moments she longed to be like them. It would suddenly strike her that they seemed very happy, very sure of themselves as they gossiped together. There was something so secure in their feminine conclaves, a secure sense of oneness, of mutual understanding; each in turn understood the other's ambitions. They might have their jealousies, their quarrels even, but always she discerned, underneath, the sense of oneness." Like Stephen, coming out for me brought the great relief of discovering others who shared that sense of being an outsider.

Whether this sense of separateness is the product of social pressures alone, or of something beyond them might be questioned; as with many homosexuals I am likely to argue at different times and on different occasions either that there is something inherently special about us, inseparable from our homosexual orientation, or that whatever that special thing is, it results entirely from social oppression. Just as we do not know just how much of what we regard as masculine or feminine is socially invented and how much inherent, so too, if less obviously, with homosexuality. In general, I believe, the homosexual sensibility is entirely a product of social pressures. Yet there are those who argue for an inborn gayness that goes beyond socially prescribed behavior.

The bitterness, irony, and amusement that go to make up the sensibility of the homosexual who moves continually between a gay and a straight world is perfectly caught in Christopher Isherwood's novel *A Single Man,* a book that is, I would argue, a much finer exploration of the homosexual sensibility than more touted works such as *The City and the Pillar, Giovanni's Room,* or *The Boys in the Band,* all of which, in the mode fashionable for homosexual literature, verge on melodrama. Isherwood's art of understatement is a valuable relief. *A Single Man* describes one day in the life of a lonely middle-aged writer who might be, and in some ways is, Isherwood, living out his life on the Southern California coast, alone after the death of his lover.

There is bitterness in the book. Giving a lecture at the local college, the protagonist says: "A minority has its own kind of aggression. It absolutely dares the majority to attack it. It hates the majority—not without a cause..." There is self-parody: "Why," laments George, "can't these modern writers stick to the old simple wholesome themes—such as, for example, boys?" There is consciousness of playacting, enjoyable at times, yet ultimately painful. When George suggests to a neighbor who has asked him in for a drink that they make it tomorrow: "Her face falls. Oh well, tomorrow. Tomorrow wouldn't be as good I'm afraid. You see, tomorrow we have some friends coming over from the Valley and...

And they might notice something queer about me, and you'd feel ashamed, George thinks, okay, okay..." Yet George has resolved his homosexuality, made it a part of his life, without any of the great Sturm und Drang that pervades most homosexual fiction.

Here Isherwood himself is an important model of one type of coming out. Though it was only in 1971 with the publication of *Kathleen and Frank,* the biography of his parents, that he wrote explicitly of his homosexuality, he gives the impression of someone who has been able to resolve without too great trauma the problem of coming out. Which is not to deny the extent to which his life, in particular his move to Berlin and, later, to California, has been affected by his sense of outsideness. "I am sure," he once said, "that it was my queerness that kept me from being a Communist in the thirties. The attitude of the Russian Communist towards homosexuals disgusted me so much that I could not join the Communist Party, though I agreed, at that time, with some of its other attitudes." Indeed the whole style of slightly ironic detachment, the "I am a camera" pose that made Isherwood famous in the thirties, is in part the response of a sensitive man to his stigma. As Isherwood has aged that pose has been relaxed, and his later novels, particularly *A Single Man* and *A Meeting by the River,* tell us increasingly more about Isherwood the man. There is a slight priggishness in the young man who wrote of Sally Bowles in pre-Hitler Berlin; the much older man who wrote the two later novels is less afraid to reveal both lust and pain. Perhaps for this reason these books are less well known than they ought to be: they embarrass the straight world because they reveal clearly what de Mott sees as the universal experience available to the homosexual outsider.

It is fitting, in a way, that it is in writing about his parents that Isherwood makes an open affirmation of his homosexuality, for it is in relation to one's family that the peculiar nature of our stigma cuts most deeply. Unlike those stigmatized by color or caste, our homosexuality is not shared by our family; unlike physical defect, there remains always the suspicion that we could rid ourselves of it if we wanted to enough. Most gay people feel caught in an insoluble dilemma: if we disclose our homosexuality to our parents, we will risk anger and pain; yet if we hide it, we must drift apart, avoiding any contact that might uncover our essential selves. Like the problem of relationships this is barely discussed in the literature about homosexuality, which tends to consider the family only as part of the etiology of homosexuality, and not as part of an environment in which even the most self-accepting homosexual lives. (Allen Ginsberg has written that when he began "Howl" he did not think it should be published, partly because of the impact of his queerness upon his parents.) Yet this is again a clear example of how social attitudes themselves create the homosexual problem, for part of that "problem" is this very estrangement from family. It is here that the double life ceases to be a game and becomes instead a hard and painful reality.

Thus coming out for a homosexual implies a long process whereby he or she seeks to arrive at a modus vivendi in the interaction between his or her sexual and emotional needs, the stigma with which these are branded, and the gayworld through which one can meet others with similar needs. This world can be seen both as possessing its own particular characteristics and as sharing many of the features of the larger society; far from being a genuine community, providing a full and satisfying sense of identity for homosexuals, it consists predominantly of a number of places which facilitate contacts with other homosexuals. At best the gayworld can be seen as a pseudo-community, held together largely by sexual barter, and this, as I shall argue, explains its rejection by gay liberationists.

The key factor in being a homosexual in contemporary society is that very few of us do not feel, at least in part, the need to live a double life. All evidence suggests that the majority of those who identify as homosexuals fear disclosure—Martin Weinberg's study to which I have already referred, and which included a disproportionately large number of men prepared to identify with homosexual organizations, suggested that even among these some three-quarters feared disclosure of their homosexuality. It is this vulnerability that both binds and separates the gayworld and helps explain why it is no more than a pseudo-community. But why is it that we fear so greatly to reveal ourselves? To understand that one must turn to a discussion of oppression.

2. Oppression: The Denial of Identity

In contemporary rhetoric, oppression has become a highly over-worked word. Yet its sheer fashionableness should not lead us to deny the existence of oppression. Strictly speaking, it results from the fact that societies are divided along class, race, and caste lines and that some groups occupy positions from which they are able to dominate others. In these terms oppression is a concept whose applicability to societies like Australia, Britain, or the United States runs counter to the liberal myth of a society of autonomous individuals, a myth that has maintained itself despite quite remarkable evidence to the contrary.

But even when one concedes that, in these terms, oppression exists, it may seem difficult to conceive of groups being oppressed for their sexuality. This is, I think, largely because our concept of oppression has tended to be based upon a crude sort of Marxist model that envisages oppression as essentially a class or economic phenomenon, and many still seek to incorporate all oppressed groups into such a unidimensional economic model. It is precisely the discovery that oppression is multidimensional, that one may be simultaneously both oppressed and oppressor, that underlies the analysis of the sexual liberation movements. Thus sexual oppression is probably, as feminists insist, the oldest of all dominance/subordination relationships, though this is often clouded by the fact that while women form a caste which is oppressed by men, they themselves divide along class and ethnic lines, and so oppress others, both men and women, in turn.

A similar approach needs to be made in the case of homosexuals. That is, if we restrict ourselves to a primarily political or economic definition of oppression, it will be difficult to fit homosexuals into it. A failure to recognize that the oppression of gay people is somewhat different in kind from the oppression of other groups—women aside—lies behind some of the more inaccurate statements of participants in the gay movement. There exist, for example, gay ghettos, in the sense of areas where there are large concentrations of homosexuals, and where homosexual behavior is largely accepted. In such areas, rents may well be higher than in comparable but nongay sections of the city, and there will probably be a number of exploitative (that is, overpriced) bars, etc. But such areas do not suffer from the same constricting socioeconomic features as do ethnic ghettos, and it is poor analysis and bad politics to ignore the difference.

Which is not to minimize the real oppression we suffer, nor to argue, as Dave McReynolds has done, that "it is a basic mistake to think of the queer as another variety of Negro, Catholic or Jew." It is to stress the quite peculiar nature of our oppression which results from the fact, already discussed, that we are, by and large, visible at will.

Do not believe those who argue "the queers are taking over," or "it's *in* to be gay nowadays." It isn't, not in real life. "Try an experiment," urged one girl at a rally at New York University. "Wear a button saying 'I am a lesbian' and watch how people react." The much vaunted sexual permissiveness of our time has not eradicated the oppression homosexuals suffer, though it may replace being largely ignored with being subjected to prurient voyeurism. Gore Vidal wrote recently: "When the rewritten edition of *The City and the Pillar* was brought out a few years ago I was startled to find that the popular press was quite as horrified by the subject as it was twenty years ago."

Oppression can take many forms; when it is most insidious, it is not always recognized. Most whites, for example, still conceive of racism as synonymous with lynching and enforced segregation; it takes an act of imagination to realize that racism rests on a certain set of assumptions that permeate virtually all of Western society, and whose effect is felt even by those who disavow it. The oppression of homosexuals has often taken very blatant forms. In the Middle Ages homosexuality was regarded as "the unspeakable crime." To quote from a poem written by the (New York) Flaming Faggots Collective, a group of gay men associated with gay liberation:

When witches were burned in the middle ages,
the Inquisitors ordered the good burghers
　　(all of them men, of course)
　　to scour the jungles for jailed queers
　　drag them out and tie them together in bundles,
　　mix them in with bundles of wood
　　　at the feet of the women,
　　　and set them on fire
　　　　to kindle a flame
　　　　foul enough for a witch to burn in
The sticks of wood in bundles like that
　　were called faggots
and that's what they called the queers; too,
and call us still,
meaning our extinction, our complete
　　extermination,
anthrocide and gynocide their one response to
any heretical blasphemy against
a god-given manliness.

The death sentence for sodomy lasted in Britain until 1861, but was used relatively sparsely. We have advanced beyond this, but not much. In five states of the U.S.A., "the abominable crime against nature" is punishable by imprisonment up to life; in another thirty-two, the maximum punishment is at least ten years. A number of American states have recently abandoned such laws, as have the vast majority of European countries and Canada. It is likely that some moves will be made soon in Australia, at least in the federal territories. In both Chicago and London, however, experience has shown that the absence of specifically antihomosexual laws does not materially change the hostility encountered by most homosexuals.

Coming out, as we have seen, involves the homosexual in a process of developing some way of dealing with his or her sexual identity. Part of this adjustment involves a recognition of the way in which homosexuality is stigmatized by society, and the adoption of a means to manage the stigma. The oppression faced by homosexuals takes on a number of forms, and at its most pernicious may be internalized to the point that an individual no longer recognizes it as oppression.

Persecution, Discrimination, Tolerance

Homosexuals encounter oppression of three kinds: persecution, discrimination, and tolerance. The first of these is based for the most part on the illegality of homosexual behavior. Now it is obvious that as long as society attempts to legislate morality, millions of citizens will fairly constantly and consciously break the law, and in this sense the homosexual is rather like the marijuana smoker or the woman seeking an illegal abortion. In fact most homosexuals know that they are reasonably safe from police action, certainly in private, for no society could afford to enforce fully the antihomosexual laws that remain in most Australian and American states,

Scotland, Ireland, and New Zealand. Accurate figures are hard to find, yet it is clear that many more homosexuals are harassed by the police than is ever reported—and also that these represent only an infinitesimal proportion of all homosexual "criminals." Nonetheless knowledge of one's lawlessness has certain implications.

The gayworld, because it is semilegal at best, must constantly interact with the police. Homosexuals learn the places to be avoided because they are commonly visited by the vice squad in search of an easy arrest; homosexuals pay, too, for the protection that many bars, etc. have to purchase. The situation in public places is more dangerous. Men have been shot by police, not because they were involved in sexual acts but because they were suspected of being so. In an incident at the end of 1970 outside one of San Francisco's best-known gay bars, police moved in to "clear the sidewalks" as people were leaving, and ended by shooting a kid who had "got in the way of" police, but who, witnesses agreed, was only trying to get away as quickly as possible. (After recovering from bullet wounds, the young man in question was prosecuted for attempting to run down police.) The case of Dr. Duncan, who was drowned in Adelaide's Torrens River at a spot used by homosexuals to make contacts became a *cause célèbre* in South Australia in 1972, and allegations about police involvement have not been fully answered. In Britain the National Council for Civil Liberties has involved itself in a campaign against police harassment, which has continued despite the 1967 Sexual Offences Act. While this Act removed penalties from "private behaviour" between "consenting adults," it by no means established homosexuals as enjoying the same rights as heterosexuals, imposing an age limit of 21 and rigid definitions of "private behaviour."

Treatment of homosexuals by the police and jail officials appears in many cases barbaric, despite the widely held beliefs that homosexuality is rife in prisons, and jail a comparatively good place for a homosexual to be. This view has been questioned—see for example the article by John Gagnon and William Simon, "The Social Meaning of Prison Homosexuality"—and I suspect that there is some truth in the first point and virtually none in the second. Homosexuality in jail usually involves considerable brutality and, quite frequently, rape. Known homosexuals are often victimized by both inmates and wardens, as suggested in the picture of constant cruelty and taunting contained in John Herbert's play *Fortune and Men's Eyes* and Floyd Salas' novel *Tattoo the Wicked Cross*. In the jail situation, homosexuality becomes brutalized and takes on the crudest forms of dominance/subordination role playing, as Genet's novels of prison life illustrate. It is unfortunate that there are those like Norman Mailer who tend to draw conclusions about homosexuality in general from the peculiarly distorted conditions existing in prisons, as he does in his book *The Prisoner of Sex*.

Like other stigmatized groups, homosexuals do not enjoy equal protection of the law. Robbery and blackmail of homosexuals are common, partly because our legal status makes us uneasy about going to the police. Lack of equal protection is most threatening in regard to the violence from which homosexuals, particularly men who are at all effeminate, or women who appear too butch, suffer. Beating up queers, or as it is known in Australia, "poofter bashing," is a common way for some men to assert their masculinity, and the police cannot be relied upon for assistance in such situations. Indeed anyone in a position where he is likely to be suspected of being a homosexual can expect rough police treatment. I was once stopped and searched—groped would be a more accurate word—by two policemen because they saw me walking with a friend along a street known as a homosexual beat. Nor are gay women immune from police harassment, though the much more restricted nature of their world tends to limit it. The worst persecution is probably that encountered by transvestites, though it is interesting that in San Francisco (and perhaps elsewhere) the police department has sought to expand its contacts with and understanding of transvestites.

In some American states the law allows for compulsory treatment and even castration of "sex offenders," a high proportion of whom are homosexuals. One recent castration involved a twenty-four-year-old UCLA law student charged with "child molestation"—he was having an affair with a sixteen-year-old boy. Nor, with some exceptions, have liberal civil rights groups been very concerned with police and judicial excesses against homosexuals and transvestites.

Usually persecution of this sort is encountered only by homosexuals acting as homosexuals; that is, it is only in overtly homosexual situations that I am likely to encounter it. If I walk arm-in-arm with my lover, I need fear persecution; if I walk beside him without physical contact, I needn't. But if I am simply *known* as a homosexual, I will encounter discrimination even at times when no one seriously believes my sex life is directly involved. This is most obvious in the field of employment, and there are homophile leaders who believe that job discrimination is the greatest single reason why homosexuals fear disclosure.

Outside certain areas of work, of which entertainment and some personal services, such as hairdressing, are the major examples, one's career can only be adversely affected if one is known as—or suspected of being—a homosexual. It is as much this situation as the camp characteristics of certain jobs that lead to the high number of homosexuals commonly believed to be found in certain occupations. The military seeks to bar homosexuals and dismisses anyone found engaging in homosexual acts, a fact that many, including nonhomosexuals, have used to avoid the draft. A recent book by Colin Williams and Martin Weinberg, *Homosexuals and the Military,* details how the American military pressures suspected homosexuals so as to isolate them and place them in a position where they fail to take full advantage of their legal rights. There are no equivalent studies for other countries. Interestingly, when Britain legalized homosexuality, it exempted the military and merchant marine. One wonders—and this is only partly facetious—whether the intent was to maintain a sufficient level of sexual repression and hence aggression.

In many branches of the civil service homosexuals are similarly barred, particularly where security checks are involved. Gore Vidal has claimed that "two government workers living together in Washington D.C. would very soon find themselves unemployed. They would be spied on, denounced secretly and dismissed. Only a bachelor entirely above suspicion like J. Edgar Hoover can afford to live openly with another man." Schoolteachers have been dismissed in both America and Australia for being homosexual, even when there was no more reason to suspect them than their heterosexual colleagues of sexual interest in children. (In California at least the state supreme court has ruled that homosexuality by itself is not sufficient to debar somebody from teaching.) It is ironic that while the possibility of blackmail is often used to defend such discrimination, homosexuals who come out, and hence are hardly vulnerable to this, are not thereby guaranteed job security.

One can be refused a job, of course, without the real reason being stated; who knows how many men are refused promotion because they lack a respectable family image, how many women because they seem "too masculine." With the increasing information available to employers, often purchased from private investigating agencies, the problem increases. In my case I realized some years ago that I was precluded from entering conventional politics, because I was not prepared sufficiently to hide my homosexuality. There are, of course, a number of politicians who are in fact closeted homosexuals, but I would not be prepared to live the quite tortured life of secrecy such men must suffer. We have probably moved beyond the senator in *Advise and Consent,* who committed suicide out of fear that his one-time homosexual act would be divulged. We have not yet reached the point, I suspect, where an overt homosexual could run for office and hope to win.

One of the most bizarre cases of discrimination on the basis of homosexuality was the refusal in late 1970 by the Connecticut Commissioner of Motor Vehicles to issue a licence to a man because his "homosexuality makes him an improper person to hold an operator's licence." Admittedly this was an odd exception, but it illustrates how far-reaching discrimination can be.

Social discrimination against homosexuals helps produce a further variant of oppression—and one that most nearly approximates economic oppression—best summed up in the term "exploitation." The existence of a separate gayworld is in large part the product of the stigma that surrounds homosexuality. The strength of social pressures against any overt homosexual behavior has made us particularly vulnerable to businessmen prepared to provide specialist services—for example, somewhere to dance with another man or woman. To this extent, the ghetto analogy *is* accurate, for as in ethnic ghettos, "homosexual" restaurants, bars, shops, hotels etc., tend to be overpriced and of inferior quality. Housing, too, can be a considerable problem, and gay couples in particular sometimes encounter hostility that limits their ability to rent or even buy. In a society organized relentlessly around the norm of the heterosexual family, the single gay or straight, or homosexual couples encounter continual problems, particularly in matters concerning life-style.

It is impossible to be both a self-accepting homosexual and live a conventional life in Western society. This is the problem encountered by Stephen, the central (female) character in *The Well of Loneliness*. "Could you marry me Stephen?" asks Angela, her first lover, underlining the nature of Stephen's outsideness. This form of discrimination may be of declining importance as marriage itself becomes less important, yet there remain important legal and taxation difficulties that result from the inability of homosexuals to establish legalized relationships. These difficulties can be of major consequence. In Isherwood's *A Single Man* the hero experiences the death of his lover of many years, and realizes that he has less status for the man's family than would a casual girlfriend. And if their relationship had been open, what then? If his lover died intestate, what court would treat him as it would a widowed *de facto* wife? A London report in the *Times* referred to a lesbian dying in a hospital who "was only allowed visits from her immediate family, and her partner of twenty years was excluded. When a lesbian loses her partner she can expect little or no comfort from conventional sources of support like neighbours, a priest or doctor who would try to ease the hurt of a heterosexual faced with bereavement or divorce."

The most common form of oppression to which we are exposed tends to be neither outright persecution nor discrimination but rather the patronizing tolerance of liberals, or what Isherwood has referred to as "annihilation by blandness." (I realize that my experience, for reasons of class and race, is more sheltered than most.) Certainly liberals would not wish to see me arrested for sleeping with another man nor even for cruising for one; they might, of course, send me to their therapist; more likely they will ignore my homosexuality, rather as some liberals will say anything rather than describe a black by his color. The difference between tolerance and acceptance is very considerable, for tolerance is a gift extended by the superior to the inferior: "He's very tolerant," one says, which immediately tells us more about the other person's social position than his views. Such an attitude is very different from acceptance, which implies not that one pities others—and pity has become the dominant emotion expressed in our society toward homosexuals— but rather that one accepts the equal validity of their style of life.

Thus most liberal opinion is horrified by persecution of homosexuals and supports abolishing antihomosexual laws, without really accepting homosexuality as a full and satisfying form of sexual and emotional behavior. Such tolerance of homosexuality can coexist with considerable suspicion of and hostility toward it, and this hostility is reinforced in all sorts of ways within our society. Plays and books on the subject are popular insofar as they reinforce the stereotype of the faggoty, unhappy homosexual. *Boys in the Band,* by playing to every stereotype, proved that in our liberal era homosexuals are as good a subject for ethnic theater as Jews and hippies. To the best of my knowledge no film depicting homosexuals as anything but pitiful and scarred or at least pathetic and ridiculous has come out of Hollywood, and where necessary the movies falsify history to preserve accepted notions of morality. The *Life* review of Twentieth Century Fox's *The Agony and the Ecstasy* commented:

> The movie stresses the love . . . between Michaelangelo and the teen-age daughter of Lorenzo the Magnificent. . . . Though it may seem strange to the conventional minds of moviedom, this amorous relationship is more offensive to the knowledgeable spectator than the truth about Michaelan- gelo's homosexuality. Throughout his life he formed passionate attach- ments to men, most of which were well known to his contemporaries . . .

While European filmmakers have tended to be more open in their approach—note for example Visconti's movie of Thomas Mann's *Death in Venice* and John Schlesinger's *Sunday, Bloody Sunday*— the homosexual remains a figure of pathos/fun in American movies, not least in the films of such underground pop heroes as Andy Warhol, and for the most part an invisible person on television, except as an object of breathless investigation. The 1972 Australian film *The Adventures of Barry McKenzie,* based on the comic strip of that name, used "poofters" as a running joke; one of the lesbians in the film is converted to heterosexuality, as if to show that all lesbians really need is a good fuck.

We are fair butt for jokes—"Would you want your son to marry one?"—and the peculiar pain of the closeted homosexual is most marked when he finds himself laughing a bit too heartily at fag stories. There is a parallel here with the black experience. Stokely Carmichael spoke of black kids cheering as they watched Tarzan beat up the "savages." A friend of mine was considerably upset by an English teacher who insisted, with some vehemence, on the de- generacy of Marlowe and Wilde.

While the media have recently devoted considerably more space to homosexuality, this increased attention has not necessarily meant greater acceptance. *Time* used Kate Millett's avowed bisexuality as a fact with which to belabor her claiming that this betrayed her dislike of women. *Newsweek*'s (approving) review of *Oh! Calcutta!* congratulated it on its "bracing heterosexuality"—a notice that was reprinted on the theater's billboards. More space about homosexuality has not necessarily meant more space *for* homosexuals to express their position, and articles by avowed homosexuals remain few in number. A notable exception is the *New York Times,* which printed the Merle Miller article already referred to, and has commissioned homosexuals to review gay books. There are few similar examples outside the realm of the underground press.

To complain about the scarcity of open homosexuals writing in the media may seem unreasonable, just as similar complaints by blacks once seemed unreasonable. But given the enormous social pressures that exist against homosexuals, the absence of the open homosexual makes for distortions, misunderstandings, false concepts of balance (that is, pro-homosexual statements need always to be combined with anti-). As Stuart Byron, a journalist and member of the Gay Activists Alliance, wrote of the *New York Times'* coverage of the riots that would lead to the emergence of gay liberation and of the paper's failure to understand the significance of the riots: "you had to be gay to know just what 'coming out' in public meant, how protesting in the streets and risking still and film camera exposure and police arrest was something entirely different and new." Of course, there are homosexuals employed by the *New York Times.* Given the pressures to conceal themselves, they were the least likely to provide adequate coverage.

Thus it is a common complaint among homosexuals that the media ignore their political activities, and even refuse space to homosexual organizations for advertisements, apparently regarding these as unfit to be printed. One of the earliest gay liberation protests in New York occurred because *Village Voice* refused to allow the word "gay" in its classified ads—but printed "dykes" and "fags" in its news columns. This in 1969, in the mouthpiece of swinging, with-it journalism. Similarly in Britain, the lesbian publication *Arena III* has had its ads, which identify the publication as homosexual, refused by a number of papers including the *Times* and the *Observer,* and the House of Lords ruled in 1972 that homosexual personal ads were illegal, notwithstanding the law changes of five years before. Similar refusals have been made to homosexual organizations in Australia, particularly by the *Sydney Morning Herald* (which refused even to review this book).

When they are not specifically concerned with homosexuals, the media merely ignore our existence. The *New York Times,* for example, ran a long feature article (31 January 1971) on "people who live alone." Now a large proportion of young singles, particularly in New York City, are gay. In a half-page article, this is not mentioned. A similar approach is found elsewhere; the Women's Electoral Lobby, which investigated candidates' views on "women's issues" in the 1972 Australian elections, ignored lesbians altogether. Even among sympathetic "movement" people one finds the same avoidance: in an article written by a number of women in Chicago, "A Woman Is a Sometime Thing" (in Priscilla Long's *The New Left*), the plight of the unmarried woman is discussed without any suggestion that lesbians exist. Similarly the burgeoning literature on travel always assumes that it is heterosexual couples, or, at best, "swinging singles," who are making the trip. As the travel industry makes considerable money from homosexuals, who, not having families, are often freer to travel than many heterosexuals, one can only instance this as an example of morality overriding economics. Or, to move from the mundane to the terrible: how many people know that the Nazis sent known homosexuals, with pink armbands, to the gas chambers? Among the signs of mourning for the Jews, the Communists etc., where are those for the fags?

The real mark of tolerance is its failure to imagine the experience of others. I am constantly made aware that even the most liberal of straights think of a world that is entirely heterosexual, in the same way as there are few whites who really comprehend that for millions of Americans theirs is not a white country. I lunched some time ago with a male graduate student who was researching men's attitudes toward women's liberation. Angry in his enthusiasm for the movement, it had never occurred to him that there were men, like me, who viewed women in a quite different perspective from that of the average straight.

Tolerance, too, tends to result from an ideological position which overrides an emotional attitude; that is, most intelligent heterosexuals reject, intellectually, their hostility to homosexuals while unable to conquer their emotional repugnance. The outward result is tolerance. I have played enough games with self-styled liberated straights to have discovered the hate that lies behind the mask and it is perhaps this experience that explains how frequently such games occur in homosexual literature. Indeed many of the plays by writers such as Albee, Genet, and Tennessee Williams are built around this device.

The Ideologues of Oppression

Social attitudes toward homosexuals in Western societies reflect a deeply imbued fear and hatred of homosexuality. I shall seek to explore some of the psychic roots of this in the next chapter. For the moment let me note the role played in legitimizing oppression by both churches and psychiatrists, the latter having come to supplant for many the role of the churches in defining what is desirable or permissible behavior. Until recently the dominant position of both church and psychiatry was to advocate the repression of homosexual behavior; the demand that it should be eradicated as far as possible has led some gay militants to charge both churches and psychiatrists with advocating genocide.

Opposition to homosexuality is particularly bound up with the nature of our religious heritage, and the Christian church has traditionally viewed it as a sin, and a sin, moreover, to be punished in this world as much as the next. As with all moral issues there is of course a broad spectrum of theological views, and to fully discuss Christian positions on a matter of such complexity would demand more space and expertise than I possess. The most significant position is perhaps that of the Catholic church, and here I rely on the "vulgar" teachings of the Church, that is, the position on homosexuality communicated to the laity through those pamphlets made available at church information centers.

The predominant view appears to be that homosexuality is a condition for which the individual himself is not responsible, and the homosexual is not, therefore, per se a sinner. To give in to homosexual impulses may be sinful; the Church however makes a distinction between objective and subjective sin:

> Homosexual acts...are objectively sinful. But for the particular individual concerned the degree of guilt may vary with any given act. It is impossible to establish a rule of thumb guide for judging the morality of these acts. It is therefore not wise for anyone to speculate about the subjective guilt of an individual homosexual, let alone homosexuals in general. One can neither accuse them of mortal guilt, nor can one free them from responsibility from their acts; for to know anything about the true nature of the allegedly irresponsible impulses of the homosexual one should know all about his total personality. (John Kane, *What is Homosexuality?* Claretian Publications, 1966)

The homosexual is counseled continence and assured that with effort and Grace he or she can live a fruitful, meritorious, and happy life. This is consistent with the general Catholic view of sex, which after all counsels continence to everyone outside marriage, and Kane states that "the desires [the homosexual] feels are not more free or more sinful than the spontaneous desires of the heterosexual." Unlike the situation regarding heterosexual desires, however, the Church offers no way in which those of the homosexual can be legitimized, and its prescription becomes therefore one of total repression. Those Catholic publications that I have read do not seem particularly sanguine about the possibility of "cures."

The church has, of course, lived long with homosexuality, and it is often claimed that homosexuality is a "vice" much practiced by members of the clergy. Among the Protestant churches there is a broad range of opinions, from some sections of the Anglican, Unitarian, and Quaker churches who accept the validity of homosexual love, to the fire and brimstone of fundamentalists conjuring up technicolor threats of Sodom and Gomorrah. (Modern Jewish teaching tends to hover uneasily between the two.) As institutions, churches have been largely unsympathetic to their homosexual members; even R. E. L. Masters, whose book *The Homosexual Revolution* represents patronizing liberalism at its best—Masters, I believe, invented the term *Homintern*, but spoiled the joke by believing it—condemns the churches for either rejecting homosexuals or else insisting that they "practise hypocrisy and deceit" in their worship. In recent years there has appeared on the fringes of the churches a new acceptance of homosexuality, and churches catering specifically for homosexuals have been established, sometimes manned by ministers debarred from more orthodox congregations for their homosexuality. In general, however, the bulk of organized religion continues to contribute to the hostility that supports oppression of homosexuals, and opposition to homosexual law reform was expressed by ten leading Protestant clergymen just before the 1972 Australian elections.

With the growth of secularism, fewer people regard homosexuality as a sin, and the more popular image of it is as an illness. Dr. Irving Bieber's definition of homosexuality has already been mentioned, and his view is widely shared by many psychiatrists—though it hardly represents the view of Freud, who wrote in his "Letter to an American Mother": "Homosexuality is assuredly no advantage, but it is nothing to be ashamed of, no vice, no degradation, it cannot be classified as an illness; we consider it to be a variation of sexual functions produced by a certain arrest of sexual development." Though this is not the place, nor I the person, there is need for a history of how Freud's views have been corrupted, so that the contemporary psychiatrist Charles Socraides can now write of homosexuality as a *medical* problem.

Among homosexuals, psychiatry is particularly distrusted, for it is often viewed as seeking to enforce standard heterosexual normality on gay patients. This attitude is a considerable exaggeration, for many psychiatrists seek to help homosexuals overcome social pressures, rather than advocate changing them into heterosexuals. Psychiatry, after all, embraces a wide range of views of human behavior and experience. That all psychiatrists regard homosexuality as a malady to be cured is an impression fostered by those practitioners who do in fact advocate such "cures," the most objectionable of which, however, are those of the behavioral therapists, who sometimes rely on very crude forms of conditioning (including, for example, the use of drugs that induce a sensation of suffocation and drowning, electric shocks, and emetics to induce vomiting). D. J. West, who discusses these methods in his book *Homosexuality,* reports at least one death resulting directly from such aversion therapy.

Luckily there has recently been an increasing tendency to question both the ethics and techniques of aversion therapy, influenced, in part, by the film *A Clockwork Orange.* It is not merely that the infliction of pain in order to "cure" is seen as unacceptable by many, it is, more importantly, that "curing" homosexuality is coming to be recognized as the imposition of conformity that it really is. Aversion therapists claim that their "patients" come to them voluntarily. They do not seem to understand how far their acts are responsible for leading homosexuals to see themselves as sick.

To be viewed as ill rather than evil is not much consolation, for it represents an attempt to destroy an individual's identity that is as brutal in a subtle way as is imprisonment. It is my impression that today there is a decline in the extent to which homosexuality is viewed as an illness, and growing acceptance of the more sophisticated version that sees it as a pathology, the word used by Edward Sagarin, a sociologist who has spent considerably energy investigating the gayworld. Or, for those more metaphysically inclined, as a curse, which was the term used by Joseph Epstein in a remarkably confessional article in *Harper's Magazine* (Sept. 1970). Our model is no longer the witch or the invalid, but rather the crippled and disturbed—"He's gay you know," they whisper about us and, as to the blind, offer us pity. For, after all, as Edward Sagarin argues, we are men and women who are somehow incomplete, unsatisfied, deserving of help.

Epstein seems to go further, and echoes with approval the remark of Mailer that anyone who has succeeded in repressing his homosexuality—both men seem largely uninterested in lesbians—has earned the right not to be called a homosexual. That the struggle to inhibit homosexual impulses might do considerable psychic harm, that it leads to great bitterness and unhappiness, is apparently of little concern to these latter-day rabbis. It is interesting that Epstein, an avowed liberal writing in one of American liberalism's more prestigious journals, adopts a position similar to that of the Catholic church—if not, indeed, one that is cruder and more hostile—but this is, perhaps, a reflection of the narrowness of the very liberalism he represents.

Straight attitudes toward homosexuality are often the product of quite amazing ignorance, ignorance which so-called experts help foster. Such an "expert" is David Reuben, whose *Everything You Always Wanted to Know About Sex . . . But Were Afraid to Ask* sets out to dispel myths about sex and assiduously creates some of its own. Because of its wide circulation, it is worth looking at the image of homosexuality this book presents. The book has sold several million copies in the past couple of years and has been hailed, in the words of a *McCalls'* article, as part of a new wave of books with "no prudery, no moral judgement, no provoking of guilt." I imagine that *McCalls'* seven and a half million readers include some lesbians, who may be less inclined to accept this judgment when they read that they are disposed of in three pages in the chapter on prostitution. "The majority of female prostitutes are female homosexuals anyway," Reuben says, which makes one wonder about his earlier comment that "most girls become prostitutes because they like it."

Gore Vidal wrote of Reuben: "[He] is a relentlessly cheery, often genuinely funny writer whose essential uncertainty about sex is betrayed by a manner which shifts in a very odd way from nightclub comedian to reform rabbi, touching *en route* almost every base except the scientific." This is most apparent in his chapter on male homosexuality which deserves some credit for its yellow press prurience, if at the same time leading one to wonder what is actually taught in psychiatry classes in Reuben's alma mater, the University of Illinois. Having dismissed all proposed theories about the causality of homosexuality without providing any of his own, Reuben goes on to tell us that homosexuals can be cured—if they "find a psychiatrist who knows how to cure homosexuality." It is perhaps fortunate that Reuben, who at other times is so confident about his ability to "cure" frigidity, nymphomania, and premature ejaculation, does not suggest that he is such a psychiatrist. One is reminded of his comment that "exhibitionists need psychiatric treatment badly, but they are a puzzle to most psychiatrists."

All homosexuals, he claims, spend their time compulsively searching for partners whose names they rarely know: "They all have this in common: the primary interest is the penis, not the person." One might have thought that this statement would need to be modified by the fact, which Reuben acknowledges, that some homosexuals live together for long periods, but he quickly dismisses these by telling us that they are not really happy. Real life must not be allowed to disrupt the symmetry of his prejudices.

But Reuben has the true soul of a drag show comedian, and he gleefully develops his theory that "food seems to have a mysterious fascination for homosexuals." Why? Well, he tells us, "many" great chefs, "some" good restaurants, even "some" fat people are homosexual. (Who, I wonder, ever suggested homosexuality as an antidote to obesity?) Food, he claims, is used by homosexuals as a lubricant and, literally, as a masturbatory device: 'The homosexual who prefers to use his penis must find an anus. Many look in the refrigerator. The most common masturbatory object for this purpose is a melon. Cantelopes are usual, but where it is available, papaya is popular." Dr. Reuben's book must rank with Philip Roth's account of "making it" in the family liver (heterosexually, of course) as one of the classics of gastro-pornography.

Since Reuben has been widely touted as an expert on matters sexual, his views on homosexuality can be expected to do considerable harm. He writes as if totally uninterested in the problems faced by homosexuals and their relatives (other, perhaps, than the strange disappearance of melons from the family refrigerator); rather he sets out to titillate his heterosexual readers while assuring them how much better off they are. His writing is both vicious and careless; the first mention of transvestites implies that they are all homosexual, and only fifty pages later is there the admission that this is not so. Reuben seems blissfully ignorant of virtually all contemporary psychiatric literature, while amazingly conversant with esoteric details of the more unhappy fringes of homosexual life. It is worth noting that in the Netherlands the book was withdrawn from publication after protests by gay groups about its distortions.

More subtly, the standard psychology texts reinforce Reuben's views. D. J. West's book on homosexuality, for example, which is a major survey of the psychological literature on the subject, is far more sophisticated than Reuben's. Yet however able a psychologist West may be, he is a poor logician, and a man too apt to confuse social prejudice with natural laws.

"No one in his right mind," he says, "would opt for the life of a sexual deviant, to be an object of ridicule and contempt, denied the fulfillment of ordinary family life and cut off from the mainstream of human interest." There are debatable points in this proposition, but it at least is one that sees homosexuals, like blacks and women, as suffering from social disadvantages rather than inherent disabilities. Indeed West goes to considerable lengths in his early chapters to point out that in a number of societies "some form of homosexual activity [is] considered normal and acceptable" and that "a certain amount of homosexual feeling is natural to the human being." Yet despite this, his use of words like "natural," "perversion," etc., powerfully reinforces conventional morality. At several points he talks of homosexuality as being of the same order as bestiality and other "perversions." Like too many psychologists, West is strongly conformist, even where his own expert knowledge tells him that social norms are not necessarily sensible.

Yet the social disadvantages of homosexuality—the "ridicule and contempt," the divorce from "the mainstream of human interest"— are as much the product of opinion makers like West and Reuben as of the homosexual condition per se. Society having defined us as deviant, it is likely that we will exhibit all the traits of deviance. And, indeed, the sociologists of deviance—the "zoo keepers of deviance" as Jock Young referred to them—play an important role in reinforcing homosexual oppression. It is not merely that criminologists and sociologists accept unquestioningly the view that homosexuality is deviant behavior. (One should note that deviance is itself a political definition and not merely lack of adherence to a statistical norm; sociologists do not, by and large, study the sexuality of priests and nuns, though statistically they are further from "the norm" than homosexuals.) But their discussion is usually based on a static view, one that ignores the reasons for homosexual behavior but seizes upon such behavior to justify the stigma that causes it in the first place.

Thus writing in a book edited by two leading sociologists, Merton and Nisbet, with the giveaway title of *Contemporary Social Problems,* Kingsley Davis says: "The few who turn into *true* homosexuals are presumably like the few drinkers who turn into confirmed alcoholics; they do so because they cannot make the normal adjustments in life." Such judgments are common in sociological literature, and so too is a general neglect of lesbians, a heavy stress on the exotic as against the day-to-day experiences of homosexuals, and a preoccupation with etiology. All these together make sociology as it is usually taught in Western universities part of the general indictment of homosexuality.

Guilt and the Internalization of Oppression

Insofar as society teaches its children about sex, and most of this teaching is indirect (which, considering most people's hang-ups on the subject, is probably fortunate) it presents a model that is totally heterosexual in orientation. Look, for example, through advertisements in any glossy magazine. Thus the difficulty of coming out: most of us become aware of vaguely homosexual feelings before having any model to help understand them. And from society's refusal to acknowledge homosexuality as a valid part of the human experience stems the most destructive aspect of oppression, the fact that it becomes internalized and affects the self-image of the oppressed. "You can only be destroyed," James Baldwin wrote to his nephew, "by believing that you really are what the white world calls a *nigger*." So it is with the homosexual.

Because society's attitudes are internalized, homosexuals develop a great sense of guilt about themselves; for myself, however much I try, I doubt if I shall ever totally lose that. Guilt, in turn, produces self-hatred, and those who hate themselves will find it difficult not to despise others who share their guilt. Such a syndrome, Martin Hoffman argues in *The Gay World,* is the major reason for the difficulty so many homosexuals have in relating to each other, the obsessive search for new partners, the one-night stands. This picture of unrelieved promiscuity can be overdrawn—as it is by Dr. Reuben—and there are other reasons, such as social pressures for secrecy, that often prevent homosexuals from developing lasting relationships, for such relationships threaten them with discovery. One should note, also, the considerably greater number of lasting relationships that appear to exist between female than male homosexuals, though how far this is merely a reflection of the social conditioning to which men and women are subject is impossible to say. Nonetheless, the cycle of guilt and self-hatred is a vital factor in explaining much about the gayworld.

There are few homosexuals who have not felt at some time the various attitudes—sin, crime, illness, curse—with which society brands us; few indeed are those who do not wonder, at times and in the more dismal hours of lonely nighttime, whether these may not in fact be right. There is a lurking sense that maybe our experience is not in fact the equal of the straight, that however much pleasure and love we can take from each other, something is still denied us. Similarly the sense of isolation and being excluded which, I have suggested, many homosexuals feel as children, may remain an obstacle to the development of full relationships in later life.

Guilt and self-hatred has been reflected in most overtly homosexual literature. "Show me a happy homosexual," says Michael in *Boys in the Band,* "and I'll show you a gay corpse." Indeed a remarkable number of corpses dot the pages of homosexual literature, which traditionally has used most literary clichés except the living-happily-ever-after one. The typical homosexual novel—I speak now neither of those with real literary merit nor of those written for purely pornographic effect, but rather those that fall in between, the Irving Wallaces and John O'Haras of the gayworld— are full of guilts, agonies, and melodramatic peaks of momentary happiness before the final reckoning. Few have a happy ending; even fewer dispute that homosexual love must be a guilty love and that considerable effort should be spent in hiding it. Perhaps the best of this genre is Gore Vidal's *The City and the Pillar* whose hero, Jim, never fully accepts his homosexuality, but sees his love for his school friend—by whom he is, of course, ultimately rejected—as somehow placing him apart from other homosexuals. It is interesting that the original ending, in which Jim kills his childhood friend, was later altered by Vidal to remove the melodrama he himself came to regret.

One of the more significant ways in which self-hatred reveals itself is through the hostility that many homosexuals have for any kind of homosexual movement, a hostility that often seems irrational in the strength with which it is voiced. Yet this is hardly surprising, for such movements threaten too closely the manner in which most homosexuals have arranged their lives. Self-hatred shows itself, too, in the way in which homosexuals "objectify" each other, that is, see each other purely as physical objects rather in the manner of *Playboy* centrefolds. (Gay men should understand at least one of the aims of women's liberation—the one against sexual "objectification"—for we have experienced it ourselves.) In the preceding discussion of the gayworld, I examined the degree to which that world is organized around sexual barter and its dehumanizing effect. Most male homosexuals at least, myself included, pass through a period during which we seek to protect ourselves by refusing any contact other than the purely physical one. To move beyond this is an important stage in rejecting the internalization of oppression.

As already discussed there are a number of good reasons for leading a double life, reasons connected with self-preservation, careers, and family. Yet beyond these reasons, the need to conceal homosexuality is often a psychological one, product of the self-hatred born of guilt. For reasons of self-esteem many homosexuals—though this is now changing—seek to spend as much of their life as possible as straight, seeking to deny the longings that determine their sexual lives. I lived such a life for several years, and looking back on it, I can only wonder at the complicated tissue of half-lies, evasions, and deceits I involved myself in. (To say nothing of the boredom and discomfort I suffered in forcing myself to imitate a straight life.) Yet even now there are times when I flinch from being identified as a homosexual, for I feel the contempt that the identification brings. It requires a self-assurance that very few, either gay or straight, possess, to be fully immune to the effect of social disapproval.

Like the black, the homosexual suffers from a self-fulfilling stereotype. Tell people long enough that they are inferior, and they will come to believe it. Most of us are "niggers" because we believe that we are in large part what society constantly brands us as; in response we come to exhibit the characteristics that justify our stigma. There are a large number of neurotic, unhappy, compulsively promiscuous homosexuals whom one might well regard as "pathological." Their pathology is, however, the result of social pressures and the way they have internalized these, not of homosexuality itself. If people are led to feel guilty about an essential part of their own identity, they will in all likelihood experience considerable psychological pressures.

As I have already suggested, much of the campness of the homosexual world is a reflection of social pressures, and it is precisely because so much of the gayworld is a product of social ostracism, forcing together people who have only this one part of themselves in common, that it makes up what I have already called a pseudocommunity. Most homosexuals, given a fully accepting society, would, I suspect, eschew constant gay company; one has interests that extend beyond sexual orientation. Yet there are very few straights who seem able to fully accept us, to treat us, that is, without pity or fascination or condescension but—and I hesitate to write something so corny-sounding—simply as people. Which is not to deny that there are straights who are capable of such acceptance; many homosexuals have one or two such friends, often of the opposite sex, who occupy a special importance in their lives, perhaps because they provide the reassurance which I fear we all need, that there is nothing so terrible or peculiar about our gayness.

Often unconsciously, homosexuals internalize the expectations that popular psychology and psychiatry have of us—homosexuals are by and large vociferous readers of books that purport to explain them—and come to believe these expectations. (When homosexuals are surveyed for research purposes, they tend to echo these beliefs, and thus the stereotype becomes self-reinforcing.) It takes little imagination to see how corrosive such internalization can become, for it is difficult to withstand the conventional wisdom even when it contradicts our own experience. I know in reflecting on my own experiences how far popular beliefs about homosexuality, and the guilts that I felt, prevented me from accepting that I had fallen in love. Indeed, with memories of those myths that deny the homosexual the experience of love, I fled the first man who might have become my lover and sought an unsuccessful affair with a woman—whom I seduced, with some irony, by telling her of my homosexual urges. Most straight women seem to value the possibility of converting a fag even above preserving their virtue.

Of course, homosexuals *are* denied some experiences, most particularly parenthood. Indeed the desire to have children is probably a major factor explaining why a number of homosexuals marry. Not all such marriages are necessarily failures, though aside from exceptional circumstances one would hardly counsel them. But there is no reason why gay men and women could not adopt and raise children, for children would certainly be happier in such a situation than in the sterile institutions which are the usual alternative for unwanted kids. There are, of course, a number of homosexual mothers and, more rarely, fathers, who do raise children, either by themselves or with a homosexual partner.

Beyond this, however, homosexuals are denied the right to publicly express their love. "All the world loves a lover"—yes, a heterosexual one. It is impossible to know to what extent love is strengthened by being public, yet romantic ideals of secret love notwithstanding, I suspect that after a time lovers have a real psychological need for the support that comes from being recognized as such. (Commonly, heterosexuals need only hide their love when deceit is involved, but even without deceit, the very concealment of love tends in time to produce strains a more open relationship could better handle.) We are all social animals, and highly dependent on the approval of others. Each time one's lover need be hidden, and jokes or excuses need be made about living with another man or woman, homosexuals feel the denial of what virtually all straights can take for granted—and thus usually miss out on its importance. There is real pain in not being able to walk hand-in-hand with one's lover, a pain perhaps akin to that felt by a black who is constantly made aware of his color.

And even if we are unaffected by social disapproval, the knowledge that others close to us are not becomes a difficult burden. In this way the hurt of one's family becomes part of the homosexual's oppression, and one most difficult to resolve. Most parents are not only unable to help their homosexual children deal with their stigma, they themselves are sometimes more affected by it than the children themselves. There is something to the idea that the parents of a homosexual rather than the child itself should seek psychological help—or there would be if more psychologists and psychiatrists could be relied upon to understand "the problem," which is not the child but the attitude of the parent toward what the child is.

Some homosexuals will, of course, respond to oppression by hating in turn; it is a liberal delusion that those who are oppressed will be more accepting of others than are the oppressors. Indeed one might expect them to be worse, and thus one finds the stereotypic dyke who hates men or the fag who detests women and considers heterosexuals as sick. Others react by excessive self-pity, the dominant emotion in Crowley's *Boys in the Band.*

These reactions make us open to accusations of paranoia—we say there is hostility so that we can feel sorry for ourselves—and indeed some psychiatrists maintain that we are, by definition, paranoiac. Again the metaphor of "the faggot as nigger" seems valid. It is the basic argument of Grier and Cobbs' psychiatric study of the Negro, *Black Rage,* that "for a black man survival in America depends in large measure on the development of a 'healthy' cultural paranoia." This is obviously an extravagant statement, not meant to be taken too literally. Clearly Grier and Cobbs—who are both black—do not mean that all blacks, or all expressions of black life, are paranoid. What they are suggesting is that in a hostile environment the kinds of defence mechanisms people will develop may seem paranoid by the standards of the broader society. Like the black, the homosexual will exhibit a greater number of "unhealthy" character traits. But the remarkable fact about most homosexuals is not that they seem paranoid, but that they appear remarkably able to function in an antihomosexual world.

The Function of Oppression

In so far as oppression is in large part psychological and, thus, internalized, it must be understood existentially, and can hardly be charted by the arid techniques of poll-takers. Yet for those impressed by such data, a survey undertaken by the sociologist J. L. Simmons and reported in his book *Deviants* suggests that homosexuals are considerably more disliked by the American public than ex-convicts, ex-mental patients, gamblers, or alcoholics. To explain why this should be so requires a full discussion of social attitudes toward sexuality and in particular the way in which masculine and feminine are evaluated in our society, topics that will be taken up in the next chapter.

It does seem clear that a good part of the hostility toward homosexuality derives from repressed homosexual urges. Discussing Sartre's view of Genet, Laing and Cooper wrote in *Reason and Violence:* "The honest people are able to hate in Genet that part of themselves which they have denied and projected into him." Those who are sexually insecure will often bolster up their confidence by directing hostility at homosexuals who threaten their own egos.

Yet it is too easy to attribute all hatred of homosexuals to the fear of the homosexual that lies within each of us—just as simplistic an argument in its way as the one that homosexuals are all victims of a crippling fear of the opposite sex. There are other possible sources of the hatred of homosexuality. It is a common theory of social deviance that persecution of deviants is in part a ritual devised to maintain the boundaries of what is socially approved. "The majority exercises its power by creating an atmosphere which makes life uncomfortable for those who disregard accepted precepts of conduct and it enforces these sanctions not only on deviant outsiders, but also over its own members," wrote Andrew Hacker in *The End of the American Era.* Presumably, neither he, nor his mentor, Tocqueville, were thinking of the attitude toward homosexuals but the description fits. In many ways we represent the most blatant challenge of all to the mores of a society organized around belief in the nuclear family and sharply differentiated gender differences. Moreover, there seems to me some envy in the very condemnation of homosexuals, for while we are denounced as promiscuous, fickle, and sex-crazed, there is a sense too in which our apparent freedom is envied by the average straight, as confused as we are in his or her competing desires for personal freedom versus emotional security.

Beyond this we are hated because we are different and Donald Cory has suggested that it is from this difference that there springs the word "queer." Many societies have linked homosexuality with magic. The witches of the Middle Ages, as much as the shamans of some Indian tribes and the court jesters who gave their name to the Mattachine Society, are all examples of this linkage. Some of the hostility to homosexuals is born of the same fear and dislike of outsiders that mark ethnic prejudices, and those who hate and fear homosexuals are likely to hate and fear other outsiders. Although there is some oversimplification in the statement, it is generally true that what has been termed "the authoritarian personality" does display a consistent hatred of all out-groups, and that the homosexual, under some circumstances, becomes a convenient scapegoat who can be accused of responsibility for all sorts of moral degeneracy.

The taboo on homosexuality has considerable social importance and this, I suspect, underlies much of the conservative opposition even to token tolerance. If Freud is right about the major institutions that dominate society, they are based upon the channeling of libi-dinal energies into nonsexual paths, thus maintaining group ties while displacing any overt sexual feelings outside the group. Add to this Lionel Tiger's observations about the power of male-bonding and it becomes clear that homosexuality, particularly between males, has to be prohibited. The power of men in society is main-tained by denying the existence of sexuality between them and turning women into sex objects, either to be used or honored. In societies where, as Kate Millett observed, "sex role is sex rank," homosexuality is a threat to the whole caste structure.

One Australian police chief used to be fond of warning that homosexuals were "the greatest menace facing society." By which he probably meant that they threatened *him*, for unlike other mi-norities, we lie within the oppressor himself, and our very invisi-bility, the fact that we represent a human potential that has been realized, makes the need to draw the line against us that much sharper. As Martha Shelley, the gay liberationist wrote: "We are the extrusions of your unconscious mind—your worst fears made flesh." The oppression of homosexuals is part of the general repres-sion of sexuality, and our liberation can only come about as part of a total revolution in social attitudes.

3. Liberation: Toward the Polymorphous Whole

Liberation implies more than the mere absence of oppression. Obviously there is a need to end laws which discriminate against homosexuals, to proscribe police harassment, to break down the psychiatric ideologies that see us as sick and maladjusted. Yet to remove the obvious forms of oppression is only an immediate necessity, rather than a sufficient step toward liberation. Liberation, as Marcuse has pointed out in another context, will come only with a new morality and a revised notion of "human nature."

Thus in any talk of gay liberation we need a fuller examination of sexual mores, not merely discussion of the attitudes toward homosexuality, for the liberation of the homosexual can only be achieved within the context of a much broader sexual liberation. What is needed in fact is a theory of sexuality and of the place sexuality occupies within human life. Inevitably any such theory will rely heavily on Freud, and despite the hostility of many of those in the sexual liberation movements to parts of Freudian—and particularly of neo-Freudian—thought, these movements are also part of a contemporary revival of Freudian thought, and in particular of its emphasis on the central and paramount role of sexuality in both social and individual life. This revival, in which Herbert Marcuse and Norman O. Brown have played a leading role, is part of a more general attack on positivistic social science and a resurrection of metaphysical speculation, and I am particularly indebted to Marcuse for his explorations of repression and liberation.

The current anti-positivism of the social sciences is also expressed in the writings of anti-psychiatrists such as R. D. Laing and David Cooper, who draw on the existential tradition to argue against the conventional assumptions about normality. While it would be perfectly possible to derive a theoretical argument for gay liberation from existential and Laingian precepts there seems little evidence, except in the Toronto paper the *Body Politic,* that this has been done. This may be partly due to the fact that R. D. Laing, despite his concern with the family, almost totally ignores sexuality in his writings. Cooper, however, has written to *Body Politic* that "the disease is not homosexuality but the terrified lack of adequate homosexual experience"; future theorists may well develop a fully fledged gay liberation analysis drawing on both existentialism and anti-psychiatry.

Patterns of Sexual Repression

Western societies are remarkable for their strong repression of sexuality, a repression that has traditionally been expressed and legitimized in the Judaeo-Christian religious tradition. This repression is expressed in three closely related ways. Above all, sex is linked with guilt; despite theological refinement the fall of Adam and Eve is popularly viewed as being caused by their discovery of sex. Sex becomes sin, and the strong repression of sexuality that our society has traditionally demanded gives rise to strong feelings of guilt about enjoying sexual pleasure. Today this concept of sin has been modified, but it is by no means dead. Indeed one may still find traces of an Elmer Gantry concept of sin, as in the decision of the Tennessee Baptist Convention in 1970 to ban dancing in its colleges. One preacher, it was reported, was cheered for his comment that: "Any man who says he can dance and keep his thoughts pure is less than a man or he is a liar." Women's thoughts were not mentioned.

America has a particularly strong fundamentalist tradition in which sex-as-sin is expressed in these sorts of terms, and it is probable that its current boom in pornography and permissiveness feeds on the feelings of guilt so imbued in the American consciousness, reinforcing, as it does, the whole feeling that sex is dirty and secretive. But guilt about sex is expressed in far broader terms than these. It may be profitable to regard the whole Western mystique of love as a means of resolving guilty feelings about sex, which is an approach that Germaine Greer hints at in her attacks on romantic love in *The Female Eunuch*. Nor is it only in the United States that politicians find it more profitable to talk about pornography than poverty, or tolerate unwanted births, bungled abortions, and syphilis epidemics rather than to provide proper education about contraception and venereal disease. Attitudes toward sex in prisons and hospitals—where authorities prefer to deny that sexual feelings exist rather than provide proper facilities and opportunities for sexual activity—underline just how far general repression of sexuality remains in the so-called permissive society.

Secondly, sex has been firmly linked, and nowhere more clearly than in Christian theology, with the institution of the family and with child-bearing. Sex is thus legitimized for its utilitarian principles, rather than as an end in itself, and marriage becomes a sacred partnership entered into for the purpose of begetting children. Even where sexual pleasure is accepted as a complementary goal the association of marriage and sex still remains, and is reinforced by countless television advertisements and magazine articles. It is from this form of sexual repression, Wilhelm Reich has argued, that the repressive nature of modern society stems.

How strongly this view of sex is held is suggested by the fact, already mentioned, that many homosexuals mold their behavior essentially on that of heterosexual couples, even, in some cases, playing out socially prescribed roles of husband and wife. Indeed Dotson Rader, a journalist and novelist who has written frequently about homosexuality, has claimed that many homosexuals have a desire for pregnancy, and those who have sought to explain *Who's Afraid of Virginia Woolf?* as a homosexual play manqué make much of the imaginary child that Martha and George have created. I think that Rader makes the point far too strongly, but to the extent that he is correct, it suggests how deeply the view of sex-as-procreation has permeated.

Thirdly, and as a consequence of the utilitarian view of sex, there is a particularly strong repression of all sexual urges other than those that are genital and heterosexual. It was a belief of Freud's that the infant is polymorphous perverse at birth, that is, enjoys an undifferentiated ability to take sexual pleasure from all parts of the body. As part of this view Freud also believed in the essential bisexual nature of our original sex drive. This is a view supported by considerable historical and anthropological evidence. "The Greeks," wrote the British anthropologist G. Rattray Taylor, "recognized that the sexual nature of every human being contains both homosexual and heterosexual elements." In restressing this, Freud was to link it to a linear concept of sexual development that made heterosexuality more mature than homosexuality. One of his more sophisticated followers, Sandor Ferenczi, whose paper "The Nosology of Male Homosexuality" introduces a subtle, if unconvincing distinction between "subjective" and "objective" homosexuality states: "The extension of object homoeroticism is an abnormal reaction to the disproportionately exaggerated repression of the homoerotic instinct component by civilized man, that is, a failure of this repression." He goes on to argue: "It is thinkable that the sense of cleanliness, which has been so specially reinforced in the past few centuries, that is, the repression of anal eroticism, has provided the strongest motive in this direction, for homoeroticism, even the most sublimated, stands in a more or less unconscious associative connection with pederastia, that is, anal-erotic activity." Which brings to mind Rattray Taylor's comment, that "the Greeks distributed their sexuality and were as interested in bosom and buttocks as in genitals," a polymorphousness that declined with the development of guilt and the justification of sex as procreation.

The traditional libertarian view of sexual repression tended to stress the first two forms, while ignoring the last, and this is most clearly expressed in Reich's concept of sexual liberation as demanding a perfect orgasm which could only be achieved through genital heterosexual coupling within the same generation. It is from Reich's views that Norman Mailer has derived his cult of the orgasm, and hence his suspicion of homosexuality and of contraception which are seen as preventing full sexual freedom. The importance of Marcuse and Norman O. Brown is that they have stressed the third of these forms of repression, and reminded us that any real theory of sexual liberation needs to take into account the essentially polymorphous and bisexual needs of the human being.

There exist a number of explanations of how sexual repression of the sort I have discussed came into being. The simplest is a theory that attributes sexual repression to a need, developed early in the history of humankind, to beget large numbers of children for both economic and defense purposes. This would explain why homosexuality and nongenital sexuality came to be subordinated to heterosexual coupling organized in the patriarchal family. Women for biological reasons were seen primarily as bearers of children, and by extension as their rearers as well. In this view both repression of our polymorphous instincts and the creation of the patriarchal family can be linked to the importance attributed to procreation. Freud himself advanced a partly anthropological argument, in which repression stems from the assertion of domination of one individual over others, that individual being the father. Thus the patriarchal form of society is established, based both on strong repression of sexuality into socially approved forms and on the inferiority of women. Freud argued that even when the sons banded together to overthrow the father, thus ushering in a new period in which women played an increasingly important role, they were unable to escape fully from the domination of the father, and patriarchal authority came to re-assert itself. Marcuse quotes Otto Rank's version of this argument: "The development of the paternal domination into an increasingly powerful state system administered by man is thus a continuance of the primal repression, which has as its purpose the ever wider exclusion of woman."

Freud himself linked his theory with the rise of religion, and in particular the triumph in the Western world of monotheism. Support for this view is found in Rattray Taylor's argument that "a remarkable psychological change" emerged in the classical world after 500 B.C. This, he claims, led to increasing repression of sexuality and the development of a sense of guilt, both of which facilitated the triumph of the more repressive Jewish view of sex over that of the early Greeks.

Another explanation of sexual repression places its stress on just this fact, and sees it as largely the product of the Western Judeo-Christian tradition. Unlike Freud's view this stresses the particular as against the universal forms of sexual repression, seeing religion as not merely a rationalization and legitimization of sexual repression but as a major cause. Certainly there is considerable evidence that the Western religious tradition has placed great stress on sexual repression. At times indeed, especially during the Middle Ages, to totally repress sexual desire was considered a mark of virtue, and the resulting hysteria, masochism, and persecution set the tone for much of the underside of life in medieval Europe. Continence for all was hardly a practical policy for an entire society, leading as it does to its own self-annihilation, but the next best thing was the development of the view that sex exists merely as a means of procreation—hence continuing Catholic opposition to birth control and masturbation, and the institution of clerical celibacy. To the best of my knowledge the church has advanced beyond its teachings that made sex illegal three days each week and eleven weeks each year; yet the rhythm method, when followed conscientiously, has a similar effect.

Religion may well have been a particularly important influence on the repression of bisexuality, for as the Jewish view of sex came to supplant the Greek in the Western world, homosexuality was more and more frowned upon, and biblical evidence was produced to show its inherent sinfulness. Thus the story of Sodom and Gomorrah has long been used (probably inaccurately) as proof of the homosexual's sin; in Leviticus 20 we read that: "If a man also lie with mankind as he lieth with a woman, both of them have committed an abomination; they shall surely be put to death; their blood shall be upon them." To which Paul, never one to encourage sexuality, added his condemnation in the Epistle to the Romans.

To the Jewish heritage, so much bound up with the whole history of the patriarchal family, was added the Christian theology of "natural law," whence a long line of popes (denied, one assumes, any firsthand experience) have derived the Catholic views on sex. The linkage of sexuality exclusively with procreation made homosexuality (plus a considerable number of heterosexual acts) unnatural and hence sinful. The concept of "natural" sex has affected even those who are not practicing Christians, and this provides the argument most often advanced against homosexuality. But there is no necessity to link sex exclusively with procreation, and few societies have applied this ideology as rigidly as the Western Judeo-Christian. Even the most repressed admit the dual function of the (male) sex organ: sex and bodily evacuation. It is theoretically no more difficult to admit that the sexual act itself has more than one function, and that sensual gratification is as much its purpose as is procreation.

There is finally the attempt to link Marx to Freud and relate sexual repression to a theory of economic development. In this view

Freud's theory of the origin of patriarchal authority is taken as having symbolic rather than anthropological reality, and is related to the organization of society around certain forms of productive relationships. Something of this approach is expressed in an article by Roxanne Dunbar in a collection of women's liberation articles, *Notes from the Second Year:*

> The patriarchal family is economically and historically tied to private property, and under Western capitalism with the development of the national state. The masculine ideology most strongly asserts home and country as primary values, with wealth and power an individual's greatest goal. The same upper class of men who created private property and founded nation-states also created the family.

Yet the patriarchal family long preceded Western concepts of property and nation-states, and is indeed very much in evidence in societies that are in no real sense capitalist. Furthermore, most civilizations of which we have any knowledge have defined male and female as sharply differentiated categories, and one might in fact argue that the subordination of women under Western capitalism, while certainly real, has been less than in, say, precapitalist Chinese or Arab society. The eagerness to wed Marx and Freud has too often ignored the realities of both history and anthropology.

Nonetheless it is undoubtedly true that sexual repression was to prove highly functional for the rise of capitalism and industrialization which, at least in its early stages, demanded very considerable repression in the interests of economic development. In the light of this analysis one can make connections between, for example, the rapid industrial growth of nineteenth-century England and the ideology of the Victorian era vis-à-vis sex. Thus it is hardly surprising that countries seeking rapid industrialization, from Russia under Stalin to much of the Third World today, adopt rigid puritanical codes similar to those now being rejected in the West.

Marcuse has argued that the sexual repression brought about under the primal dictatorship is linked to economic subordination as the sons come to channel their energies into unpleasant but necessary activity. However, as Paul Robinson has pointed out in his book *The Freudian Left,* Marcuse neither makes clear whether sexual repression causes economic subordination or vice versa, nor, most important for our purposes, does he connect his use of Freud's image of the primal crime with his ideas about the repression of nongenital and homosexual drives. Indeed one of the primary differences between Freud and Marcuse is the latter's belief in the desirability of overcoming the repression of polymorphous perversity.

For Marcuse the homosexual occupies a particular role—Robinson interprets his writings as suggesting that "in a certain sense, then, the social function of the homosexual was analogous to that of the critical philosopher"—and it is perhaps surprising that Marcuse's works, and in particular *Eros and Civilization* to which Robinson is referring, are rarely referred to in gay liberation literature. Marcuse seems to suggest that the homosexual represents a constant reminder of the repressed part of human sexuality, not only in his or her interest in their own sex, but also in the variety of nonconventional sexual behaviour that homosexuality implies. Sodomy, of course, recalls repressed feelings of anal erotocism, as Ferenczi suggests—not that sodomy is restricted to homosexuals, as Rozjak in Mailer's *American Dream* should remind us. Even more do female homosexuals disturb the myth that sex need be phallus-centred, which underlies what Mailer has called the "peculiar difficulty" of lesbianism. "Man we can do without it and keep it going longer too!" wrote Martha Shelley in the gay liberation newspaper *Come Out!*

Anatomy has forced the homosexual to explore the realities of polymorphous eroticism beyond the experiences of most heterosexuals, for we are denied the apparently natural navel-to-navel coupling. There is among most homosexuals, I suspect, an awareness of their body, a knowledge of human sensuality, that is one of their strengths, although this is too easily distorted in the body-building cult among men or the disregard of physical appearance among women.

Because homosexuality cannot find its justification in procreation nor in religiously sanctioned marriage, it represents an assertion of sexuality as an expression of hedonism and love free of any utilitarian social ends, and it is this very fact that may help explain the horror with which homosexuality is regarded. Marcuse observed in *Eros and Civilization* that: "Against a society which employs sexuality as a means for a useful end, the perversions uphold sexuality as an end in itself; they thus place themselves outside the domination of the performance principle"—Marcuse's term for the particular variety of repression necessary for the organization of capitalism—"and challenge its very foundations." This is spelled out in detail in the case of Orpheus, traditionally associated with the introduction of homosexuality, who "like Narcissus... protests against the repressive order of procreative sexuality. The Orphic and Narcissistic Eros is to the end the negation of this order—the Great Refusal." In the context of a society based on rigorous repression of polymorphous and bisexual urges, the homosexual thus comes to represent a challenge to the conventional norms that make him or her a revolutionary.

Still, even in the Marcusian variation of Freudian thought, exclusive homosexuality represents as great a repression as exclusive heterosexuality even if, because of the legitimization of sex-as-procreation, it places the homosexual outside society in a way that is not true for the heterosexual. Homosexuals who like to point out that everyone is queer—"either latent or blatant," as one girl put it—rarely concede that everyone is equally straight, and that to repress the one is as damaging as to repress the other. It may be the historic function of the homosexual to overcome this particular form of repression, and bring to its logical conclusion the Freudian belief in our inherent bisexuality.

Sex Roles and Repression

The repression of polymorphous perversity in Western societies has two major components: the removal of the erotic from all areas of life other than the explicitly sexual, and the denial of our inherent bisexuality. The latter in particular is bound up with the development of the very clear-cut concepts of masculine and feminine that dominate our consciousness and help maintain male supremacy, and this dichotomy underlies the analyses of sexuality and sex roles associated with women's liberation.

The de-eroticizing of our lives is the primary concern of Norman O. Brown, who ascribes the grand neuroses that he associates with organized civilization to the subordination of the generally erotic to the specifically genital urges. It is argued too by Marcuse, though he is less willing to move to the ultimate conclusion favored by Brown. Marcuse sees modern industrial society as being particularly repressive of our nonspecific erotic instincts; thus in *One Dimensional Man*, his major critique of modern society, he writes of the "reduction of erotic to sexual experience and satisfaction":

> For example, compare love-making in a meadow and in an automobile, on a lover's walk outside the town walls and on a Manhattan street. In the former cases, the environment partakes of and invited libidinal cathexis and tends to be eroticized. Libido transcends beyond the immediate erotogenic zones—a process of nonrepressive sublimation. In contrast, a mechanized environment seems to block such self-transcendence of libido. Impelled in the struggle to extend the field of erotic gratification, libido becomes less "polymorphous," less capable of eroticism beyond localised sexuality, and the *latter* is intensified.

There is a strong romanticism in Marcuse's views, and one that is echoed in the moves to establish rural communes that have become so marked in the United States in recent years.

If we are all at birth polymorphous perverse, the whole process of socialization acts so as to break this down and channel our instincts into the narrow but socially approved norms. These involve not only a repression of general eroticism, but also of bisexuality. Why a minority reject this socialization is, as I have already suggested, a mystery beclouded by vast quantities of psychological research. Most difficult to understand perhaps is why genuine bisexuality is comparatively rare, though as I have already suggested it often appears a threat to exclusive homosexuals and heterosexuals alike. Thus one finds that even those who accept the Freudian notion of inherent bisexuality are hostile to its manifestation in practice; D. J. West, for example, in his book on homosexuality, appears to regard it as "betraying an underlying defect of character."

There is a marked connection in our society between the repression of bisexuality and the development of clearly demarcated sex roles. Now this is not a necessary connection. There are few societies which have not held up models of masculine and feminine into which recalcitrants were to be forced and a sharp distinction between the two does not of itself produce repression of homosexual urges. The ancient Greeks extrolled both bisexuality and the supremacy of men, and homoeroticism thrives, in fact, where men and women are kept apart and sharply differentiated (as for example in the Arab custom of addressing love songs to boys because women are regarded as too inferior to be objects of such praise). Unlike Greek society, however, ours is one that defines masculinity and femininity very much in heterosexual terms, so that the social stereotype—and often indeed the self-image—of the homosexual is someone who rejects his or her masculinity or femininity. Thus, as already suggested, one finds the two extremes of male homosexual role playing: the drag queen who tends to accentuate the image of the homosexual as a man who would be a woman, and the leather type who seeks to overcome it. To a lesser extent comparable stereotypes exist among lesbians.

It is in fact probably true that individuals are often forced into exclusive homosexuality because of both the way in which society brands those who deny its roles and the penalties meted out to those who are unwilling to accept them. Whether it be the educational system—boys are naturally good at math and science, girls at languages and arts—or the jeweler's notice—"We do not, nor will we in future, carry earrings for men"—sex roles are a first, and central distinction made by society. Being male and female is, above all, defined in terms of the other: men learn that their masculinity depends on being able to make it with women, women that fulfillment can only be obtained through being bound to a man. In a society based on the assumption that heterosexuality represents all that is sexually normal, children are taught to view as natural and inevitable that they in turn will become mummies and daddies, and are encouraged to rehearse for these roles in their games.

The way in which our concepts of sex roles are bound up with making it with the opposite sex illustrates how far our definitions of these roles are influenced by the fears of homosexuality that most straights have repressed. Proving one's man- or womanhood is in the popular imagination bound up with the rejection of any fag or dyke characteristics; if this seems more obvious in the case of men, it is because women have traditionally been defined as inferior, and whereas there is some grudging respect accorded women with masculine qualities, none is given to womanly men. Even among children tomboys are more acceptable than sissies.

That lesbianism is stigmatized less than male homosexuality is one of the clichés about homosexuality, and to the extent that it is true it reflects the inferior position of women in our society. (Reports of group sex activities—see for example an article in *Newsweek*, 21 June 1971—suggest that sex between women is far more easily accepted by "middle Americans" than that between men.) Nor, despite apocryphal stories about Queen Victoria's disbelief in lesbianism exempting it from legal sanction, is this lesser condemnation of lesbians restricted to modern times. Derrick Bailey, in his book *Homosexuality and the Western Christian Tradition*, points out that this difference was equally true of early and medieval Christianity, and argues it is due to the inferior position of women, in particular to the fact that homosexual acts, and particularly sodomy, involves "degradation, not so much of human nature itself as of the male, since in it he simulates or encourages or compels another to simulate the coital function of the female—a 'perversion' intolerable in its implications to any society organized in accordance with the theory that woman is essentially subordinate to man." Indeed, female homosexuality may well touch on that deep-hidden fear in men, the suspicion that women are in fact more capable of sexual enjoyment than they, which helps explain the male-created ideology that for a long time denied sexual feelings to women.

Gay women are, after all, doubly oppressed, and suffer particularly from the social norms that expect women to repress not only their homosexual but even, to a considerable extent, their heterosexual urges. In some ways the equivalent of the compulsively promiscuous male who never dares know his partners may well be the woman who cannot admit the sexual component of her love for another woman; both are victims of the sexual expectations of a society that perceives masculinity as making it with a woman, femininity as preserving one's purity. It is often claimed, for example, that men react more to physical stimuli than women. Yet if the media were to bombard us constantly with pictures of pretty boys and nude men, who knows whether heterosexual women might not in fact "objectify" beautiful men with all the single-mindedness of the *Playboy* male. And, by extension, whether lesbians might not behave more like men, both straight and gay, than like straight women.

The major way in which children are socialized into particular forms of sexual repression and concepts of sex roles is through the family, and indeed this may be the only major socialization task that the family retains in modern society. (This may explain the strength of opposition to sex education in schools, which might usurp even this role of the family.) The patriarchal family as we know it is essentially a nuclear family; indeed the transformation from the extended (or stem) to the nuclear family has been one of the major effects of industrialization, irrespective of whether industrialization is achieved through capitalist or noncapitalist means. Nonetheless, the family still retains one of its original functions, albeit in a modified form, which is to teach children to make clear-cut role distinctions between the sexes.

Equally, the institution of the family as we know it contributes very importantly to the persistence of the repression of homosexuality. As all parents are either fully heterosexual in behavior—or, except in special cases, will appear so to their children—it follows that children are exposed to models of sexual role playing that are fully heterosexual, and denied virtually all contact with homosexuals, for even friends or relatives who are gay will by and large conceal this in front of children. A social system that provided instead an opportunity for children to grow up regarding *both* homo- and heterosexuality as part of the human condition, a system perhaps approximated—for men—in ancient Greece, would be a far better one for enabling children to come to terms with their own diverse sexual impulses. As long as homosexuals are denied any role in child-rearing—in which numbers, of course, participate through their careers, while concealing in almost all cases their homosexuality—it is unlikely that children can grow up with other than a distorted view of what is "natural."

The Effects of Sexual Repression

It is basic to the whole psychoanalytic approach that repressed desires appear elsewhere and it is from the concept of repression or sublimation of sexual urges that Freud derived his theory of civilization, and Brown, and to a lesser extent Marcuse, their explanations of human aggression. Sexual repression, as I have already stressed, takes a number of forms, but I am particularly concerned with the repression of nongenital and homosexual desires. This is not to deny the significance of the repression of heterosexuality, which I have already suggested is of comparable importance *for the individual.* For a society based on the ideology that heterosexuality is the only normal form of sexual behavior, repression of homosexuality has particular social consequences. Largely, I think, because of the different ways in which society regards hetero- and homosexuality, the repression of the latter is much more widespread and has many more implications.

This is a problem that few social theorists have been prepared to take seriously. Despite the undercurrent of jokes and comment about repressed homosexuality—which is held to account for a large variety of social phenomena, from behavior in British public schools through Australian mateship to sexual attitudes among American cowboys—there has been little exploration of the consequences for society of the enormous amount of libidinal energy devoted to repressing our inherent bisexuality. Protestant Anglo-Saxon cultures are remarkable for the extent to which they seek to deny all and any homosexual urges; thus the embarrassment of Protestant Anglo-Saxon males when faced with the Mediterranean custom of men embracing. (Our societies are also noted for the prevalence of overt and exclusive homosexuality, nor is this coincidence accidental.) Many men are so concerned to deny any homosexual feelings that they tend to adopt extreme postures of aggression, to reject feelings of tenderness or love as well as sexual desire for each other. Lionel Tiger has observed:

There are important inhibitions in much of Euro-American culture—if not elsewhere too—against expressing affection between men, and one result of this inhibition of tenderness and warmth is an insistence on corporate hardness and forcefulness which has contributed to a variety of tough-minded military, economic, political and police enterprises and engagements.

Now Tiger, as already mentioned, tends to see homoeroticism as a development from the basic male bonding, and has indeed used this theory to argue against some of the assumptions, if not the aims, of women's liberation. Yet what if it is the reverse that is true?

What if male bonding, far from being basic, is indeed the product of repression of those same homoerotic feelings? Organized sports—again, particularly important in Anglo-Saxon societies—have quite remarkably obvious homoerotic overtones. (I remember the headmaster of one of Australia's most prestigious private schools talking with nostalgia of "the boys" showering together after the rugger matches at Oxford.)

"Except for sex, and my wife's very good at sex, I like you guys better," says Ben Gazzara to his buddies in John Cassavetes' film *Husbands,* a comment very revealing of the extent to which men are haunted by the fear of homosexuality in their close relationships. Both male bonding and the "inhibition of tenderness and warmth" may be the results of repressed homosexual feeling, and the dialectic between the two is one of the staples of contemporary fiction and cinema.

To Leslie Fiedler relationships between men are the dominant theme of the American novel, and women such as Ellen Willis and Betty Friedan have claimed that this theme illuminates much current cinema. As Betty Friedan wrote in the *New York Times:* "In one after another of the sickly slick latter day Hardy Boys that have filled the Best Ten movie lists and occupied the movie houses the last few years—*Easy Rider, Midnight Cowboy, Little Fauss and Big Halsy,* etc.—ageing boys toddle two-by-two down the vacant road to nothingness—a road somehow as void of human life or human value as it is devoid of women." In our time the most significant figure to explore this relationship is Norman Mailer, who is one of the few contemporary writers prepared to take seriously the effects of sexuality on social and political behavior. (Eldridge Cleaver, whom I shall consider later, seems to me to be within this tradition.) Mailer has stated that "being a man is the continuing battle of one's life; and one loses a bit of manhood with every stale compromise to the authority of any power in which one does not believe." This is one of the major leitmotivs in Mailer's work, nor is it less present in the whole consciousness of America.

For "being a man" is so bound up with the problems of relating to other men while denying any sexual interest in them that it has become a major preoccupation of the American male psyche. Mailer's preoccupation was echoed in the words of a conservative candidate for the New York State Senate in 1970 who was quoted as speaking of his antipathy to homosexuals thus: "I think a guy who sells out his manhood sells out the most important thing he has. And if he'll sell that out he'll sell out anything." Which brings to mind all those presidential statements about the need to prove ourselves by standing firm in Vietnam.

Mailer's views on the relationship between sexuality, aggression, and males together is best revealed in his novel *Why Are We in Vietnam?*, a book whose scatological brilliance reveals a vision of America as cursed by the complex and hidden relationships between repression, dread of homosexuality, and violence. Such women as appear in *Why Are We in Vietnam?* are, in the narrator's terminology, "cunts": the focus of the book is the male relationship of father and son, of D.J. and his mate Big Tex, or rivals and lovers. The culmination of the book, a savage fantasy based on a bear hunt in Alaska, is a lone night in the wilds between D.J. and Tex— teenage studs and fearless cuntsmen—in which sex and love merge in that dread-love-hate that Mailer sees as underlying America, both maiming and strengthening her.

Why Are We in Vietnam? is a book that is obsessed both with masculinity and with homosexuality, for Mailer speaks in the dark voice of our Judeo-Christian guilt in seeing one as the enemy rather than the complement of the other. Masculinity for Mailer is measured by one's sexual prowess, for women exist in his universe largely as the ultimate challenge against which men must prove themselves. (On this see Kate Millett.) Yet, too, masculinity is constantly challenged by underlying homosexuality; the girl in Mailer's story "Time of her Time" becomes a "real killer" to Sergius O'Shaunnessy when she exits on the line: "You do nothing but run away from the homosexual that is you."

I am reminded of a remarkable Australian television documentary on pack rape, in which one of the boys interviewed said that the real thrill in it was "doing it with your mates." Mailer would understand and applaud; Tex and D.J. even "prong" each other's girls. When they can. For him homosexuality is a threat to be mastered, yet he is also aware of the costs of this battle. There is within Mailer a conflict between two heritages, the Judeo-Christian guilt metaphysic and the libertarian, socialist rationalist, and it is the almost unbearable tension between the two that makes him great. However objectionable he is as a dispenser of morality one must admire Mailer's comprehension of the dynamics of sexual fears and fantasies.

The sublimation of homosexual desire into both aggression and mateship between men seems a particular characteristic of frontier societies—it is evident, also, among white Australians and South Africans, and Ronald Conway in his book *The Great Australian Stupor* claims there is "latent homosexuality on an astounding scale" in that country. It is a common observation that Englishmen feel less threatened by homosexuality than Australians or Americans, and while this may often be overstated I think there is an element of truth in it. It would be interesting to compare attitudes in the frontier societies of Latin America, where the white settlers brought with them a strongly developed sense of "machismo," and where homosexual oppression remains very strong.

Men in such societies are drawn together, yet the more this happens the more they need to repress their feelings, and thus the undercurrent of violence that exists between men which is turned outward in the assertion of masculine dominance, whether vis-à-vis foreigners (Vietnam?), women, or other inferiors. The argument that men fight each other because they are unable to love each other is a version of Marcuse's formulation that aggression results from a failure to give sexuality free reign. I find this argument persuasive, in part because of my observation of homosexuals. Violence seems on the whole remarkably absent among self-accepting homosexuals, while particularly prevalent among those who have strong homosexual desires that they seek to repress. This argument is explored in James Purdy's horrific novel *Eustace Chisholm and the Works,* which ends with the sadistic murder of a man who becomes the perfect victim through his inability to accept the love of another male. Like Herbert's play *Fortune and Men's Eyes,* the novel suggests the extent to which our society distorts homoeroticism into cruelty and viciousness. Homosexual sadism, as found for example in late Imperial Rome, is often the product of the interplay of guilt and partial repression, and it requires little imagination to see how these are involved in the homosexual cult of leather with its strong stress on punishment and authority. ("Young man seeks discipline, experienced master" reads a fairly typical ad in the underground press.) On the other hand, concentrations of gay men seem largely quiet and nonviolent. Gay bars, for example, with the exception of those catering for "rough trade"—often homosexuals trying to disguise themselves by a parade of toughness—are relatively free of the hints of suppressed violence that seem so often to hover over straight bars.

Violence is a characteristic very strongly linked with sex roles in our society, and it may be that homosexuals, because they have rejected the need to suppress affection toward other men, are also able to reject the idea that violence is a means of proving one's manhood. It is not, I think, accidental that Mailer as well as regarding homosexuals as "cursed" is also much enamored of physical conflict between men—thus his enthusiasm for boxing—while Cleaver, who echoes Mailer's denunciation of homosexuals, is strongly attracted to the mystique of violence. To argue that violence is often the product of sexual frustrations and insecurities finds considerable support in contemporary literature and film; the gun, as the film *Bonnie and Clyde* suggested, is a substitute penis, and the extraordinary passion with which many defend the right of the individual to possess a gun may suggest deep psychological motives. Watching clashes with the police one is struck—here one is again indebted to Mailer—by the strongly sexual overtones of their brutality, by the fury with which they seize upon effeminate and long-haired boys, the almost orgiastic way in which they fondle their nightsticks.

Because violence is regarded in our society as a far more acceptable form of behavior among men than among women, one would expect sexual repression to reveal itself somewhat differently in women. Indeed it seems likely that if repression in men is often externalized into violence, among women it is often internalized, and here, indeed, one can see parallels between male homosexuals and women. One of the more frequent clichés in standard writings on homosexuality is that because it is more socially acceptable for women to display affection toward each other they are able to deal with their homosexual needs more easily than are men. Yet the testimony emerging from the writings and consciousness-raising sessions of women's liberation suggests strongly that women feel estranged from each other, highly competitive, and unable to establish genuinely close relationships. In the early days of women's liberation the most hurtful accusation was that they were a bunch of lesbians, and feminists such as Betty Friedan took considerable pains to show that they really were "feminine" (i.e., liked men).

Women far more than men are trapped in a social view that suggests that their ultimate worth is derived from a suitable heterosexual attachment, and the result of this is that they come to despise both themselves and other women. Germaine Greer's *The Female Eunuch*—which largely ignores the lesbian, though whether because she is in Greer's view not female or not a eunuch I am not sure—suggests strongly that the failure of women to establish close relations with each other is based on this self-denigration, and it is to overcome this that women's liberation stresses the need to develop a sense of sisterhood.

I have already argued that women are taught to repress aggression as much as sexuality, and to this extent the stereotypical butch lesbian is quite consciously rejecting this part of her socialization. Among women, sexual repression often reveals itself in the bitterness, possessiveness, and petty tyranny that seems to be associated with so many of them in our society. This is most obvious in the case of American "momism," and in a society that teaches women that they should find almost total emotional satisfaction in their family it is not surprising that maternal love becomes a smothering one, in which women seek not only emotional but sometimes barely disguised sexual satisfaction from their children. There is some truth in the idea that American women often seek to destroy their children's, particularly their son's, sexuality: Albee's vision of the mother in *The American Dream* or the quite fantastic mysogyny of William Burroughs—"I think that the whole anti-sex orientation of our society is basically manipulated by female interests" he said in an interview with Daniel Odier—is the ultimate expression of this. Nor would I deny that it may be an important "cause" of homosexuality, though it is far from sufficient, as I have already argued.

Ultimately what we conceive of as human nature is in large part the product of the nature and extent of sexual repression, and if one accepts the analyses of radical Freudians like Marcuse and Brown one can also accept the thesis, implicit in much of the writings of gay and women's liberation, that human nature is mutable. Now this is ultimately a belief for which we do not yet have empirical evidence; just as we do not know how far there are inherent differences between men and women beyond the purely anatomical ones, so also we do not know how far repression of our sexual instincts is responsible for aggression and competitiveness. The theory of sexual liberation that I shall advance rests on a belief that it is possible through the removal of at least some of the restraints on human eroticism to develop a greater sense of warmth, affection, and community between people.

Toward Liberation

Any discussion of sexual liberation involves some concept of overcoming sexual repression, although there is considerable debate as to how far we can in fact dispense with any form of repression at all. Freud distinguished between repression and sublimation, and argued not only that the latter was a healthy variant of the former but that it was in fact essential for the maintenance of civilization. Norman O. Brown on the other hand appears to be arguing for a total end to repression, and a return to the infantile state of polymorphous perversity, a position that is more utopian than programmatic. If one accepts the centrality of the sexual urge it is difficult to argue for a total relaxation of repression without answering the claim that this would mean an end to all forms of socially necessary activity. Marcuse seeks to overcome this objection with his concept of "surplus repression," that part of sexual repression which acts so as to maintain the domination of the ruling class but which is not necessary for the maintenance of a genuinely cooperative human community. He also suggests the possibility of eroticizing everyday life, including work. I would further argue that there are other basic human needs and urges apart from the erotic and that because of these some forms of sexual repression would be freely accepted even by an individual totally untouched by social conditioning. At the very least I suspect one has to accept the need for some form of postponed gratification.

Kate Millett in *Sexual Politics* defined a sexual revolution as requiring "a permissive single standard of sexual freedom," which would follow an end to patriarchy and to what she refers to as "separate sexual subcultures." Millett, like most women's liberationists, is primarily concerned with sex roles, which she sees as underlying the nuclear family structure which in turn, as Reich saw, "forms the mass psychological basis for a *certain* culture, namely the *patriarchal authoritarian one* in all of its forms." I would not dispute this claim. Yet is seems to me that liberation requires, as well, a general eroticizing of human life and a move toward polymorphous perversity that includes more than reassessment of sex roles.

Let me make clear at once a point to which I shall have reason to return: liberation as a concept embraces far more than sexual liberation. Moreover, the concepts of liberation with which we shall be concerned relate almost entirely to affluent Western societies; as Susan Sontag and others have pointed out, changing consciousness in an underdeveloped and once neocolonial state like Cuba must in some ways reverse the changes applicable to North America, Western Europe, or Australasia. (However, I am less willing than she, writing in *Ramparts* in 1969, to excuse Cuban treatment of homosexuals.) Were I concerned with broader concepts of liberation I should, of course, need to concern myself as much with the nature of Western capitalism, imperialism, consumerism, bureaucracy etc., as with sexual repression and freedom. How far the latter can be conceived without coming to grips with the former is one of the key ideological concerns of both the women's and the gay movements. Yet there is a sense in which we should be constantly suspicious of attempts to deny the centrality of sexuality in any discussion of liberation. "I do not believe in a nonerotic philosophy. I do not trust any desexualized idea," wrote the Polish writer Witold Gombrowicz in his diary. It is the desexualization of the concept of liberation that accounts for much of the abstruse intellectualism of sections of the Left—and the common tendency of revolutionaries to become vicious and puritanical on winning power. As the song goes in *Marat/Sade:*

What's the point of a revolution
Without general copulation?

The more difficult question with which we have to come to grips is what's the *possibility* of a revolution without ...

Liberation, then, in our restricted context implies freedom from the surplus repression that prevents us recognizing our essential androgynous and erotic natures. "Originally," wrote Marcuse in *Eros and Civilization,* "the sex instinct has no extraneous temporal and spatial limitations on its subject and object; sexuality is by nature 'polymorphous perverse.' " And as examples of surplus repression Marcuse notes not only our total concentration on genital coupling but phenomena such as the repression of smell and taste in sexual life. For both him and Brown, liberation implies a return to original sexuality.

Yet this definition is perhaps too narrow. Liberation entails not just freedom from sexual restraint, but also freedom for the fulfillment of human potential, a large part of which has been unnecessarily restricted by tradition, prejudice, and the requirements of social organization. If it is true that social needs still demand a certain degree of repression of sexuality, it is also true that affluent, postindustrial societies, such as those of the developed Western world, offer an unparalleled opportunity for freedom. Technology, which too often becomes restrictive, in fact allows the individual far greater liberty from toil and opens up the possibility that work might truly become play, not just for a small minority as at present but for the vast majority. Which in turn opens up the possibility of breaking down the rigid lines our society draws between art and life, or in other words the possibility of eroticizing everyday living. Developing countries are not in this position, which is why they must define liberation differently; on the other hand, the degree of affluence in the West, if properly distributed, is far greater than would be needed for an immediate and considerable decrease in personal restrictions. Liberation demands a renunciation of the traditional puritan ethic, so successfully imitated by communism, that sees hard work and expanding production as goods in themselves: indeed ecological demands mean that there is an increasing urgency to slow down the rate of production. Instead it requires a new examination of the basic erotic instincts that we have repressed in the name of morality and production:

As human beings we are unique among animals in having a largely unspecified potential. Besides the basic biological needs for food, water and rest, we have needs which are specifically human and subject to conscious development: the need for relationship, the need to create and build. We are all erotic beings. We experience our lives as a striving for realization and satisfaction. We experience our lives sexually, as enlivened by beauty and feeling. At base we have a need for active involvement and creation, the need to give form and meaning to our environment and ourselves. [From *Gay Liberation*, a pamphlet of the Red Butterfly movement, a group of revolutionary socialists within gay liberation.]

One of the problems involved in discussing liberation is that we live at a time when traditional sexual restraints are apparently collapsing, and the individual's freedom for sexual expression appears greater than ever before. As Abbie Hoffman put it, society is "simultaneously more repressive and more tolerant," a truth Marcuse attempts to explain through the concept of "repressive tolerance."

The present experience of the homosexual, in particular the liberal tolerance of which I have already written, seems to bear out all Marcuse's fears of "repressive desublimation," that is, greater apparent freedom but a freedom manipulated into acceptable channels. Thus most of the Western world has abolished legal restrictions against homosexuality while maintaining social prejudices. It is instructive to examine the position of the homosexual in the Netherlands, a society often held up as a model of enlightenment, to realize the falsity of the idea that existing bourgeois society has in fact permitted full personal liberation.

In an article with the typical snideness of most that deal with homosexuality, *Newsweek* described Amsterdam in 1968 as the "Mecca of homosexuals." What this means in practice however is that homosexuals are not bothered by the police and that they are allowed to meet freely in their own clubs and organizations. Men may dance with men and women with women—but only in certain specified places, and attempts to break this down have led to scuffles, for example at a dance in The Hague in May 1970. Some extremely progressive social measures, for example in regard to housing, have been achieved. Yet the entire bias of the media and of education remains heterosexual—Dutch schools, for example, do not teach the equal validity of homosexual and heterosexual love—and the prevailing social climate is one of tolerance rather than acceptance. Opinion polls have shown that dislike of homosexuality remains strong, so it is not surprising that other studies have revealed that Dutch homosexuals, particularly teenagers, are oppressed by the same feelings of guilt and social ostracism as are American or Australian ones.

"Repressive tolerance" underlies contemporary permissiveness. Sex in our time has become increasingly used as a commodity and the first principle of advertising appears to be to imply that your product enhances sex appeal. It takes little imagination to see how this helps maintain the capitalist need for continuing production: "If you work hard and earn lots of money then you too can have a beautiful man or woman," is the barely concealed message. Indeed we are so programmed into accepting fashionable standards of beauty that the more permissive the society becomes—meaning the more that standardized bodies are displayed—the more discontented we become with the inevitable flaws of our own, and our lovers' bodies, and the more unable to perceive any beauty in those unlike the current stereotype.

But the gap between sexual freedom and repressed eroticism is wider. "In America," Kate Millett has said, "you can either fuck or shake hands," and this sums up the situation. The ability to feel, to hold, to embrace, to take comfort from the warmth of other human beings is sadly lacking; we look for it in the artificial situations of encounter groups rather than accepting it in our total lives. From the rock musical *Salvation:*

> If you let me make love to you
> Then why can't I touch you…

Perhaps there lies the difference between sex and eroticism.

The cartoonist Jules Feiffer is reported to have said that "the love ethic went to Chicago, was polarized and came out as the fuck ethic" and it is certainly true that the permissive society with its high component of voyeurism, sexual objectification, and "dildo journalism" is hardly a liberated one. Nonetheless I am less sure than Marcuse that growing sexual freedom is totally illusionary. Without it movements like women's and gay liberation could hardly have come into being. It is necessary now to transform sexuality into eroticism; as Marcuse writes in *Eros and Civilization,* there must be "not simply a release but a *transformation* of the libido: from sexuality constrained under genital supremacy to erotization of the entire personality. It is a spread rather than an explosion of libido—a spread over private and societal relations which bridges the gap maintained between them by a repressive reality principle."

Liberation would involve a resurrection of our original impulse to take enjoyment from the total body, and indeed to accept the seeking of sensual enjoyment as an end in itself, free from procreation or status enhancement. To quote Marcuse again: "The full force of civilized morality was mobilized against the use of the body as mere object, means, instrument of pleasure: such reification was tabooed and remained the ill-reputed privilege of whores, degenerates and perverts." Which is why whores, degenerates, and perverts become the new antiheroes and heroines of books such as *Last Exit to Brooklyn.* There are, I think, some reservations to Marcuse's argument which he partly avoids by the sheer abstractness of his writing. That is, if there were in fact an erotization of the entire personality this would act *against* the use of the body "as mere object, means, instrument of pleasure." A concept of liberation that involves a transformation of the libido would not, I would argue, include sex based solely on the objectification of the body. (The clearest example of this is necrophilia but it would also include bestiality and some forms of sadomasochism, and indeed much of the depersonalized sex of the permissive society.) Sex would be seen as a means of expanding contact and creating community with other persons, and would demand some reciprocity other than the purely physical. Sex as much as everyday life would be eroticized and would become a means of human communication rather than purely physical gratification or consummation of a sacred union. One of the implications of this, of course, is that sexual activity among children would be encouraged rather than, as now, frowned on.

Affirmation of the total body involves, as Norman O. Brown puts it in *Life against Death,* "a union with others and with the world around us based not on anxiety and aggression but on narcissism and erotic exuberance." It involves, too, an acceptance of the "funkiness" of the body, a rejection of the plastic, odorless, hairless, and blemishless creations of *Playboy* and its homosexual equivalents, and a new sense of play and spontaneity, a move toward what Brown, perhaps unfortunately, called "a science of enjoyment rather than a science of accumulation." "The underground," claims Richard Neville in *Play Power* is "turning sex back into play."

Paul Goodman has suggested that the homosexual has, in fact, already partly achieved this:

A happy property of sexual acts, and perhaps especially of homosexual acts, is that they are dirty, like life: as Augustine said, *"inter urinas et feces nascitur."* In a society as middle-class, orderly and technological as ours, it is essential to break down squeamishness, which is an important factor in what is called racism, as well as in cruelty to children and the sterile putting away of the sick and aged. Also, the illegal and catch-as-catch-can nature of many homosexual acts at present breaks down other conventional attitudes. Although I wish I could have had many a party with less apprehension and more unhurriedly—we would have enjoyed them more— yet it has been an advantage to learn that the ends of docks, the backs of trucks, back alleys, behind the stairs, abandoned bunkers on the beach and the washrooms of trains are all adequate samples of all the space there is. For both good and bad, homosexual behaviour retains some of the alarm and excitement of childish sexuality.

Undoubtedly there is a positive side to the sordidness of traditional gaylife, in that it represents an acceptance of sexuality in a way that perhaps fewer heterosexuals have experienced. There is a positive side to casual sex, particularly when it is free of the guilt so pervasive in the sort of encounters Goodman writes about, and *some* "one-night stands" can be rewarding, just as *some* lasting relationships can be disastrous. I am certainly not extolling some new form of puritanism that would deny the possibility of transitory sexual encounters nor would I want to uphold monogamy as either necessary or, indeed, desirable. Casual sex can be a good way of getting to know people though it is hardly sufficient. Goodman was attacked in *Come Out!* by the poet Milani for advocating "lust without the rhythms of Eros," and the accusation has some point. Promiscuity, even selective, hardly equals liberation, nor is the ability to appreciate the varieties of human eroticism—unlike Reich, I am a firm believer in nonorgasmic sex in certain situations, and the extension of sexual play to large areas of life appears to me a necessary part of liberation—a substitute for the creation of real relationships.

Nonetheless we need to move toward a full acceptance of the erotic qualities of humankind and of the many different kinds and levels of sexual encounters that are possible. As part of this an acceptance of our basic androgyny is needed. To turn again to Brown: "The 'magical' body which the poet seeks is the 'subtle' or 'spiritual' or 'translucent' body of occidental mysticism, and the 'diamond' body of oriental mysticism, and in psychoanalysis the polymorphous perverse body of childhood. Thus, for example, psychoanalysis declares the fundamentally bisexual nature of human nature; Boehme insists on the androgynous character of human perfection; Taoist mysticism invokes feminine passivity to counteract masculine aggressivity; and Rilke's poetic quest is a quest for a hermaphroditic body." There is a danger in Brown of the realities of the body dissolving into metaphysical flights, so that his concept of polymorphous perversity becomes ultimately an asexual one and he seems to envisage this not as a move to expand sexuality from its obsessive genitality but rather as the total supplanting of that genitality. It is often, indeed, difficult to relate Brown's writings to the real world of sexuality in which bodies tend to impose on us in more than "spiritual" or "translucent" ways. Nor am I as concerned as he to break down all differences between the sexes. Although liberation certainly demands an end to the false dichotomies imposed by social roles, removal of these dichotomies will not by itself end our repression of bisexuality; as will be discussed in a later chapter, the apparent blurring of sex roles among, say, hippies does not necessarily mean any greater acceptance by them of homosexuality. Yet the existence of these dichotomies and the repression of bisexuality are of course interrelated. In an article on the importance of feminism Theodore Roszak observes: "The woman most desperately in need of liberation is the 'woman' every man has locked up in the dungeons of his own psyche. *That* is the basic act of oppression that still waits to be undone, though the undoing might well produce the most cataclysmic reinterpretation of the sexual roles and of sexual 'normalcy' in all human history." And, equally, there is need to unlock the "man" every woman has in the dungeons of *her* psyche.

With liberation, homosexuality and heterosexuality would cease to be viewed as separate conditions, the former being a perversion of the latter, but would be seen rather as components of us all. Liberation would also, as women's liberation theorists have pointed out, mean an end to the nuclear family as the central organizing principle of our society. It would not, emphatically, mean an end to the importance of human relationships, although it would suggest an end to legalizing them, to compulsory monogamy and possessiveness, to the assumption, often echoed by homosexuals, that it is "natural" to divide up into couples who live isolated by and large from other couples. Perhaps it is our cult of acquisitiveness that makes us feel that love needs to be rationed. I suspect, in contrast to such a view, that the more one gives the more one is replenished, and that humans are capable of many more love relationships, both sexual and nonsexual, than social norms prescribe. It is this realization among young people that underlies the considerable experimentation with communal living that is already occurring.

In a situation of liberation there would develop radical changes in the attitude toward bearing and rearing children, changes related—but only in part—to the fact that for the first time in human history it is technologically possible to control childbirth.

Brown, relying largely on Nietzsche, argues that the desire for children is often a product of suffering, of a need to reject oneself. "Joy," he quotes Nietzsche as saying, "does not want heirs or children—joy wants itself, wants eternity, wants recurrence, wants everything eternally the same." Free from a sense of guilt and of the social pressures toward procreation, with a decline too in the institution of the patriarchal and monogamous family structure, one might expect both a substantial number of women to consciously decide against having children and, conversely, an increase in communal child-rearing which would involve nonparent adults, including homosexuals. Both for society—which faces the specter of overpopulation—and for individual children, who hardly benefit from the smothering effect of the present family, the changes would be an improvement. "Being sole focus of attention for an adult who has little to worry about but your psyche is too much burden for an adult, let alone a small child," Marge Piercy argued in the first issue of the radical quarterly *Defiance*. There are great advantages for children in communal living, representing as it does a compromise between the tyranny of overpossessive parents and the repression of the typical educational system. It is also probably the only really effective way to break down the sex role sterotypes into which the family structure tends to force us. The idea that a child "belongs" to his parents is a logical extension of the cult of property, only exceeded in horror by the concept that the child "belongs" to the state.

Ultimately, as Marcuse insists, liberation implies a new biological person, one "no longer capable of tolerating the aggressiveness, brutality and ugliness of the established way of life." Speaking to the 1967 Congress of the Dialectics of Liberation, Marcuse argued that this new person would be "a man [one assumes also a woman] who rejects the performance principles governing the established societies; a type of man who has rid himself of the aggressiveness and brutality that are inherent in the organization of established society, and in their hypocritical, puritan morality; a type of man who is biologically incapable of fighting wars and creating suffering; a type of man who has a good conscience of joy and pleasure, and who works collectively and individually for a social and natural environment in which such an existence becomes possible." And elaborating on this in *An Essay on Liberation,* he argues that as such new men [women] appear, they will redefine the objectives and the strategy of the political structure.

Those who seek to relate sexual to total liberation tend often to argue that the two are interdependent in some chicken-and-egg manner. This has been put strongly by the gay revolutionary socialist group, the Red Butterfly, who claim: "To break our chains and become free we are going to have to work for fundamental changes in the institutions which oppress us, such as the existing family system with its web of supports: male chauvinism, sex typing of personality traits and arbitrary labels such as 'gay' and 'straight.' But to change any one basic institution will require changes in related ones. Change in family patterns would mean changes in education, in the economy, in laws, etc. This will mean coming up against vested interests, those who gain at the expense of our oppression. It will mean a struggle to free ourselves." In the Red Butterfly perspective, the upshot would be some genuine form of socialism.

It seems to me that the connection between sexual liberation and total liberation should be made somewhat differently. Liberation is a process that individuals strive toward, and part of this striving involves a recognition of the way in which oppression is implanted in the very structures of our society. To overcome the stigma society places on homosexuality, for example, requires radical alterations in the way in which we order the socialization process. More than this, as individuals come to a greater acceptance of their erotic/sexual being they tend spontaneously to reject the "performance principle" that underlies the dominant ethos of property, competition, and aggression. Thus, between individual and social liberation there is a dialectic relationship, and as Marcuse puts it in his *Essay on Liberation* "radical change in consciousness is the beginning, the first step in changing social existence: emergence of the new Subject." (Brown's views on the other hand seem to me less acceptable, for he seems to posit a personal liberation within a social vacuum.) Only a socialism highly flavored by anarchism would seem to me consistent with sexual liberation, for conventional notions of socialism do not contain sufficient protection for the individual vis-à-vis the collective. One might note, however, that individual rights are not the same as property rights, and that those who most ardently extol the latter are often those most willing to impinge on the former.

One of the most important early statements of the gay movement was Carl Wittman's "The Gay Manifesto," where he argues—a position with which I would basically agree—that a change in individual consciousness is a basic requirement for any qualitative social change. To talk of liberation for others, i.e. society, is meaningless until we have come to grips with the meaning of liberation for ourselves. In terms of social actuality I find most persuasive the argument of the American antipsychiatrist Jo Berke in *Counter-Culture* that:

As more and more groups associate with each other we shall see the large-scale creation of "liberated zones" within bourgeois society, who will have the same relationship to themselves and established institutions as "liberated areas" of Mozambique and Vietnam have to each other and to the Portuguese or Americans.

Such "liberated zones" will be defined, however, more by a shared consciousness than a geographic base, although the commune movement attempts to combine the two.

One last point, and here I may seem to be contradicting myself: any theory of liberation needs to take into account the problem of aggression. I have already argued that much violence is the product of repression and that the disappearance of the latter would lead to a sharp decline in the former. Yet just as I would argue that there are instincts other than the sexual with which we need come to terms, so I would argue that an end to repression does not automatically mean an end to human aggression. Aggression is partly a product of sexual restraints and of socially imposed sex roles, but it most likely has an existence within the individual independently of these two factors. What I would argue is that liberation both from sex role stereotypes that force men to prove their masculinity through violence and from the repression of erotic impulses that both sexes are taught to restrain would make the management of human aggression far easier than it now is. Liberation does not imply some insipid state of languid flowerdom. Yet if we were less hung-up sexually, aggression might be expressed not through guns, wars, and suicidal automobile driving—remember all those pop songs about "chicken" drivers—but through less violent means, perhaps through increased creativity or, as Goodman seems to hope, through raucous play and athletics. (The play, one hopes, would be individual feats like Horatio's bike ride in *Empire City*, or communal activities, like the street softball match in *Making Do*, rather than the authoritarian and conformist qualities of competitive spectator sports.) It is impossible to know to what extent aggression is innate or a product of particular social forms and economic scarcity. It would be dishonest to say otherwise.

I argued at the beginning of this chapter that gay liberation as a concept makes sense only within a broader context. Yet my concern is basically with the homosexual, and the move from tolerance to acceptance. While one would expect a liberated society to regard bisexuality as the norm, this view would not mean that all persons would behave bisexually—or at least not in the symmetrical way suggested by Gore Vidal when he wrote that "it is possible to have a mature sexual relationship with a woman on Monday, and a mature sexual relationship with a man on Tuesday, and perhaps on Wednesday have both together." The nonrepressed person recognizes his bisexual potential; he is not some ideal person midway along the Kinsey behavioral scale. People would still fall in love and form relationships, and these relationships would be homosexual as well as heterosexual. What would be different is that the social difference between the two would vanish, and once this happened we would lose the feeling of being limited, of having to choose between an exclusively straight or exclusively gayworld. The lack of any available sense of identity for the bisexual in present society, and the pressures on him and her from both sides—for bisexuality threatens the exclusive homo- as much as heterosexual—probably explains why it is relatively uncommon. Given a change in social repression we would all be less uptight about the whole thing and probably accept some experimentation with each sex as natural.

Liberation would mean the end of the gayworld as we now know it, with its high premium on momentary and furtive contacts. It would involve a breakdown of the barriers between male and female homosexuals, and between gays and straights. Masculinity and femininity would cease to be sharply differentiated categories, and one would expect an end to the homosexual parodies of role playing in the cult of leather and of drag. The nuclear family would come to be seen as only one form of possible social organization, not as the norm from which everything else seems a deviation. This would mean an end not only to the oppression of gays, but major changes in general consciousness. Sexuality, once it became fully accepted, would be joyful, spontaneous, and erotic, and with that one could hope for a withering away of both *Playboy* and Leagues of Decency. Above all liberation implies a new diversity, an acceptance of the vast possibilities of human experience and an end to the attempt to channel these possibilities into ends sanctioned by religious and economic guidelines.

If homosexuals cannot achieve full sexual liberation within society as it exists, for this can only be achieved through a revolutionary change in both social attitudes and structures, they can achieve liberation from at least much of the internal oppression imposed by social stereotypes and roles. To overcome this is not sufficient for liberation, but it is an essential step toward it for those who have been so deeply stigmatized. And by overcoming this part of their stigma homosexuals are able to move toward liberation, as well, from the restraints of sex roles and the repression of eroticism.

One cannot prescribe liberation, for it arises out of the individual consciousness and demands a greater sense both of autonomy and of community than at present exists. Above all there is need for a new sense of sister- and brotherhood, a willingness to fully accept one's own erotic and sexual being, and an attempt to form new sorts of human relationships. It may indeed be profitable to regard liberation as a process rather than an attainable goal, to regard the writings of men like Marcuse and Brown as providing us with aims for which we strive. Liberation does not mean an end to struggle, but it does alter the ends for and the means by which we struggle.

4. The Movement and Liberation: Confrontation and the Community

As with all social movements, much about gay liberation is ephemeral; organizations are formed and collapse, newspapers cease to appear, people drift away to new preoccupations. Much of the detailed material that is available on gay liberation movements is now superseded; in many cases there is little contact between groups in different countries, particularly where there is a language barrier. Yet the cry "Out of the closets and into the streets" that emerged in America in the summer of 1969 has spread through most of Western Europe, Canada, Australasia, and parts of Latin America and has affected far more people than those who have participated directly in the gay movement. There exist already several accounts of the American gay liberation movement. I am concerned however with the basic direction and activity of the movement, in London, Toronto, and Melbourne as much as in New York or Los Angeles, and when I speak of organizations and incidents it is mainly to illustrate the wider points I wish to make.

I start with two incidents that occurred in New York at the end of summer 1970. They are not in themselves particularly remarkable; similar incidents have since occurred in a number of countries. Their main interest for the present discussion is that they illustrate many of the issues important to any analysis of the gay liberation movement and its significance. Both revolved around New York University whose campus surrounds Washington Square, of which Henry James wrote: "This part of New York appears to many people the most delectable. It has a kind of established repose which is not of frequent occurrence in other quarters of the long, shrill city; it has a riper, richer, more honorable look than any of the upper ramifications of the great longitudinal thoroughfares—the look of having had something of a social history." The Square, too, is the focal point of the West Village often, like Earl's Court in London, referred to as a "gay ghetto," and indeed New York University is encountering in its relations with the gay community some of the same tensions that Harlem has presented to another New York campus, Columbia.

In September, then, two confrontations took place involving the university and the "community." The first was a good example of the direct action that gay groups were increasingly undertaking and involved the university only peripherally, as a peace rally was being held there featuring Mayor John Lindsay. Now while John Lindsay was well known as a liberal, a model example indeed of Spiro Agnew's "radical liberals," his popularity was declining among more radical homosexuals who were not particularly impressed by the city's liberality toward them. Over the summer, as gay militancy had increased, so too had police harassment. Bars used by homosexuals were raided frequently on all sorts of pretexts and during August over 300 homosexuals were arrested on charges such as loitering, disorderly conduct, unlawful assembly, and soliciting. One of the results was a large rally and march that led to some street fighting in the Village on the last weekend of August. More recently, even that most respectable of organizations, the Daughters of Bilitis, had been bothered by police harassment.

How far Lindsay was to blame for this was uncertain; it is my view that his control over the police force was shaky and he wished to avoid any public showdown that would demonstrate this. It was alleged however that the mayor had been unsympathetic to homosexual complaints and certainly he had been virtually inaccessible to gay organizations seeking an end to harassment.

Thus it was decided to "zap" the mayor, that is, directly confront him at the meeting. This decision was made at the weekly meeting of the Gay Activists Alliance, a group that had broken away from the Gay Liberation Front, after disagreement with the Front's support for the Panthers. About 150 people were present at this meeting, most of them men and young but a handful of gay women as well, and almost all of them traveled down to Washington Square to confront Lindsay.

But this was 1970, and New York University had some experience with campus disorder. When the group arrived shortly before Lindsay himself they found the doors barred; all seats, said the police at the door, were taken. The Gay Activists circled the building, uncertain what to do next, while inside the hall students and earnest workers for peace listened to a folksinger fill in until the mayor arrived.

His arrival, accompanied by several siren-shrieking police cars, was hardly inconspicuous, even by American standards, but he slipped through the circling gays. A flash of his toothpaste smile at the demonstrators and he was inside the hall. But one of the GAA members managed to get inside and onto the podium. At such a well-behaved gathering—John Lindsay's people are, after all, not Mayor Daley's—the reaction was surprise more than anything else, and the GAA member was able to read a prepared statement in which he detailed the gay complaints of harassment and called on the Mayor to reply.

"I believe everyone has the right to express their grievances," said Lindsay on his return to the mike, and then proceeded with his speech as planned, with a few vague references to the need for orderly protest and his desire to meet all dissenting groups. Outside, the Gay Activists had formed picket lines at all entrances: "Answer the question... Answer the question," they chanted. And "Gay, gay power to the gay, gay people." As Lindsay left they surrounded his car, chanting, yelling, angry and jubilant both. The mayor drove off with a final toothpaste smile for the newsmen. End of incident one, which, though minor, was something that would not have occurred two years earlier. (Two years later, when seeking the Democratic presidential nomination, John Lindsay was to firmly support gay rights.)

The next week gay militants were back at New York University, but this time in direct confrontation with the university. Over the summer, the university's Gay Students League had arranged to sponsor dances in a residence hall, open to the surrounding community. The university intervened to stop this on the grounds that it had first to determine whether homosexuality was "a valid lifestyle," and talked of impressionable first-year students who would presumably be impressed by all those men and men, and women and women dancing together.

Given the new mood among homosexuals, this was a red flag for action: "Out of the closets and into the streets." A few of the university's gay students sought help from the Gay Liberation Front's regular Sunday night meeting, and once again there was almost unanimous response. The result was a week-long sit-in in the basement of the residence hall where the dance was to be held. The group occupying the basement was joined by local homosexuals, some sympathetic students, and street people, the general term used to describe kids without permanent homes who spend much of their time on the streets. The occupiers were almost all young and numbered perhaps a hundred over the course of the week.

At which point the situation became somewhat confused. It appeared for a time that the university had handed over the power to decide the issue to the residents of the hall, who duly decided to let the dance go ahead and to support an occupation until after the dance. Someone in the school administration, however, apparently changed his mind and on the afternoon before the dance was scheduled a number of men from the Tactical Police Force arrived at the basement and demanded its immediate evacuation. Faced with forty or so armed men, the kids remaining in the basement went away.

But not very far. As they gathered outside the dorm—girls in granny glasses and long hair, boys unshaven in boots and jeans, street people in an exotic mixture of elaborate and casual garb— they began to attract a crowd. By early evening several hundred people, largely local gays, were milling around on the street and a decision was made to march to Christopher Street, home of the street people and symbolic focus of the gay protest movement since the riots of the previous summer at the Stonewall bar out of which had sprung the Gay Liberation Front.

Arm-in-arm, hand-in-hand, led by the street transvestites (of whom more later) they marched down Eighth Street, ogled and gaped at by passing tourists and shoppers and accompanied by the Tactical Police Force. "Join us, join us," they chanted at the passersby and, yes, along the way people slipped into the line, some of them veterans of other gay marches, some of them making their first public commitment as homosexuals, some sympathetic straights. ("Why are we marching?" hissed one girl as she flung her arms around two of the boys.) Down they went past the corner of Sixth Avenue, where the sellers of Black Panther and Young Lords newspapers gave a salute of greeting; left opposite the Women's House of Detention ("Free our Sisters" called the marchers); into Christopher Street where campaigners for Bella Abzug, who was running for Congress, flashed peace signs. They were herded along by the tight-mouthed, short-haired members of the Tactical Police Force, a couple of whom seemed to be fingering their night sticks as if in contemplative masturbation.

Then back to the dorm, but this time on the street rather than the sidewalk. But the drive, if not the anger, was going out of the protest, despite a short burst of spasmodic chants: "Gay Power!" and "Today's pig is tomorrow's bacon!" Still there was real fury in that crowd, and none were angrier than the street transvestites, victims of constant police harassment and of ridicule by the straight (and often the gay) world, part-time hustlers, united by a strong sense of mutual love and suddenly up there in front, marshaling the protesters and now accepted by men who would have put them down only a week ago as "street queens." But the fury lacked direction, for no one knew what to do next.

So when the police ordered the crowd to disperse it did, drifting off to cafés and beds and the nearby Alternate University. Over the weekend large meetings of radical gays were held to work out future action. These meetings were notable for the numbers they attracted and for the increased feeling of solidarity. There was an erosion of at least some of the tension between various groups in the movement, and more significantly the continued acceptance of the street transvestites as a key part of the gay liberation movement symbolized by the formation of a new group, the Street Transvestite Action Revolutionaries, made up, largely, of street people. With time, however, doubts would be raised among members of the Gay Liberation Front as to whether transvestism was not really just another form of sexism, a parody of straight society's concept of sex roles.

But despite fiery rhetoric at the weekend meetings, a planned demonstration the following Monday at New York University and at the New York University-operated Bellevue Hospital (referred to, in gay literature, as "a butcher shop," "a psychiatric prison") attracted very few people. Half-hearted attempts to win the support of the student body foundered on the almost total ignorance among the organizers of the campus scene and despite sympathetic coverage in the student newspaper, the question of the university's attitude to homosexuality quietly submerged with apparently little trace.

Not entirely, however, for the university took enough notice of the incident to initiate contacts with the Gay Students League to discuss "gay studies," and its School of Continuing Education now offers a course entitled "Homosexuality: A Contemporary View." One only hopes that those administrators who were uncertain about the "validity" of the homosexual life-style are attending the course to find out. Thus the original issue of allowing dances on university property had acted as a catalyst for other much more far-reaching issues that questioned the whole nature of homosexual oppression in American society and the way in which this oppression is maintained. The people who participated developed a view that went beyond the original civil libertarian position to one that identified their oppression as furthered and legitimized through the structures of society, of which universities are, of course, an important part. Demands were made of New York University that went far beyond the dance, and included the introduction of "gay studies" and "open enrollment and free tuition for gay people and all people from the communities New York oppresses." The first seems to me to make some sense in view of the education system's role in the oppression of homosexuality. The second does not, as gay people per se do not suffer the same sort of inferior schooling as ethnic minorities. The events affected not only the university; more importantly they radicalized those few hundred people, predominantly of course homosexual, who became involved.

The Movement Has Many Forms

While such incidents have become much more common since 1969–70, they do not mark the beginning of homosexual organizations in America nor even the first use of militant tactics by such organizations. It is not my intention to write a history of the movement; there is a short one contained in the collection edited by Ralph Weltge, *The Same Sex,* and an unconsciously very funny one, complete with hints at international conspiracies, in R. E. L. Masters' *The Homosexual Revolution*. But it will be useful to trace the change in perspectives within the developing homosexual movement.

Apart from the possibly apocryphal Sons of Hamidy and the euphemistically named Bachelors-for-Wallace (Henry, not George), the first important American homophile group, the Mattachine Society, was founded in California in 1948. This was an important year for homosexuals, for it also saw the appearance of the Kinsey Report—*Sexual Behavior in the Human Male*. In the furore that the report caused, the figures that perhaps most shocked, confronted, and titillated Americans were that 37 percent of white American males had had at least one overt homosexual experience to the point of orgasm; 18 percent had as much homosexual as heterosexual experience over a period of at least three years; while 4 percent were exclusively homosexual. Whatever meaning one chooses to ascribe to such figures, for the homosexual they served to break down the fear of total isolation.

The postwar period was one of increasing liberality toward sex, and even some of the taboos against homosexuality seemed to be relaxing. "For perhaps ten years after World War II," wrote Leslie Fiedler in *Love and Death in the American Novel*, "the work of such fictionists as Capote and Carson McCullers profited by a detente in the middle-class, middlebrow war against homosexuality ..." To which list should be added Gore Vidal (*The City and the Pillar* appeared in 1949), James Baldwin (*Giovanni's Room*, 1956), and Tennessee Williams, plus the rather maudlin, yet important, personal account, *The Homosexual in America* (1951) by Donald Cory.

Not surprisingly the homophile movement grew, albeit slowly— this was, after all, the time of McCarthyite purges—and Mattachine was joined by One, Inc. and the specifically lesbian Daughters of Bilitis. Like the early organizations of the civil rights movement, these groups were marked by caution, moderation, and, often, a sense of their own inferiority. (The movement had its Booker T. Washingtons in those who saw themselves as pathological, and sought to adjust to this.) The fifties were the era of Eisenhower, of the man in the grey flannel suit, and, above all, the early groups sought to show that they too were respectable, that homosexuals could live restrained lives in station-wagon suburbia. Their emphasis was on individual counseling and assistance, although One, Inc. occasionally went beyond this, as in the article they published by Norman Mailer, "The Homosexual Villain." Another similarity with the early civil rights movement was the emphasis on winning church support; in California the Council on Religion and the Homosexual was established to provide such support. (California has also produced more recently the Reverend Troy Perry whose Metropolitan Community Church, set amidst the pink bungalows and gay bars of flatlands Hollywood, skillfully combines high camp religion with a muted assertion of gay rights. Perry himself tends to be far more militant than his congregation and has participated in demonstrations with the Californian Gay Liberation Front.)

The sixties saw a decline in the apathy of Disneyland-America, and even homophile organizations benefited. Not only did their numbers grow—the major addition perhaps being the Society for Individual Rights in San Francisco which used social events to build up a large membership—but the groups became more open and more militant. The Mattachine Society of Washington, under the lead of Dr. Frank Kameny, began to directly confront federal government discrimination against homosexuals; in 1966 a group in Los Angeles, led by Henry Hay, organized a motorcade to protest exclusion of homosexuals from the armed forces.

But the militancy had not yet reached the point of liberation: homosexuals were still seeking integration into society, the right to work for the Defense Department in Washington or serve it abroad. There was still a certain apologetic tone, as if homosexuals were agreeing that homosexuality was abnormal, while pleading to be given a chance to show others just how square—if not straight—they could be. Men like Kameny and Hay deserve enormous admiration for their courage in publicly coming out and organizing other homosexuals. Their style, however, was that of a pressure group rather than of a movement for liberation.

In 1968 the fourth annual meeting of the North American Conference of Homophile Organizations, with some two dozen affiliated groups, adopted as its slogan "Gay is Good" and by 1969, Edward Sagarin has estimated, there were some 150 organized homophile groups in America. But by 1969 these groups seemed suddenly supplanted. Simultaneously, and apparently independently of each other, gay liberation groups emerged in California and New York.

In San Francisco the Committee for Homosexual Freedom was founded, and became quickly involved in direct action after one of its founders, Gale Whittington, had been fired from a shipping company because a photo of him hugging another man had appeared in the *Berkeley Barb*. The company was picketed, and this was soon followed by demonstrations against the San Francisco *Examiner* because of the way in which it referred to homosexuals, and by a sit-in at the mayor's office. Under the impact of events in San Francisco a gay liberation movement was launched across the Bay in Berkeley.

That summer there occurred in New York the Stonewall Riot—the Boston Tea Party, as it were, of the movement. The Stonewall was a homosexual dance bar on Christopher Street, and the riots took place over a period of three days, following a police raid over alleged infringement of the liquor laws. This was a common occurrence: what was unusual was that the customers fought back. Not only that, but they shouted their pride in being gay. It seems possible indeed that the slogan "Gay Power" was born here, opposite the small square commemorating General Sheridan and now nighthome for the old and alone, and for the street people.

Sheridan Square this weekend looked like something from a William Bur-roughs novel as the sudden specter of "gay power" erected its brazen head and spat out a fairy tale the likes of which the area has never seen.

The forces of faggotry, spurred by a Friday night raid on one of the city's largest, most popular, and longest lived gay bars, the Stonewall Inn, rallied Saturday night in an unprecedented protest against the raid and continued Sunday night to assert presence, possibility, and pride until the early hours of Monday morning. "I'm a faggot, and I'm proud of it!" "Gay Power!" "I like boys!"—these and many other slogans were heard all three nights as the show of force by the city's finery met the force of the city's finest. The result was a kind of liberation, as the gay brigade emerged from the bars, back rooms, and bedrooms of the Village and became street people. (Lucien Truscott IV, "Gay Power Comes to Sheridan Square," *Village Voice*, 3 July 1969)

It was amidst the exuberance that followed the riots—they began, almost too symbolic a coincidence, the day Judy Garland, favorite of so many "queens," was buried—that the New York Gay Lib-eration Front was founded. By November the newspaper *Come Out!* had begun to appear.

With the emergence of gay liberation, the movement was deci-sively changed. It would be tedious for the reader and near impos-sible for an author to trace the splits, the regroupings, and above all the growth of gay liberation groups since their beginning three years ago in the Bay area and New York. There are groups iden-tifying with gay liberation in such unlikely places as Tallahassee, Florida, and Lawrence, Kansas; since 1970 numerous gay liberation papers have appeared, more or less regularly. In universities and colleges gay student organizations have sprung up with enormous rapidity and there is now a National Gay Student Center financed partly by the American National Student Association.

Nor has there been any corresponding decline in old-line groups; if anything they have been strengthened by the new. Yet between, say, San Francisco's Society for Individual Rights or the Mattachine Society on the one hand and the gay liberation groups on the other, are large and significant differences.

The basic difference is not, as is often implied, just one of militancy. Certainly the gay liberation groups are prepared to take a militant position—to picket, demonstrate, fight back—but this is becoming true also of some of the more traditional groups who have been forced into revising their methods under the pressure of events. The basic difference is rather that gay liberation advances beyond the civil rights liberalism of the earlier groups; it is in some ways what Black Power is to the civil rights movement. No longer is the claim made that gay people can fit into American society, that they are as decent, as patriotic, as clean-living as anyone else. Rather, it is argued, it is American society itself that needs to change. Not everyone who identifies with gay liberation would accept the vision of liberation outlined in the previous chapter. None would deny that liberation implies change going far beyond the vision of the older groups.

Like groups espousing Black Power or women's liberation, the gay movement is directed both inwards and outwards: inwards to its own constituency, ranging from drag queens and butch dykes to businessmen terrified of discovery and ageing women unable to face the sexual foundations of their friendships; and outwards to society at large. The earliest groups tended to act as mutual-support groups for homosexuals who half believed the stereotypes about themselves; during the sixties there was a development toward more open demands, even confrontation and protest against social discrimination. But gay liberation represents a new self-affirmation and a determination that if anyone will be "cured," it is those who oppress rather than those oppressed. As Tom Maurer, then president of the Society for Individual Rights wrote: "What they (the gay liberationists) are doing is declaring themselves for what they are—human beings, persons, to be sure, with certain sexual proclivities, but courageous people who are beginning adult life being themselves—unwilling to live a life that is a lie. I admire and respect them more than I can say."

The older groups were always conscious of the need to create a favorable public image, one, that is, that portrayed homosexuals as appropriately "manly" or "feminine"—no drag queens or braless girls in jeans for *them*—just as the civil rights groups were scared of "bad niggers," insisting always that given the chance no one could be better citizens, more patriotic, more WASP-like than the Negro with an integrated education and the right to vote. Gay liberationists, like black radicals before them, have reversed this: there is almost perverse delight in playing up to the stereotypical image, of shocking rather than persuading society.

> BLATANT IS BEAUTIFUL!
>   Oh, how I love that saying! The Age of Blatantness is up on/in us Brothers and Sisters. Take a stand and show your Fairy Wings or Construction Helmets!...
>   Straight society is really down on Blatant Gays, and that affects and oppresses all Gay people, because Gays won't be treated as beautiful human beings until even the most "Flaming Faggots" and "Diesel Dykes" are respected in our community, as well as in Straight society...
>   It's time, NOW, for ALL Gay people to stand up and kick out the JAM. Straights have ruled us too long. It's time to be YOURSELF! Don't blend in with Straight people—that's oppressing yourself.
>   BLATANT IS BEAUTIFUL!
>
> ("sister" Brian Chavez,
> *Gay Sunshine*, San Francisco, October 1970)

Now this attitude, in the view of the older groups, is self-defeating, and so it is if one believes that homosexuals can win their rights within the existing social framework. To the traditionalists the model for action might be that of trade unionists or farmers: organize, prove ourselves, according to accepted community standards, and we, too, will get our share of the cake. If, however, one accepts the far more radical analysis already suggested, that only a total transformation of society will free the homosexual, then the kind of calculus involved in working within the system no longer makes sense. This acceptance has two major implications: that there is a need for alliance with other alienated groups and a need to transform the consciousness of homosexuals, to develop the revolutionary potential that I have already suggested is inherent in our condition. For without such a transformation homosexuals will remain too much the prisoners of old stereotypes and guilts to seek either personal or social liberation.

Obviously there is no absolute distinction between the two positions; in practice a Mattachine Society and a gay liberation group might do similar things. Further, few individuals in the movement are likely to adopt rigid stances: even conservatives have experienced the oppression that goes beyond law reform, and radicals are aware that there are real, if insufficient, benefits to be derived from certain legal changes (though if Chicago and London are any guide, not very much from merely ending the antisodomy laws). Essentially, however, gay liberation, to a much greater extent than is true of the older homophile groups, is concerned with the assertion and creation of a new sense of identity, one based on pride in being gay.

There are enormous difficulties in forging a new identity, in overcoming an oppression as deeply internalized as is that of the homosexual. The very act of rejecting conventional social roles and norms is a disturbing one, and produces considerable confusion for both individuals and movements. Indeed the extent to which gay liberation means a revolutionary change in consciousness is demonstrated by the sheer messiness and sometimes apparent paranoia of its groups, and the fact that it attracts, as will any revolutionary movement, numbers of people seeking to resolve all sorts of personal difficulties. For this reason too its appeal to older homosexuals is likely to be much less, for they have already established an identity and a way of coping with the world. Indeed to such persons, gay liberation is as much a threat as it is to straight society, for it undermines the whole complex set of roles and social relationships they have built up. The real importance of gay liberation may be for those just realizing their homosexuality. A schoolboy I knew was greatly helped in accepting his gayness by listening to the gay radio programs now broadcast in New York and by reading the gay press. A few years earlier he would have had no other models to follow than the bland assurances of popular psychiatry that he would "grow out of it," or, perhaps worse, the masochistic self-hate of much gay literature. Moreover, gay liberation is not an organization, though there are many organizations which use its name; it is rather a state of consciousness, expressed thus in the first Gay Liberation Front statement as published in the first issue of *Come Out!*:

Gay Liberation is a revolutionary homosexual group of women and men formed with the realization that complete sexual liberation for all people cannot come about unless existing social institutions are abolished. We reject society's attempt to impose sexual roles and definitions on our nature. We are stepping outside of these roles and simplistic myths. WE ARE GOING TO BE WHO WE ARE. At the same time, we are creating new social forms and relations, that is, relations based upon brotherhood, co-operation, human love and uninhibited sexuality. Babylon has forced us to commit ourselves to one thing...revolution.

To illustrate the difference between the perspective of those whose model is essentially the liberal pressure group and those who adopt a more revolutionary attitude, one might contrast the two major "radical" gay groups in New York, the civil libertarian Gay Activists Alliance and the revolutionary Gay Liberation Front. The following description, though accurate as of early 1971, has changed considerably since then, but I am concerned to illustrate certain broad points rather than describe or analyse any particular organizations.

The Gay Activists Alliance is a hip, with-it, political pressure group, highly structured organizationally, and proclaiming itself "a militant (though nonviolent) homosexual civil rights movement," and as such it is a logical extension of the Mattachine Society. It has a strong sense of political realities, as befits an organization whose members enjoy politicking. Watching a GAA meeting in progress one feels that the leadership would, in other circumstances, have all been presidents of their student councils. Like the old-line groups, particularly the Washington and New York Mattachine Societies and the Society for Individual Rights, GAA is concerned with questions of tax laws, of fair employment, and of elections. GAA, as one might expect from a civil rights organization, has directed considerable energy to getting homosexuals to register to vote and to publicizing candidates' views on the homosexual issue. During the 1970 senatorial campaign, the three major candidates were invited to address GAA. Two of them sent representatives; the third, James Buckley, the Conservative party candidate and ultimate victor, conscious no doubt of all those antifaggot hard hats, refused the invitation.

In its political concerns, GAA is close to the old-line groups: the concept of organizing a homosexual voting bloc is an old one. (Mailer claims that when he was approached in the early fifties to write for *One,* they offered him the possibility of running for Congress with homosexual support.) The same conference meeting of homosexual organizations in 1968 that proclaimed "Gay is Good" also asked that all Congressional candidates should take a stand on homosexual rights. San Francisco's Society for Individual Rights has for several years mobilized homosexual voters, and in 1968 may—for, despite the pretensions of political scientists, one can never prove such things—have aided Alan Cranston to defeat Max Rafferty for the Senate. (Rafferty, then state superintendent of Public Instruction, had proclaimed that he would "oppose any change in the present laws against homosexuality except to make them more severe," and later followed this up with the statement: "I favor letting homosexuals serve in any branch of the government, after they have received proper medical and psychiatric treatment to remedy their sad affliction, and have been pronounced cured by competent medical authorities." These statements were widely publicized by the Society throughout the California gayworld.) The

Society for several years has also invited candidates for local offices to attend meetings and in 1970 even gave a testimonial dinner for Willie Brown, a black state assemblyman who has sought to end California's antisodomy laws.

The logical extension of pressure through the ballot box was the 1970 candidature of Dr. Kameny for election to Congress from the District of Columbia. As he received only 2,000 votes, one may say fairly safely that a majority of Washington's homosexuals did not vote gay. However at the 1972 Democratic Convention a number of openly gay delegates attended, and pushed—unsuccessfully—for a pro-gay platform. In both Canada and Australia overt homosexuals have also run for political office.

Where the Gay Activists Alliance differs from groups like Mattachine and SIR is in its far greater willingness to engage in direct action, such as the direct confrontation of Lindsay, and an earlier sit-in at Republican party state headquarters that led to the arrest and subsequent prosecution of a group known as the Rockefeller Five. The organization straddles a wide range of life-styles: a meeting will include both an elegant, fortyish man, hair carefully groomed and a voice modulated in the best tradition of Broadway, reporting on a successful raffle, *and* a twenty-year-old boy, in denim jeans and jacket announcing plans to confront television figure Dick Cavett or Mayor Lindsay.

Such diversity makes for a large membership, and so do the GAA dances which offer an alternative to the bars and bathhouses and draw very large numbers. (Since late 1971 GAA has had its own building in New York.) At least in part because of GAA pressure, laws have been introduced in New York's State Assembly and City Council to remove discrimination against homosexuals, and there has been a significant change in the attitude of the New York media to homosexuals, which of course affects the whole country. My comparative neglect of such traditional political activity is not meant to suggest that it is unimportant. A proliferation of groups, as sociologists are now coming to see, serves some purpose, and may indeed be a sign of health in a movement. Social movements, after all, serve expressive as well as instrumental ends and must cater to a wide variety of personalities and needs. That no one group can speak for "the homosexual"—one is reminded of Robert Penn Warren's plaintive question in the title of his book *Who Speaks for the Negro?*—is less important than the fact that different groups can cater for different sorts of homosexuals.

The style of the Gay Liberation Front is totally different. Members of the GLF are no more likely to describe theirs as a civil rights organization than is the Black Panther party. Their meetings, as is true of most in the (white) radical movement, are largely unstructured with a very heavy stress on personal declarations and revolutionary sentiment. Unlike GAA, which has rigid requirements for membership (including attendance at a number of meetings), GLF defines itself as open, unencumbered by structure, and as a movement rather than an organization.

Here, as in other features, GLF has borrowed consciously from the women's liberation movement. There is a strong feeling in both movements that traditional rules of debate and procedure tend both to polarize opinion and to preclude the shyer and less verbally agile from full participation. Thus devices are adopted like choosing chairmen or women by lot, rotating discussion around the room so that no one may speak twice until everyone has been heard, avoiding any formal motions in favor of a search for consensus, etc. GLF meetings, as a result, are often something of a cross between a Quaker meeting and an informal rap session, infuriating to those who want to "get things done" but important in raising the level of self-awareness and acceptance of those with less experience and less self-confidence. Or, at least, this is the theory. In some cases, I suspect that the very lack of structure gives an enormous advantage to a few charismatic figures who are able to dominate the meeting as totally as in any rigorous debate-by-the-rules gathering.

Both the Gay Activists Alliance and the Gay Liberation Front are open to men and women and both of them, GAA in particular, are predominantly male. Each contains a small number of blacks and Spanish-Americans, each has a few transvestites and transexuals. ("No member may be discriminated against because of personal appearance, style or behavior or sexual taste" reads the GAA manifesto, and in both groups there is a very conscious effort to avoid stigmatizing anyone for whatever their thing may be.) But inevitably the Liberation Front, though less than the Activists Alliance, seems to be dominated by gay men of a certain type—white, middle-class, educated, closer to straight movement types than to the homosexual of the popular imagination—and this has led to a number of breakaway groups. Women, youth, Third World, and transvestite organizations have all been set up, part of gay liberation as a movement but distinct from the GLF. At a time when people are becoming aware of the many ways in which they can suffer oppression, there seems almost a competition as to which group can identify itself as the most oppressed. Is the transvestite who is harassed for wearing women's clothes more oppressed than the black lesbian? The need to explore multiple oppression is expressed in this statement by a group of Third World gays. "We, as Third World gay people suffer a triple oppression: 1) We are oppressed as people because our humanity is routinely devoured by the carnivorous system of capitalism; 2) We are oppressed as Third World people by the economically inherent racism of white American society; 3) We are oppressed by the sexism of the white society and the verbal and physical abuse of masculinity-deprived Third World males."

Yet if there is a proliferation of groups that adopt a liberation perspective there is also a common sensitivity and a number of common activities. One of the more interesting activities that grew out of the movement was Gay Night at Alternate University—the now defunct successor to the Free Universities of a few years ago which was established to provide revolutionary education: "We must create and expand revolutionary values, visions of alternate structures, and analyses of history and existence. And as our un-derstanding changes, we must change ourselves. As everywhere else, in our workshops and classes we must combat élitism, sexism, racism and liberalism—and fear (from the 1970 fall prospectus). Along with the classes on organic foods and revolutionary Cuba, on self-defence, squatter movements, Marxism and social practice, Gay Night provided a time for gay men and women to come to-gether, to pool experience, knowledge, and wounds, and to develop a new sensibility and community, a concern far less pronounced in the civil libertarian focus of the Gay Activists Alliance.

One Friday night at Alternate University: in one side room a few transvestites are rapping with a group of gay men and women, trying to discover the essence of their own experience. Diane, who had previously been Roger, is dressed in burlesque style in a short, submini frock of black net, buttocks rounded by black lace pants, face heavily powdered and eyes lovingly formed. He insists that he is passing as a woman, to which the gay women, women's-liberation-clad in heavy slacks and shirts, respond indignantly that he is in fact only acting out the male fantasy of what a woman is. In the main room a short girl in black slacks is briefing a group on first aid during demonstrations: "If there's heavy bleeding," she says, "stop it, and worry about infection later."

Back in the transvestite classroom, Sylvia, one of the leaders of the street transvestites, is explaining a decision to have "the" op-eration. "But what," expostulates Dusty—a tall lean boy with wild Afro hair who has played opposite Jackie Curtis in an Andy Warhol movie—"what does cutting your penis off change? Isn't the whole thing all in your head?" And in another room the Third World gay people having completed their discussion, a discussion gets under way on roles, led—dominated—by Pat, a (genital) woman with two kids who likes to play at being a man.

This, then, is part of gay liberation. And if a Fellini or a Warhol might make it grotesque in film, there is a deadly seriousness to it, a straining to comprehend other people's experiences and fantasies and fears, as when a tall black, who until now had been irritating everyone by uncalled-for wisecracks, talks of his/her problem as a hermaphrodite with no clear concept of which sex to identify with, raising problems whose dimensions one can scarcely grasp. There are wounds opened in such exchanges that have rarely been opened before, but there is as well a real feeling for each other, a common sense of belonging and identity.

The Gay Liberation Front has also been identified with the commune movement, and this sets it apart from the more conventional life-styles of GAA members. While the traditional homophile groups are seeking to institute homosexual marriages—in Los Angeles, the Reverend Troy Perry, the Billy Graham of the homophile movement, is in fact performing such marriages and two women in Kentucky fought a court case to have such a marriage recognized—the kids in Gay Liberation Front, like their counterparts in the rest of the movement, are searching for new forms of communal living, rejecting the traditional one-to-one relationship as selfish and constricting. The Gay Activists Alliance seeks to find acceptance in present society; the gay liberationists are committed to a transformation of that society.

Activists and Radicals Elsewhere

The New York Gay Liberation Front no longer exists; the Gay Activist Alliance, as at the end of 1972, carries on much as before. But the differing approaches of the traditional groups, with their stress on public education and persuasion; the activist militants, concerned with direct confrontation of oppressive institutions; and the radicals, who seek not just acceptance by society but instead a transformation of that society, remain and they exist also in comparable countries.

Early groups like Mattachine and One, Inc. had their counterparts in many European countries; in 1951 an International Committee for Sexual Equality met in Amsterdam with delegates from thirteen countries. (Holland has become one of the strongest centres of the homosexual movement, and its major traditional organization, COC, is known all over the world.) Travelers from Anglo-Saxon countries brought back copies of *Arcadie* (France) or *Der Kreis* (Switzerland) and these publications influenced early movements at home.

Compared to Western European countries, Britain experienced a slow development of homosexual organizations. The fifties saw a proliferation of male homosexual prosecutions and convictions for private behavior—one of the more notorious cases is described in Peter Wildeblood's *Against the Law*—leading to the establishment of the Wolfenden Committee which was to recommend reform of the then antihomosexual laws.

Although it was not until 1967 that Wolfenden's recommendations (which by no means established homosexual behavior as able to enjoy comparable freedom to hetrosexual) were passed into law, acceptance of these recommendations was being urged by a number of very eminent persons. Thus in 1957 the Homosexual Law Reform Society was established, including six Anglican bishops, numerous lords, and a group of famous writers; the following year they were responsible for the formation of the Albany Trust as a counseling, educative, and research body concerned primarily but not exclusively with male homosexuals. In a similar manner the Minorities Research Trust was established to cater for the problems of lesbians.

The major difference between Britain on the one hand and the United States (and Australia) on the other is that in Britain pressure for law reform came largely from members of the elite who in most cases were not themselves homosexual; indeed it was not until the seventies that any overt homosexual organizations became prominent. The nature of the British establishment meant that the prevailing atmosphere was one of patronizing tolerance, whereas in countries where opposition to change was widespread homosexuals themselves have had to organize pressure even for legal change.

While homosexuals were numerous among sections of both the social and intellectual elite, as in the Bloomsbury Group which included both Lytton Strachey and John Maynard Keynes, their very integration into such groups and the extent to which homosexuals were divided along class lines tended to prevent the appearance of self-conscious homosexual organizations. Interestingly New Zealand seems to be following the British pattern and its Homosexual Law Reform Society (founded in 1967) has equally prestigious membership.

Law change in Britain allowed for the opening of a number of clubs, particularly outside London, although even now police harassment seems fairly common. But it was not until 1970 that the major homosexual organizations, the Committee for Homosexual Equality (CHE) and the Gay Liberation Front came into existence. The former is rather akin to SIR or COC, combining pressure for social reform with the provision of club facilities; the latter; begun after two London School of Economics students returned from a summer in the United States where they had become involved in the movement, resembles its American counterparts in organization and activity.

A similar American influence is evident in Canada, particularly in the Toronto gay liberation paper *Body Politic* and the Vancouver Gay Activists Alliance. In Australia, although there had been several not very successful attempts to establish law reform societies and a lesbian group had existed semiunderground for several years, the first major homosexual organization also came into being in 1970. Known as CAMP (Campaign Against Moral Persecution) this grew very rapidly, basically along the lines of the traditional homophile groups; for a short time one of its state branches provided homosexual speakers who were, however, instructed to masquerade as heterosexual. Partly owing to American influence, partly to the infusion into CAMP of radicalized gays, gay liberation emerged in Australia at the end of 1971.

In the interrelations of these various groups many of the conflicts and ideological disputes that took place in America have appeared. As happened with its counterpart in New York, the Gay Liberation Front in London has undergone extensive radicalization, with considerable tension between the women and men, and argument over how far gay oppression is a result of women's oppression, which in turn has meant a heavy stress on "radical drag" as a means of destroying sex role dichotomies. Such tensions have as yet been less noticeable in Australia, though they seem likely to develop. Not only within GLF itself, but also between CHE and CAMP on the one hand and GLF on the other, many of the tensions obvious in America a couple of years earlier have appeared.

The Search for Community

The essential quality of gay liberation, it seems to me, lies in its assertion of gayness, its refusal to feel shame or guilt at being homosexual. Out of this affirmation of being gay comes an affirmation of solidarity with other gays, and the transformation of the pseudo-community of the old gayworld into a sense of real community. Here there are parallels with the black movement. Black Power is not, I would argue, a very meaningful slogan for homosexuals to imitate. Black Pride *is:* "Say it loud, we're gay and we're proud" chant the demonstrators. To the extent that homosexual oppression is internalized such self-affirmation is an act of liberation.

There was, of course, a quite conscious attempt among some American gay radicals to model themselves on black militants, and this was reflected in the confrontation at New York University. I have already stressed that there are significant differences between the position of blacks and homosexuals, for homosexuals are not immediately visible and their oppression is not interwoven in the same way as it is for blacks into the problem of distribution of resources that so bedevils America (and makes the connection between black liberation and socialism a much closer one, I would argue, than is true for homosexuals). Yet there are some meaningful similarities between the statement of the New York Gay Liberation Front, and this from Stokely Carmichael and Charles Hamilton's *Black Power,* a book that is significantly subtitled *The Politics of Liberation in America:*

We must face the fact that in the past what we have called the movement has not really questioned the middle class values and institutions of this country. If anything, it has accepted these values and institutions without fully realizing their racist nature. Reorientation means an emphasis on the dignity of man, not on the sanctity of property. It means the creation of a society where human misery and poverty are repugnant to that society, not an indication of laziness or lack of initiative. The creation of new values means the establishment of a society based, as Killens expresses it in *Black Man's Burden,* on "free people," not "free enterprise."

Out of different experiences of oppression comes a common analysis of the need for radical change.

Carmichael and Hamilton argue strongly for blacks to assert their common identity, and to develop a new sense of community, and these are essentials of the gay as much as of the black movement. "We must first redefine ourselves" they state. Exactly the same is true, I have already argued, for homosexuals. The real oppression we suffer is psychological. We accept straight society's definitions of ourselves, and the necessity these impose on us to conceal our homosexuality, and hence remain apart from each other. Now for the first time large numbers of homosexuals are coming out publicly, and seeking to integrate their sexuality into a total life-style, rather than living the traditional divided life of the gayworld. Redefinition for the homosexual as for the black is a necessary part of liberation.

It is not surprising that one of the major targets of gay liberation confrontations has been psychiatrists. Gay activists have been present at a number of psychiatric and medical conferences, seeking to present an alternative to the standard psychiatric view of homosexuality.

When we heard that Bieber and company were coming to the American Psychiatric Association convention, we knew that we had to be there. And we were—on the convention floor microphone:

"We've listened to you long enough; you listen to us. We're fed up with being told we're sick. You're the ones who are sick." "We're gay and we're proud"—bearded Konstantin running around in a bright red dress.

Andy laying it on the twenty shrinks who show up for a Gay Liberation workshop. Gay guerrillas in the balcony sailing a paper airplane down to the convention floor when the delegates voted for a two-year study of violence. (Gary Alinder, "Confrontation I: San Francisco," in *Gay Liberation Meets the Shrinks,* a Gay Flames pamphlet, New York 1970)

As Chicago gay liberation stated in a pamphlet addressed to the 1970 American Medical Association Convention: "A psychiatrist who allows a homosexual patient—who has been subject to a barrage of anti-homosexual sentiments his whole life—to continue in the belief that heterosexuality is superior to homosexuality, is the greatest obstacle to his patient's health and wellbeing. . . . We are convinced that a picket and a dance will do more for the vast majority of homosexuals than two years on the couch." One of the most effective gay liberation "actions" in Australia was guerrilla theater directed against the aversion therapy being conducted at the University of New South Wales.

Not just gay liberation groups are engaged in such acts of self-awareness. Many activities of the civil libertarian organizations serve the same purpose. The real significance of "zapping" a political figure like John Lindsay may lie less in its effect on the policies being challenged than in the new self-confidence and identity the activity gives those who participate and the new model of gayness it offers to those as yet too scared to come out. In such terms groups such as GAA can be seen as part of the liberation movement, for its actions have been highly public and its members no longer crouch behind pen names.

The argument is sometimes advanced that sexual liberation will arise out of political power. I cannot agree. Liberation, particularly for a minority as self-hating and concealed as the homosexual, requires a change in values and consciousness that transcends traditional politics. Of course it is important to change laws, to confront magazines that give inaccurate information, to demand equal time on television. But this does not add up to liberation. We are freeing ourselves through the way we live, and as long as homosexuals are oppressed, walking arm-in-arm with one's lover down the street is as much a political act as campaigning for legal reform. As Kate Millett argues in *Sexual Politics*, those of us who are oppressed because of our sex or our sexuality need a new and broader definition of politics to meet the requirements of our oppression.

A reporter asked why we considered a gay picnic political. We told him that gay oppression was different from race oppression; that tearing off the mask of anonymity is the first step in our liberation. And we must take the first step. But you can only do it once.

We thought we wore masks to hide from other people; then we found that we ourselves didn't know who we were until we took off the masks. Next year we won't need a parade. We don't know what we will be next year. (From "Christopher Street Liberation Day" by two lesbians, *Come Out!*, Sept/Oct. 1970)

The old-line groups tend to reinforce the traditional gayworld rather than seeking to supplant it. The best example of this is SIR, which is closely associated with the Tavern Guild, an organization of owners of San Francisco bars catering to homosexuals, which arranges tours of gay bars, rather like those provided by ordinary travel agencies, but similar comments can be made of most old-line groups. The more commercial of the gay papers, such as Los Angeles' *Advocate* or New York's *Gay*, which adopt a guarded position in support of gay activism while deploring its "excesses," rely heavily on advertisements from the very large number of baths, bars, restaurants, book, and clothing shops, etc. catering to homosexuals—usually only to males—and are totally unlike gay liberation papers such as *Come Out!* or London's *Come Together*. In a sense there is a "gay establishment" which, like the black establishment, benefits economically from the present system of (liberal) oppression: even after paying for protection, gay bars and baths are profitable investments.

Rather than reinforcing stereotypical homosexual behavior, as do most places in the gayworld, gay liberation offers an alternative, as, for example, in its dances. Holding a dance has become one of the most common of gay liberation activities and, despite frequent complaints that these merely duplicate (if less expensively) the dance bars, they play an important part in defining a new sense of community. The atmosphere at such dances has less of the pure sex barter found in commercial dance bars; people talk and hug and mingle and embrace without the solitary kind of anxiety that hangs over the traditional dances—will he/she ask me to dance; do I want to go home with him/her; do I look all right. (Although these dances are in a sense only an exaggeration of some straight dances, bearing out my earlier point about the similarity between much of the gay and straight world.) Gay liberation dances strive quite consciously to break down alienation, as in the circle dances which promote a new feeling of community, or in the political discussions held by London GLF at their early dances.

But what is strange to you is natural to us. Let me illustrate. Gay Liberation Front "liberates" a gay bar for the evening. We come in. The people already there are seated quietly at the bar. Two or three couples are dancing. It's a down place. And then GLF takes over. Men dance with men, women with women, men with women, everyone in circles! No roles. You ever see that at a Movement party? Not men with men—this is particularly verboten. No, and you're not likely to, while the Gays in the Movement are still passing for straight in order to keep up the good names of their organizations or to keep up the pretense that they are acceptable—and not have to get out of the organization they worked so hard for because they are queer. (Martha Shelley, *Gay Is Good,* a Gay Flames pamphlet, originally printed in *Rat*)

More important than dances are the situations provided in which gay people can come together in a totally non sex-barter situation.

(One of the main problems with the dances has been the unwill-
ingness of many gay women to come to them, and the subsequent
organization of separate women's dances.) Gay coffee houses, or
evenings like the Gay Night already described, bring together homosexuals in a new sort of atmosphere, and have been important in
linking male and female homosexuals. Writing of the Australian
homosexual group, CAMP, a reporter said: "Toward the end of
the evening one youngster confided in me how pleasant it was to
be able to meet and talk with members of the opposite sex of his
own age. Since he did not have to go through the pretence of not
being a homosexual, there was no constant fear that it might lead
to a situation which he might not want to develop." The provision
of places to meet freely is particularly important for gay women
who, as already noted, have very restricted opportunities to meet
each other.

   "WE ARE GOING TO BE WHO WE ARE": and this new
determination has helped achieve a notable relaxation of the strain
and bitchinesses of the older gayworld. The best example of this I
have encountered is ZOOS, a club established by younger homosexuals in Amsterdam. Here, in an old three-storey house alongside
one of the city's canals, homosexuals can come together in an atmosphere where their homosexuality is neither cause for disguise
nor concern, where they meet as people rather than as sex objects.
At ZOOS, more than in any club, bar, or dance I have attended,
people met and talked and danced together without constantly worrying about making it with someone. If you did, fine. If not, there
were plenty of other things to be done. Relationships are seen as
more important, more lasting, more comprehensive than in the old
gayworld.

   Part of this search for community is expressed in gay community
centers which have sprung up in many cities and offer a permanent
meetingplace to homosexuals. Perhaps the most ambitious is the
Gay Community Services Center in Los Angeles, which provides
not just a social center but also seeks to help with housing, legal,

medical, and personal problems and to provide the basis of a total community. To the people responsible for the center it is an example of the development of revolutionary life-styles into political activity. The provision of counseling services, based on the acceptance of homosexuality as a valid life-style, has become a common activity of gay groups, and in a number of cases (e.g. the Homosexual Guidance Service in Sydney) brings together gay activists and sympathetic psychiatrists.

"Our salute will be a kiss," said Greta Garbo in *Ninotchka,* and one of the best things about the new sense of community being developed by gay liberation is the considerable eroticism it releases and, as if in confirmation of the Brown/Marcuse theories of polymorphous perversity, the seeming decline in compulsive scoring and promiscuity. Men and women together will embrace, hug, march with their arms around each other: in Los Angeles, the GLF organized a "love-in" in Griffith Park, rejecting *both* conventional morality *and* the anonymous circusing described in Rechy's *Numbers;* gay festivals have become common in London parks. Thus, too, out of the new feelings among homosexuals released by gay liberation came the Christmas Eve Festival of Love organized by a number of gay groups in New York to provide an alternative to the frenetic, lonely, tinsel-time of the commercial world, both gay and straight.

Part of the new affirmation is a great stress on developing consciousness. As in the women's movement, "raising the level of consciousness" is a first priority. Again, this involves certain basic questions of identity that the gay man or woman must resolve. In a remarkable article that appeared in the *Village Voice* (10 December 1970), Vivian Gornick wrote: "For me, feminism is, more than any other single thing, not a movement, not a cause, not a revolution, but rather a profoundly new way of interpreting human experience ... thus feminism also is nothing less than a new form into which one pours all knowledge, thereby revitalizing and setting into motion anew the sources of psychic energy responsible for growth and change and altered behavior.... Feminism, for me, is the journey deep into the self *at the same time* that it is an ever-increasing understanding of cultural sexism ... and, more than any-thing, the slow, painful reconstruction of that self in the light of the feminist's enormously multiplied understanding." Like Gornick there are those who see "the heart and soul of the movement" as consciousness-raising or awareness groups, small groups of gay men or women (and sometimes both) who together explore the meaning of their lives, their experiences, their oppression.

We as gays must redefine ourselves *in our own terms,* from our own heads and experience, because no political philosophy designed by white heterosexual men can be adequate for us. Thus we use CR [consciousness raising] to arrive at policy and positions, to plan actions and projects—to evolve a politics out of our experience.

The results of our CR meetings have been many. While we began as nine isolated, alienated people, we have become a group politicized by the study of our experience. We found that our problems are not individual illnesses, but are generated by our oppression as a class. This discovery negated one of the most effective weapons of our oppressors, the false division between the personal and the political. Whether or not we'd had any previous political involvement none of us saw homosexuality in po-litical terms. The sharing of our experience has brought us to a collective consciousness as gay men.

In our CR group, we have been finding new ways of relating to each other. We approach a true functioning democracy with no leaders, pro-viding support for one another in our attempts to change our role-oriented behavior. Gays need not be isolated; strength comes from the fusion of consciousnesses. (From "On Our Own," a collective effort by a New York Consciousness-Raising Group, New York 1970)

The ultimate extension of gay community is the gay commune. The commune—which is in essence an attempt to create a new form of extended family, one that is made up of people from the same generation rather than cutting across generations—is a difficult form to develop, yet the difficulties are hardly reason to dismiss it. Perhaps for gay people, who often feel rejected by their own fam-

ilies, it is a particularly important development and it offers a so-
lution for lesbian mothers and homosexuals who wish to participate
in child care.

After observing the collective living situation for two weeks I decided
that no other life style could offer so much or could be so challenging,
rewarding and valuable. Beginning the third week as a member of this
collective, I have encountered many frustrations and difficulties. But I am
more and more aware of a new strength and positiveness that comes from
the support and understanding my collective brothers have offered.

I realize now how difficult it is to make the change from an individualistic consciousness to a collective one. Yet with each obstacle I approach,
I find I have not only my own strength (which would not be enough), but
the strength and aid of my four collective brothers. And when an obstacle
has been surmounted, I have a genuine sense of something important gained
through the experience. . . .

There are still a great many things I have to struggle with in making
the adaptations necessary in bettering my life style. But the knowledge that
I am not alone in my struggle makes the problems seem much less over-
whelming. I can't see that I have anything to lose in effecting this change,
and hopefully, will be able not only to gain, but to give more fully as a
person. (From "Five Notes on Collective Living," by a Men's Collective,
Come Out! December 1970–January 1971)

In form, communes range from fairly tightly knit small groups
with a long-term commitment to each other to large, fluctuating
bodies of people more like a crash-pad than a commune. (I visited
one such "commune" in San Francisco where nobody seemed to
know the others' names.) The attitudes toward sex are likely to be
as diverse as in straight communes; in one case that I know of there
was an attempt to develop sexual relations between all members
of the commune, as a way of bringing them closer together, but
the attempt was not particularly successful. Monogamy is largely
frowned upon—one man was excluded from a New York commune
for practicing it—as it is seen, probably correctly, as preventing
commitment to everybody in the commune. Communes that are
part of the gay liberation movement often hold their own con-

sciousness-raising sessions, partly as a device to create sufficient knowledge of each other to maintain a family-type bond, and often act as focal points for the movement. Communes—or, as they are often called, living collectives—will adopt a particular task, such as running a gay coffee house or producing a newspaper.

The Redefinition of Identity

As part of the search for identity there has emerged within the gay liberation movement a discussion about "gay culture." Not the old bogies or boasts—depending on which side of the fence you were on—about homosexuals determining the course of arts and letters (one letter to *Time,* November 1969, claimed that 95 percent of all American culture was homosexual-inspired; the letter was approving, though ironically the same claim is sometimes made by the ultra Right). Nor, please, those old stories about Michelangelo, Tchaikovsky, Proust, Whitman, Shakespeare, although, as I have already suggested, the homosexuality of a creative artist is not merely an extraneous fact, as some critics, remarkably squeamish about sex, would like us to believe, but an integral part of his or her perception of the world as long as the world insists on stigmatizing homosexuals. What is now involved is an exploration of whether a genuine homosexual culture exists, whether "camp" is in fact the equivalent of "soul."

In Baldwin's *Tell Me How Long the Train's Been Gone,* there is one very powerful passage where he talks of the way in which blacks have long expressed their anger through music and movement, and how the white world has misunderstood this. Similarly gay self-parody, the whole irony and bitter wit of camp, expresses an underlying hostility and fear. Leslie Fiedler, one of the few literary critics to possess a real sense of the world outside the books he reads, has suggested a variation of the same point in *Waiting for the End:* "Who can tell the moment at which the bluff and hearty stage-Irishman, the obsequious and hand-rubbing Jew, the mincing wrist-flapping fairy, the bland, blue-eyed, dependent girl, the faithful black servitor crying 'Yassah, massah!' cease genuinely trying to become the humble roles in which they have been cast and begin to exploit those roles subversively." *Boys in the Band* would only need to be slightly rewritten for maudlin to become ironic, and maybe I too have fallen into a trap and am taking Crowley's pathos far too seriously.

In any case, blacks and gays have for a long time acted out their expected stereotypes, and with the conversion of apathy/abjection to affirmation/pride there is a corresponding attempt to find virtue in the stereotypes and convert what was stigmatized into a positive good. Twenty years ago whites, as part of their benevolent paternalism, said "blacks have rhythm;" ten years ago such statements would have been regarded, by white and black liberals alike, as derogatory and racist; today something similar is asserted in the doctrine of "soul." And so with homosexuals. The old-line groups' insistence that we are as *manly* and as *ladylike* as everyone else is giving way for some in the movement to an assertion of faggotry as a positive good.

Germaine Greer in *The Female Eunuch* tends to do something similar in her chapter on "Womenpower," where she suggests that maybe women *are* more emotional, less rational than men after all—and perhaps this is to their advantage. What Greer, quoting Cynthia Ozick, calls "the Ovarian theory of Mind" becomes the equivalent of "soul" and "camp," a strength rather than the weakness it is commonly defined as.

To the extent that Camp accepts the conception of the male homosexual as womanly and therefore inferior to real men it is self-hate. But much of Camp is something far more positive, a guerrilla attack on the whole system of male-female roles our society uses to oppress its women and repress its men. Here the Campy Queens have acted as the vanguard guerrilla partisans of the Gay revolution. Look at the response of any red-blooded all-American Man to a Street Queen. They must have a hell of a lot going for them to get the Man all that hot and bothered.

Another example. I never understood the Camp fascination with the movies of the thirties and forties until the Cockettes finally brought home to me just what was happening. Movies and movie stars aren't trivial or peripheral to American culture. They teach people what it means to be a man or a women and how you should act as one or another—Love Amerikan style. A man is like John Wayne, a woman is like Lana Turner, and the correct relationship between them is for him to fuck her and for her to like it. If one of the basic tyrannies of this society is the roles men and women are forced into, then the popular culture of movie stars and starlets, Western heroes and popular romances enforces this tyranny. They teach people they must be brawling insensitive clods to be real men, passive simpering ornaments to be real women. (Mike Silverstein, "God Save the Queen," *Gay Sunshine,* November 1970)

Such reversing of "vice" into "virtue" could of course become as restrictive as the old insistence that we should all look more square than the squares, and there is a danger of trying to force all homosexuals into adopting certain mannerisms—e.g., wearing drag—with which they would be genuinely uncomfortable. Nonetheless there is a new style of campdom that is being mobilized against social pressures: the old-style transvestite who painfully hid his genitals and plucked out all body hair is being replaced by boys in beards and dresses who send up the whole social concept of masculine/feminine.

This style of gender confusion was made famous by the Cockettes, a group that originated in San Francisco and for a time became fashionable among the avant-garde. "Don't call us drag queens," one of them is reported as saying, "call us freaks." They include both women and men and their style is an extravagant send-up of all that is normal and respectable, as in their film *Tricia's Wedding,* where the president's daughter is raped by a baseball bat. The Cockettes have inspired similar groups elsewhere, such as Sydney's Sylvia and the Synthetics whose act is a strange *mélange* of the grotesque, the violent, and the drag show.

We have as yet seen little gay liberation art, except for some poetry:

On Saturday I gave myself to
       a woman
to breasts
  to fingers
    to musky cigarette breath and
      furry vaginal softness

On Saturday I gave myself to
      cockless sex and then
I watched
  and waited
    and dropped into the heavy
      sweet sea of woman loving
      woman.

Marlene A. Geffin

i can't give you the / but i can give
i can't give you the / but i can give
    sun-rise   (cock)
    spider-web   (love)
    night-birds   (beesting)
    ocean-power   (thighs)

i can't give you nothing / man but
  my love—

but little fox-if you ever need
  to wrap something around your
  body for heat

i promise to keep you warm in
  the winter

and burning with desire in
  the summer

at least maybe that'll fill one
  of your needs

charles p. thorp/"Trilogy for Brian"

(Both poems appeared in *San Francisco Gay Free Press*, December 1970)

But as the incident at New York University illustrated, there is some agitation for "gay studies." The first such course was offered in 1970 at the University of Nebraska—a seminar in homophile studies encompassed theology, law, psychology, anthropology, sociology, and literature—and, perhaps not suprisingly in such a conservative state, was dropped after it became an issue in state politics. Similar courses have, however, appeared on other American campuses. Homosexuals want their condition to be removed from the domain of departments of abnormal psychology and from courses in the sociology of deviance; they want the deviance of homosexuality to be regarded rather as a product of society and analyzed accordingly. Thus a gay group within the American Library Association is seeking to change the library practice of classifying homosexuality as an abnormality. There is too an attempt to establish the existence of a historic gay culture. One gay liberationist, Don Jackson, argued at the founding convention of the California Libertarian Alliance: "Gays regard themselves as a people: a cultural minority with their own traditions, customs, folkways, way of thinking and an ancient cultural heritage— literary styles and visual and performing arts forms with a three thousand year history," and Bob Martin, one of the founders of the Student Homophile League at Columbia University has referred to "the unique heritage [of the] homosexual . . . a tradition going back to the dawn of recorded history."

Even more than in the case of black studies, a powerful argument can be made that homosexuality should not be studied as a thing apart, that, for example, literature departments should consider Baudelaire, Proust, and Gide, or Wilde, Auden, and Hart Crane, paying due attention to their homosexuality, their specific as well as their universal preoccupations. This does not mean that Jackson and Martin are wrong in arguing for the existence of a gay culture, though I would contend that it is a culture produced exclusively by social ostracism. But to shunt homosexuality into a special corner of its own, whether it be a course in deviance or a pro-seminar in homophile studies, seems to me potentially dangerous.

But therein lies an essential dilemma of gay liberation. For Gay is not only Proud, Gay is Angry, and out of anger develops separatism, which bears with it the danger of merely reinforcing both apartness from the rest of humanity and the doctrine that homo- and heterosexuality are sharply defined categories rather than possibilities present in us all. Such a dilemma is inherent in the creation of a new consciousness; it bedevils the women's movement even more, perhaps, than the gay. One of the likely consequences of involvement in gay liberation, at least in the United States (this seems less true in other countries), is that individuals lose contact, other than what is absolutely necessary, with straights and become intolerant of all those who are not gay.

This can reach a point that some would see as paranoia, as when gay people claim to be "oppressed" by the presence of straights at their meetings or get-togethers. I remember vividly one GLF meeting at a New York church which exploded into a furious outburst because the pastor of the church (with whom there was some dispute over rent) entered the room. His very presence was a threat, reminding gays of all the pent-up furies against a world that had constantly put them down, and the debate that the incident sparked off nearly broke up the meeting.

I do not share this feeling but it is important to understand it. To become conscious of oppression must inevitably lead to a development of hatred and a search for a target. What was once internalized into self-disgust now seeks a new target outside the self. Again, there are parallels with Black Power. "The phenomenon of Black Power," Robert Friedrichs argued several years ago in *Yale Review* (Spring 1968), is primarily "a necessary stage on the long trek back to psychic and social health—health systematically denied the black man in America for some three hundred years. The same is true of other manifestations of verbal violence burgeoning over the last few years, starting perhaps with the hints dropped by Genet's perversely perceptive *The Blacks,* breaking out of the black underworld and a narrow Muslim cultism through the charismatic tutelage of Malcolm X, parlayed in the arts for the edification of the black bourgeoisie by LeRoi, consciously appropriated by such middle class youth as Stokely Carmichael and H. Rap Brown who, though personally temperate, saw it for the portentous weapon for mass psychic liberation it was."

It is interesting that Friedrichs points to Genet as one of the first to see the meaning of verbal violence, for Genet's sense of oppression as a homosexual undoubtedly influenced his perception of blacks (though, revealing a certain self-hatred, Genet seems more able to relate to the oppression of blacks than to that of homosexuals). The anger that gay liberation expresses is, as Fanon said about violence for the colonized, a "necessary therapy." "We must become violent fairies" was the heading of one article in *Gay Sunshine,* although the article was necessarily vague about what sort of violence was required. Nonetheless there are those in gay liberation who have been moving toward a glorification of violence—the Panther slogan "Take up the gun" is echoed by a minority of gay liberationists—and who, I would argue, are betraying the ideals of liberation for which the movement stands.

At the G.L.F. dances we have danced the circle dance as a show of community. Our circle dance is the ritual—an orgy of discharged energy—before we enter the struggle. We in our circle dance have felt our sensibilities surge close to the surface. With acute aggressiveness we have encircled ourselves with protection against our oppressor. The time has now come to move out. Gay people will no longer be oppressed. We are angry at the theft of our identity. We will collectively recapture what we know is ours and has been taken from us. (Steve Dansky, *Hey man,* a Gay Flames pamphlet)

Apart from this, however, there is a strong tendency within the gay liberation movement to reject all heterosexuals, to demand a self-affirmation that denies any contact with nongays. Some lesbians take this further and reject all contact with men, even gay men.

The furthest extension of gay separation was the strange episode of Alpine County. Under the leadership of a section of Los Angeles gay liberation, it was planned to move sufficient homosexuals into a small county high in the California Sierras to make a majority of the population and turn it into a self-proclaimed gay community. Opposition both from local inhabitants and within the gay movement caused the enterprise to collapse, although some homosexuals did actually move to the county and there has been talk of a similar attempt elsewhere. The greatest virtue of the plan was the way it exploited the institutional channels that dissenters are always being urged to use so as to make very difficult the path of those who would stop them (although Alpine County officials did begin discussions aimed at incorporating the county into surrounding ones), and it dramatized the extent to which at least some homosexuals feel oppressed within society. The plan attracted considerable publicity (*Time* reported it, and for once fairly sympathetically). It seemed less likely that it would ever in the ornate language of one journal "create a gay cultural centre where our cultural identity will become defined, strong, pliable and vastly original and creative; and seek out rosy, fresh and viable personal relationships."

Gay separatism need not adopt the extravagances of the Alpine County venture, but separatism as such does seem an inevitable development. As more homosexuals come out openly, they will seek the sense of community and protection that gay liberation groups provide. Homosexuals need the opportunity to meet and get to know other gay men and women in casual situations, for society does not provide opportunities that heterosexuals all take for granted, generally assuming as they do that all unattached women are fair targets for men and vice versa. As we become aware of our oppression, there develops a common anger that, inevitably, takes as its target the straight world that has defined the homosexual as outcast. Following a rather petulant if unclear article by *Village Voice*'s film critic, Andrew Sarris, Theodore Rauch wrote in a letter to the *Voice:* "We homosexuals would all love to think of ourselves, as Mr. Sarris suggests, as human beings first, without giving a second thought to our sexual orientation. Social attitudes, however, expressed by laws and expressions like 'fag' which Mr. Sarris chooses to perpetuate, force us to think of ourselves as homosexuals first. Until the time when these laws and attitudes change, groups like the Gay Activists Alliance will continue to fight uncompromisingly for a permanent end to homosexual oppression, a fight which necessarily focuses on each individual's sexual orientation." Talk of us all being "human sexuals" too often means ignoring the reality that, whatever we may like, society has defined homosexuals as persons apart.

Yet gay liberation, as I have stressed, involves essentially an alteration in individual consciousness and hence there will be great variety in the paths taken by individuals. Nor is the gay liberation movement free from internal tensions, in particular between women and men, nonwhites and whites. Homosexuals are no more immune from racism or sexism than straights, and if this chapter largely puts things in the perspective of a white male, this merely emphasizes the point. The tensions of racism and sexism will be explored later, for they involve the whole question of alliance with other alienated groups. Here it is enough to say that gay liberation draws members from a wide spectrum of society, and a common sense of oppression does not dissolve other lines of division. (One woman at a *Come Out!* collective meeting complained bitterly about the total middle-class bias of the meeting; some Jewish homosexuals in both Britain and America, conscious of growing New Left hostility toward Zionism which was being echoed in gay liberation, have come together to explore this particular manifestation.) For the moment I want to discuss briefly one of the most difficult problems confronting gay liberation, its attitude to transvestites and transexuals (i.e., those who seek a surgical change of genitals).

My own ambivalence on this has already been noted. On the one hand, any putdown of transvestites or transexuals must remind a homosexual only too uncomfortably of the way in which we all are put down by straights. On the other hand, the transvestite— and by this I mean someone who gets real physical enjoyment from parading as one of the opposite sex, unlike the drag queen who is often using female clothing in a mocking and ironic way—and even more the transexual, seem the ultimate victims of our stigma, people so conditioned into the male/female role dichotomy that the only way they can accept their own homosexuality is by denying their bodies. I do not dispute the fact that most are, behaviourally, heterosexual; I am questioning what self-image this heterosexuality is based upon.

Perhaps all I can do is put the two points of view as argued within the context of the gay movement. Transvestites and transexuals had already organized in a small way in California in the early sixties; with the emergence of gay liberation some were attracted to the movement and its greater acceptance of the phenomena than seemed true of the older groups. Yet, in turn, transvestites and transexuals felt a need for separate organizations, and by 1970 there were groups in several cities as well as in other countries (e.g., the Beaumont Society in Britain). Certainly there is no question that however one views the phenomena, the oppression is very real: the question is what attitude should a movement pressing for full sexual liberation adopt toward them?

On the one hand there are the demands issued jointly by the New York Street Transvestite Action Revolutionaries, the Florida Transvestite-Transexual Action Organization, the New York Femmes Against Sexism (most of whom are not, strictly, transvestites or transexuals):

1. Abolishment of all crossdressing laws and restrictions of adornment.
2. An end to exploitation and discrimination within the gay world.
3. An end to exploitative practices of doctors and psychiatrists who work in the fields of transvestism and transexualism. Hormone treatment and transexual surgery should be provided free upon demand by the state.
4. Transexual assistance centers should be created in all cities of over one million inhabitants, under the direction of post-operative transexuals.
5. Transvestites and transexuals should be granted full and equal rights on all levels of society and a full voice in the struggle for the liberation of all oppressed people.
6. Transvestites who exist as members of the opposite anatomical gender should be able to obtain full identification as members of the opposite gender. Transexuals should be able to obtain such identification commensurate to their new gender with no difficulty, and not be required to carry special identification as transexuals. There should be no special licensing requirements of transvestites or transexuals who work in the entertainment field.
7. Immediate release of all persons in mental hospitals or prison for transvestism or transexualism.

The opposite viewpoint is that of the Red Butterfly group who commented as follows on the claim for "the right to free physiological change and modification of sex upon demand," contained in a list drawn up by the Gay Caucus at the Revolutionary People's Constitutional Convention in Philadelphia in September 1970.

Stripped of the above-mentioned stereotyped role-playing, we see this demand as advocating the mutilation of the human body—and at the expense of the State! "Modification of sex" is a false concept, inasmuch as modern surgery can do no such thing as "modify" sex. No physician has ever surgically changed a man into a woman, or a woman into a man. The only change which has been known to take place so far is to "modify" a man into a eunuch. The euphemisms "physiological change" and "modification of sex" cover up a lack of real concern for the ethics involved. We are philosophical materialists, rejecting the theological concepts of soul-body dualism, and therefore, we consider an injury to the body an injury to the real person. We are opposed to surgical mutilation. Medicine should serve the people.

My personal belief (hope?) is that transvestism and transexism would disappear were our social norms not so repressive of men who exhibit "feminine" traits and vice versa. Similarly, I suspect sadomasochism is a product of a screwed-up sexuality that is also likely to pass, for it is hard to see how it can avoid playing out very sharply defined roles of dominance and subordination. The relationship between gay liberation and those who practice both transvestism and sadomasochism, usually stigmatized within as well as without the traditional gayworld, is one of the real challenges faced by the movement.

Gay Liberation and the Individual Gay

One's evaluation of any political movement will be highly colored by what it means to one personally. For me the main significance of gay liberation is that is has helped me confront and accept my homosexuality, and for this I am grateful, whether or not there is a corresponding decrease in the external oppression that I face. Not that I had not seen myself as liberated before becoming involved in the movement; over the previous years I had reached a position where I no longer lived in a closet—or, more honestly, where I kept the closet door slightly ajar—and I thought of myself, with all the smugness this suggests, as pretty well adjusted. How far I have to go in really liberating myself my experience in gay liberation has made clear. But this experience has made me glad to be a homosexual, for it has given me an insight into the human condition and the human potential I had previously lacked.

Back in San Francisco. Moratorium Day, 15 October, 1969, I danced around the Capri, danced for hours, whipped my body around, fucking and being fucked and coming. Feeling natural, feeling high, feeling free. "Oh I see you got that natural rhythm," Charles laughs.

"Those guys are gross," I heard a fellow apologize to the girl he was dancing with. A lot of people seem to feel I'm obnoxious. I'm feeling liberated.

"Come and sing a simple song of freedom
Sing it like you never sung before
Sing it for me now, sing it anyhow
We, the people, don't want more war."

I'm singing it tonight as a liberated homosexual. It's Moratorium Day.
Why aren't we arm in arm, brothers? Don't you want to dance? Doesn't
everyone want to dance? "It's a solo," a boy in blue workshirt and wire-
framed glasses answers.

Asking people to dance feels archaic. I'm dancing if I want to be, not
looking down at my beer waiting. Dancing with myself, somebody else,
everybody. But the floor is mainly closed couples who fall back into their
singular positions along the wall at the end of every dance with a polite
exchange of thank yous.

Ten to two: lights up. I shout it out. "Lights up. Out of your ghettos
into your streets." People turn angrily towards me. "I wish you hadn't said
that," says Sean.

SNAP! WHAP! Back into your closets, Queers! Or we'll put you in
cages ourselves. (Konstantin Berlandt, *My Soul Vanished from Sight*, a Gay
Flames pamphlet)

Shortly after coming to New York I wrote in an article for *Come
Out!*:

In six weeks I have been only once to a gay bar, and that was with
someone I loved for a time, and to dance. Much of my time has been spent
in the gay movement—at meetings, at rap sessions, at dances, on the streets.
I still see my straight friends, but I am open with them about my homosexuality, and when I feel oppressed by them—as when I am asked to
dinner by myself while straights are asked to "bring a friend"—I tell them.
The gay community in New York has become for me just that; I walk
through the Village and I see people whom I know, even if only by sight,
and I feel I belong. Moreover, my contacts with gay people are far richer
and more diverse than ever before, for they are no longer restricted by sex
as the sole motivating force; I know women and transvestites and I find
myself struggling to understand them and their experience in a way I never
could before.

Perhaps the most important thing that gay liberation has meant for
me is to bring me closer *both* to my gay brothers and sisters *and*

to my straight friends. For when one is no longer leading a double life, there is a sudden explosive release, a sense that one does indeed see the world differently and that one has sufficient resources to be oneself. Which, in turn, can only strengthen one's love relationships.

Most important has been the effect on my relations with women. The movement, despite the tensions between the sexes that exist within it, has also provided an opportunity for mutual contact and understanding that we previously lacked. Ultimately I think I may love both men and women, but because I come to love women more is no reason to love men less. "Sex is love" chalked up a little boy in Washington Square Park. This is hardly true, and if gay liberation has taught me anything it has taught me to love more easily and in more ways.

In a sense gay liberation is a process by which we develop a theory and a practice out of our experience, living, as it were, our liberation. As already suggested, full liberation is a product of *both* individual and social change; there is between the two a dialectic interaction and here gay liberation, by developing a new sense of community, comes close to Berke's concept of "liberated zones." Gay liberation will have achieved its full potential when it is no longer needed, when we see each other neither as men and women, gay and straight, but purely as people with varied possibilities. It is the fate of the Negro, James Baldwin once wrote, to carry the burden of both white and black Americans. It may be the fate of homosexuals to liberate both gays and straights.

5. The Collapsing Hegemony and Gay Liberation

Gay liberation is a phenomenon that exists only in modern Western industrialized countries, and like the contemporary women's movement is born of the technological and social conditions of such countries. Thus it is hardly surprising that it first emerged in the United States, nor that it has spread to societies with a similar sociopolitical base (e.g., Britain, the Netherlands, Germany, France, Italy, Australasia, Canada). For although homosexuality exists in all societies, a radical homosexual movement cannot exist where the state so rigidly enforces morality as to preclude organization (e.g., U.S.S.R., South Africa) or where traditional values result in sexuality being differently managed (most of the nondeveloped world). One exception seems to be Japan where, despite both a strongly self-conscious homosexual world (as revealed in the novels of Mishima) and a Westernized economic and political system, there is to the best of my knowledge no gay movement.

Although the organizational precursors of gay liberation date back over twenty years, gay liberation as a social movement is far more a product of large-scale social change than of any evolution from the old-line Mattachine or Daughters of Bilitis. The work of such groups, I have already indicated, was important and their courage admirable. Here that is not the point. Gay liberation, as I shall argue in this chapter, is much more the child of the counter-culture than it is of the older homophile organizations; it is as much the effect of changing mores as their cause.

The counterculture has been, I believe, the most significant development in America over the past decade, and we need first to examine it as a general phenomenon before examining its relation to gay liberation. Its emergence is intimately bound up with the two great political upheavals of the sixties—the new militancy of blacks and other nonwhite Americans, and the agony of Vietnam. What we conventionally understand as politics, the governmental institutions that preoccupy political scientists, have proven quite remarkably inflexible and unable to meet the challenge presented by these upheavals: the decade ended with the best living symbol of the fifties ensconced in the White House with—as if to underline the symbolism—an Eisenhower as son-in-law. Thus there has been an apparent contradiction between the vast growth of radical challenges to the status quo and the seeming immutability of that status quo. In both government and business, those two pillars of modern America, the same men seemed as firmly entrenched in 1970 as they were in 1960, even if businessmen now wore colored shirts and paisley ties.

More accurately, what has happened over the past decade is that there has been an increasing disjunction between politics and culture, to the point that the most revolutionary features of American life are in fact cultural. Through the country's development from an agrarian, small-town, homogeneous society to an urban, industrialized heterogeneous superpower, the dominant forces in American society were supported by a culture that was functional to their needs. The Protestant ethic of hard work, sexual repression, respect for business values and organized religion—"Worship in the church of your choice"—was internalized, not only by the original WASP Americans but also by Catholic and Jewish immigrants, who in turn were able to "make it," at least to a considerable extent, through the system. There were of course those, predominantly nonwhite, who were excluded from the benefits of the American system and white dominance was maintained by a mixture of brute force and the implantation among blacks, Indians, Chicanos, etc., of the belief that they were, as the white man said, inferior.

America exhibited by and large a situation of the sort that the Marxist theorist Antonio Gramsci has described as hegemonic, that is, a situation where "one concept of reality" is diffused throughout society so that the direction and control of the dominant class is supported by norms and perceptions that have been internalized by all classes. This concept of reality was enforced in particular through the American public school system, the family, the church, and the small town or ethnic community that mediated between the individual and the state. My analysis would not deny the persistence of ethnic and regional differences, in particular the special characteristics of the South. Yet after the Civil War even these were subsumed in the main under the prevailing hegemony. Numerous sociological studies suggest that ethnic groups have largely accepted American cultural norms without necessarily losing their social cohesion. Thus while American society came to be comprised of a complex network of different subcultures, they all accepted more or less unquestioningly the hegemonic ideas of the dominant class, in particular the necessity for hard work, sexual repression, and respect for authority.

Over the past ten years, the cultural hegemony dominating America has begun to erode as different segments of the population have come to see that America has been exclusively defined according to the needs and desires of a ruling elite of white, middle-aged, male heterosexuals. In turn blacks, the young, women, and homosexuals have challenged this hegemony and as a result America is more fragmented, more divided, and yet freer than ever before in its history. The cultural hegemony of the elite has begun to collapse, and out of this dissolution of the American identity emerge both some of its most hopeful characteristics and a growing degree of violence and repression. (As Hannah Arendt points out in *On Violence*, it is when authority, based on common cultural assumptions, begins to crumble that authorities need to resort even more to force and repression.)

The dominant ideology of America was the Dream, that amorphous combination of Jeffersonian liberalism and Horatio Alger laissez-faire that proclaimed America as the land of boundless opportunity where any man and his wife (for so were women defined) could make a fortune: "Land of the free and home of the brave"—"Log cabin to White House"—"Shoe shine boy becomes steel magnate." Even during the Depression, the Dream still remained and it was the greatness of Franklin Roosevelt that he was able to preside over a country in economic collapse and maintain the basic hegemonic structure. A recent film, *They Shoot Horses Don't They,* makes this point very clearly; in the switch from old-style to new-style liberalism, from Hoover Republicans to Roosevelt's New Deal, the essential cultural values were retained though given new clothes to fit changing conditions.

Black Americans had always been excluded from the Dream, and it was from them that the first real challenge to the hegemony came. Not through the civil rights movement, for that was in a sense the last hurrah of the American ideology—"I have a Dream," said Martin Luther King, at the 1963 march on Washington, "and my dream is the American Dream." But rather through the declaration by a minority of blacks from 1965 on that they would redefine themselves, and through their open rejection of American cultural values. When blacks assumed African names and proclaimed "Black Is Beautiful," this was a challenge to the basic cultural assumptions of American society; when H. Rap Brown said "Violence is as American as cherry pie," it was an uncomfortable reminder of the fact, hidden by the dominant school of "consensus" historians, that those who controlled America were perfectly prepared to use force if necessary.

Black protest was only the most obvious sign of what Peter Schrag termed "the decline of the WASP." His thesis is that there is a collapse of the American identity, an identity formed, defined, and guarded by WASPS: "For most of us who were born before World War II, America was a place to be discovered; it was imperfect perhaps—needed some reform, some shaping up—but it did not need to be reinvented. It was all given, like a genetic code, waiting to unfold. We all wanted to learn the style, the proper accent, agreed on its validity, and while our interpretations and our heroes varied, they were all cut from the same stock." And that stock was White Anglo-Saxon Protestant. "They were the landlords of our culture, and their values, with rare exceptions, were those that defined it: hard work, perseverance, self-reliance, puritanism, the missionary spirit and the abstract rule of law." But the landlord's control is no longer unquestioned, and "the powerful are paranoid about the weak."

Simultaneously, and in part because of the black example, there came the challenge—most critical for the analysis to follow—by the "youth culture" to the hegemonic values. As with the blacks, the demand was not for admission into the dominant society by adherence to its cultural values but rather for the right to one's own culture and one's own life-style. But while the blacks at least put their challenge to whites from outside the family, the young challenged from within—the most rebellious among the young tended to be upper-middle-class and either WASPS or Jews—and hence the hostilities and insecurities they brought forth. Men who pride themselves on their "practicality," their "business-sense," their "rationality" can now be reduced to spluttering rage by boys with long hair. And when the new affirmation of self extended to women and gays, it challenged the dominant white male within his very psyche and became the ultimate act of defiance, one that threatened the identity of the oppressor himself. Thus the current dichotomy between culture and politics. The demand for new definitions and new identities is corroding the hegemony of the ruling elite, while as yet leaving relatively untouched its political and economic control.

The youth counterculture has already been the subject of exhaustive discussion and writers as varied as Paul Goodman, Margaret Mead, Theodore Roszak, and Charles Reich are all agreed on its significance. Roszak's remains the best definition of the counterculture. It is, he wrote in an article in 1968, "a culture so radically disaffiliated from the mainstream assumptions of our society that it scarcely looks to many as a culture at all, but takes on the alarming appearance of a barbaric intrusion. . . . One thinks of the invasion of centaurs on the pediment of the Temple of Zeus at Olympus, which a stern Apollo, as guardian of the orthodox culture, steps forward to admonish. Apollo, being older than thirty, could hardly expect his authority to be trusted now. And besides, these later day centaurs while high are not drunken and most likely come behaving flames." Roszak, it should be pointed out, regards the New Left as part of the counterculture, a view with which I substantially agree.[1]

This definition is similar to Charles Reich's formulation of Consciousness III in *The Greening of America,* a remarkably respectable version of the insurgent culture (this may explain Reich's preoccupation with clothes) which at times reads, both in tone and content, as if written for the *Reader's Digest.* An example of the tone:

Its essence is the total scene: a huge and happy noon-time crowd in Lower Sproul Plaza at Berkeley, some standing, some sitting, some dancing; every variety of clothes and costume, knapsacks and rolled-up sleeping bags; piled-up Afro hair and shoulder-length golden-blond hair; a sense of everyone's sharing the values and experience that the scene represents, music by the Crabs, a local group, mostly soaring, ecstatic, earthy rock that shakes

1. This quotation is taken from "Youth and the Great Refusal" (*Nation,* 18 March 1968), which was rewritten as Chapter 1 of Roszak's book *The Making of a Counter Culture.*

the crowd, the buildings, and the heavens themselves with joy; and above the scene, presiding over it, those benevolent deities, the sun-god, the ocean breeze, the brown-green Berkeley hills.

And the content:

> For older people, a new consciousness could rest on growing a garden, reading literature, baking bread, playing Bach on a recorder, or developing a new sense of family, so long as it represents a true knowledge of self, rather than false consciousness.

No matter: Roszak, Reich, et al. are charting the outlines of a new consciousness—for inside accounts one is better advised to turn to some of the underground press, particularly its poetry, and to the music—and there is little doubt of the importance of this new consciousness. Rather than write yet another survey of the counterculture, I shall restrict my analysis to those features of it most important for an understanding of gay liberation.

To understand the counterculture one needs to recognize that it grows out of the very society it seeks to reject. In one of the more perceptive of the great flood of articles on rock, Tom Smucker (writing in Jonathan Eisen's *The Age of Rock, vol.* 2), talks of the counterculture involving "a constant process of assimilation of contradictions."

It is the very advanced state of American industrial capitalism, the features of "postindustrialism" hailed by such "mandarins of the establishment" (to borrow Noam Chomsky's description) as Herman Kahn and Zbigniew Brzezinski, that explains why the counterculture is more pronounced in the United States than elsewhere. In rejecting the "performance principle" that made the development of American capitalism possible, the counterculture does not repudiate the advantages of technology—stereos, motorbikes, the pill. What it does do is reject the cult of hard work and consumerism; the latter, one might note, has been a very important part of the traditional gayworld. Largely perhaps because of social insecurity, homosexuals have long sought to buy respectability by conspicuous consumption; at the same time, within the gayworld the whole process of sex barter tended to enhance the importance of material possessions.

Technological Change and the New Consciousness

These features of American technological development—now beginning to emerge elsewhere in the Western world—have had the effect of breaking down traditional class lines, and increasing social mobility. This does *not* mean that there is an increase in economic equality; indeed the gap between rich and poor seems to be widening. What it does mean is that the alternative of either partially or wholly dropping out has become a real possibility for large numbers of young people. Whereas previous foreshadowings of a counterculture—Greenwich Village bohemia or North Beach beatniks—were restricted to a few, the possibility of refusing to take a conventional job or go to college has now increased greatly, at least among whites, and is now apparent in other Western countries.

Now I would not argue that merely dropping out is equivalent to the formation of a genuine counterculture. Indeed, the kids who move along the international hippie trail—Tangiers, Istanbul, Katmandu—are in some ways a modern version of earlier youth who did the "Grand Tour" on Daddy's money. What does seem true is that the affluence which American society has achieved has opened up new possibilities that the young, because of their very inexperience, are best able to perceive. That is, the requirements that supported "surplus repression"—requirements for hard work, competitiveness, postponed gratification, the nuclear family, etc.—no longer make sense to kids who perceive the incredible waste, destruction, and misallocation of resources on which the American economy is based.

But my argument goes beyond this. The new technology itself bears with it certain features that tend to undermine the hegemonic values. This is, I think, what is implied in much of Alvin Toffler's book, *Future Shock*. His basic argument is that technological change is accelerating to a point where it destroys all traditional values, values which are based on a sense of permanence and a belief that much of what is in fact socially conditioned—for example, the family—is "natural." The same insight about the cultural impact of the new technology runs through much of the writings of Marshall McLuhan. In *Understanding Media*—written in 1964, it is worth noting—he set out some of the basic assumptions that underlie the emerging counterculture, which in his schema is, in effect, the forerunner of the electric age (postliterate, tribal, and inclusive) as distinct from the mechanical age (literate, individualistic, and fragmented):

The aspiration of our time for wholeness, empathy and depth of awareness is a natural adjunct of electric technology.... Electric speed mingles the cultures of pre-history with the dregs of industrial marketeers, the non-literate with the semi-literate and the postliterate.... The immediate prospect for literate, fragmented Western man encountering the electric implosion within his own culture is his steady and rapid transformation into a complex and depth-structured person emotionally aware of his total interdependence with the rest of human society...

It seems clear that many of the features of the counterculture—the stress on personal experience, on community, on sensory enhancement—are related to the impact of technology and resultant social and cultural change.

This is true, too, of those aspects of the counterculture most directly related to the gay (and women's) movements, the breakdown of the nuclear family and the rejection of traditional sex roles. Toffler's chapter "The Fractured Family" makes a number of the points I have already discussed in writing of liberation, but as prophecy rather than utopian prescription. He sees an increased diversity in "family" structures, including "childless marriage, professional parenthood, post-retirement child rearing, corporate families, communes, geriatric group marriages, homosexual family units, polyg-amy..." He sees, too, a decline in the romantic expectation of coupling "and living happily ever afterwards" and a move toward less lasting and possessive relationships. Examples of such a change are increasingly in evidence. In Denmark, a bill has been introduced to legalize group marriage, while adoption of children by homo-sexuals is possibly already in effect, albeit unofficially, in some American states as a result of the increasing number of children requiring foster parents. In early 1971 a special issue of *Look* on the family included a quite sympathetic discussion of a male couple in Minnesota, even including the fact that they were non-monogamous.

Moreover, Toffler, in a view shared by Margaret Mead, sees a rapid decline in the belief that women's main role is as child-bearers and rearers: "If nothing else, we are about to kill off the mystique of motherhood." One of the consequences of the new technology is that the physical differences between men and women decline in importance, as brute physical strength is less necessary (there is something remarkably antiquated about bodybuilding and Mr. Uni-verse competitions) and as the implications of technological war-fare, brought home by Vietnam, produce a re-evaluation of the whole "masculine mystique." Most important, women possess the means of birth control, one of the most momentous developments in the whole of human history. For various reasons, explored in Betty Friedan's *The Feminine Mystique,* there was a cultural lag in adjusting to these changing conditions during the fifties and early sixties. Now, however, the realization that we enjoy far greater freedom than ever before to redefine ourselves and our roles has become widespread.

All this is not, of course, a development that is universally wel-comed, and over the past few years there has developed something of a minor cult of attacking the collapse of American masculinity/femininity which, as if in illustration of my previous arguments, is linked to an alleged growth in homosexuality. (To be accurate, that

growth is mainly in overt and self-accepting homosexuality, although there is probably an increase in those unwilling to sweat
alongside Mailer and Epstein to totally control their homosexual
needs.) Books like Vance Packard's *The Sexual Wilderness,* Patricia
Sexton's *The Feminized Male,* or Hendrik Ruitenbeek's *The Male
Myth* are all examples of this perspective. My favorite is Peter and
Barbara Wyden's—a married couple, they—*Growing up Straight,*
a guide for all parents who want to prevent their sons and daughters
turning into fags and dykes. Their book makes very explicit the
connection between the fear of a declining sex role dichotomy and
increased homosexuality; mothers and fathers are counseled to act
out all those she-woman and he-man stereotypes as a model for
their growing children.

The counterculture is thus a product of certain social and technological preconditions which make possible the search for greatly
increased desublimation. ''Be a realist. Demand the impossible'' was
the slogan of the French students in 1968. In the context of today's
technology this makes perfect sense. The hippie ethos of love, non-
competitiveness, and a greatly reduced glorification of hard work
and continence makes much more sense in our time than the stric-
tures of Republican politicians and Billy Graham evangelists.

Yet if the developments of industrial society have provided the
basic conditions out of which the counterculture emerged, this is
not to suggest, as McLuhan is prone to, some simplified theory of
either technological or economic determinism. Socioeconomic
structures act as broad limitations on possible developments of
consciousness, not as the determinant of automatic and inevitable
reflexes. Moreover, there are special conditions about the American
situation beyond its greater technological development which affect
the character of its counterculture. No movement, no society ever
breaks completely with its past, and there is a specifically American
version of the counterculture which has differences, diffused as these
are by global communications and mutual reinforcing influences,
from the versions found in other highly industrialized nations.

Above all, for our purposes, the counterculture is still troubled by the problems of sex, race, and violence that haunt the American consciousness.

The New Consciousness and Homosexuality

Taking for the moment a broad view of what is countercultural I want to look at some of the music, theater, and literature that has been both an influence on and a product of the new consciousness, and in particular the way in which it has affected homosexuals and social attitudes toward homosexuality. I begin with rock music, which is generally and, I think, quite rightly regarded as the major manifestation of the new culture. Rock, used not as the purists define it but to cover the whole gamut of contemporary youth music, seems to me one of the major influences upon social attitudes toward sexuality and sex roles.

The first, and perhaps the major contribution of rock to the new culture was that it cut at the distinction between body and mind, between Dionysus and Apollo, that underlies the divorce of the erotic from the sexual. Rock was originally the contribution of the black to the emergent youth culture, and in *The Sound of the City* Charlie Gillett has traced the way in which black music moved out of its ghettos to affect the consciousness of adolescents who were just beginning to be defined as a separate, distinct group. As Cleaver puts it in *Soul on Ice:* "The Twist was a guided missile, launched from the ghetto into the very heart of suburbia . . . a form of therapy for a convalescing nation. . . . The stiff mechanical omnipotent Administrators and Ultrafeminines [more of Cleaver's sexual metaphysics later] presented a startling spectacle as they entered in droves onto the dance floors to learn how to Twist. They came from every level of society, from top to bottom, writhing pitifully though gamely about the floor, feeling exhilarating and soothing new sensations, release from some unknown prison in which their Bodies had been encased, a sense of freedom they had never known before, a feeling of communion with some mystical root-source of life and vigor, from which sprang a new awareness and enjoyment of the flesh, a new appreciation of the possibilities of their Bodies."

Rock music proposed a new model of sensuality, and thousands of kids—not only girls felt weak before the Stones—were exposed to an eroticized music. Little wonder that there was much disquiet among the guardians of public morality at the new music; the objections tended to be expressed about the lyrics, and too blatantly sexual allusions were refused air-time, but beneath this lurked a deeper fear, that of the whole sensuousness of rock itself. For as Plato put it, and as Spiro Agnew seems to feel it: 'Forms and rhythms in music are never changed without producing changes in the most important political forms and ways...the new style quietly insinuates itself into manners and customs and from there it issues a greater force...goes on to attack until it ends by overthrowing everything, both in public and in private.'

But rock did more than repudiate the extreme repression that maintained the American hegemony. The associated clothes and hair styles also rejected the masculine/feminine dichotomy and the big breasts and hairy chests that had defined sex appeal in the fifties. Now, it is true that rock, as women's liberationists have pointed out, was largely a male phenomenon: listen to Janis Joplin sing, "Woman Is Loser." While black female singers were accepted, of the white female singers only Janis Joplin and Grace Slick of Jefferson Airplane made any real impact. Groups tended often to be all male, occasionally with a couple of decorative females as background appendages; Lionel Tiger's "male bonding" again. Yet the masculinity of rock is one that takes itself for granted, and adopts a considerable number of once feminine features—long hair, bright clothes, considerable jewelry and ornamentation. Early rock music—one thinks of Elvis Presley with his open shirt and tight jeans— tended to combine sexuality with a very traditional cult of masculinity. The big change probably came under the impact of English groups (particularly the Beatles and the Stones) who were less "uptight" about traditional concepts of masculinity, and through the linking of rock music to psychedelic drugs with the emergence of groups like Jefferson Airplane and Grateful Dead. To these influences, one should add the production of *Hair,* whose claim to be a genuine part of the counterculture is denied only by those who cannot forgive a Broadway success.

Woof, in *Hair,* loves Mick Jagger, and Woof, in *Hair,* sings the song that the pop stations never play beginning with the words *sodomy* and *fellatio.* The sexual play in *Hair* is polymorphous perverse. No wonder that when it opened in Australia the chief secretary of New South Wales said: "I cannot possibly support the way *Hair* lampoons accepted standards of morality, and loudly proclaims every known vice; from blasphemy to drug-taking to homosexuality and draft-dodging."

Everyone loves Jagger: he has become the ubiquitous sex symbol of the new culture. Even *Newsweek* recognizes this, and in their rock cover story (4 January 1971) said:

Jagger's appeal has its deep ambiguities. "Mick definitely has a kind of bisexual charm," says his friend, film-maker Kenneth Anger. "I'm sure that's part of the appeal for the chicks. It reacts in their unconsciousness, it brings out the beast." Abbie Hoffman calls Mick Woodstock Nation's Myra Breckinridge, and rock stage manager Chip Monck remarks: "Before I saw Mick, I had this old lady. Every now and then when I look at Mick from the side he looks like her. I don't know if it puts me in the latent homosexual category but it makes me feel very warm toward him."

But if that quote is revealing of the bisexuality that much of the rock style implies, it also shows how far the traditional culture's hang-ups remain. All three of the quotations seem carefully calculated—though more, perhaps, by the author of the article than the speakers—to reinforce the masculinity of the speaker: "the chicks"; "Myra Breckinridge"; "this old lady." Heaven forbid that we might think Anger, Hoffman, or Chip Monck are *faggots.*

This attitude is generally true of the whole rock scene. There are, of course, gay rock stars, at least several of whom are very well known, yet their sexual preference is guarded with exactly the same zealousness that surrounded homosexual film stars in the fifties (those who are curious are advised to look at the London *Oz* issue of August–September 1969). Gay stars are photographed with beautiful girls, stories spread of their virility. Equally the lyrics, when it comes to homosexuality, are as coy as Bing Crosby and the boys were about heterosexual screwing back in the good old days of Consciousness II. Not only do rock songs tend to objectify women, a common complaint from women's liberation, but they almost totally avoid homosexual love, either male or female. A point that to the best of my knowledge has never been considered worthy of comment in the great outpouring of idolatry about rock.

In discussing rock's softening of the male/female dichotomy one should note that there is in contemporary pop music something of a preoccupation with the blurring of sex roles, in particular with transvestism. Again this seems the influence more of British than American groups; indeed, there is a whole tradition in Britain of "drag," often free of any overt homosexuality, as a popular form of entertainment. Two examples of rock songs will suffice (Unfortunately, copyright restrictions prevent publishing the lyrics here.) The first is the Beatles' "Ob-la-di, Ob-la-da," which tells of the ambivalent romance between Desmond and Molly. (Compare their song "Get Back," with its mention of Loretta who "thought she was a woman but she was another man.") The second example is the Kinks' "Lola," where the singer meets Lola, who "walked like a woman but talked like a man."

The most remarkable pop expression of human androgyny is the film *Performance* in which Mick Jagger plays a retired pop star, Turner, presiding over a world in which sexual distinctions and roles blur into a psychedelic haze, and which traps and conquers the pretty gangster (James Fox), who stumbles into it. Jagger's song, "Memo from Turner," mocks the macho pose that the gangster has embraced; it suggests a strangely surrealistic disintegration of our present world into a future both menacing and hopeful. The film ends violently, for the gangster shoots Turner, but it is an act of violence that Turner has willed. Jagger, more than most of the antiheroes of the counterculture, has a keen sense for its dark underlying tone of destruction, a tone that Charles Reich, a real all-American booster in the Babbitt tradition, ignores completely.

In the seventies the breakdown of sex roles and sexual norms that had been hinted at in the sixties was manifest in the mainstream of rock (if not yet in the bubble-gum radio stations). Two names stand out—the American group Alice Cooper and the Englishman David Bowie. Bowie in particular suggests both androgyny and gender confusion; he claims to be bisexual and his songs reflect this. Ultimately one must conclude that the music of the counter-culture has reflected *both* the new sensuality with the accompanying breakdown of blue/pink sex role dichotomies, *and* the uptightness about homosexuality that remains. Yet is there not something a little strange, perhaps sad, that gays in the rock world remain closeted while they are coming out in the much more traditional, Consciousness II and literate worlds of theater and literature?

Homosexual themes have been important in a number of recent plays, though as in earlier works (for example, Lillian Hellman's *The Children's Hour* and Tennessee Williams' *Cat on a Hot Tin Roof*) most of them reinforce the stereotype of the guilt-ridden, unhappy homosexual. Think not only of Crowley's *Boys in the Band* but of two contemporary British plays, both made into films, Frank Marcus's *The Killing of Sister George* and Charles Dyer's *Staircase*. Not only have such plays traded on the popular view of homosexuality, in theatrical terms they have been very conservative. More interesting have been the suggestions of polymorphous perversity in a number of experimental performances, mostly confined to noncommercial theater.

It is not surprising that in a country with the puritan heritage of the United States, much of the avant-garde theater has been preoccupied with breaking down barriers against sexuality. Stage nudity has also reached the commercial theater, but its use only rarely questions the basic assumptions about sex roles that underlie Western society. That it may be possible to break down these roles has been explored in some recent avant-garde theater, most notably Richard Schechner's Performance Group. In the productions of both *Dionysus '69* and *Commune,* the first a revision of Euripides' play *The Bacchae,* the latter an allegory of contemporary America that uses the Manson murder cult as a symbol of the way in which the counterculture risks being perverted by the very things it seeks to escape, the Performance Group has attempted to eroticize human relationships, an eroticism that is both more sensual and more innocent than the voyeuristic prurience of the commercialized stage.

At times there is in Schechner's vision a strong sense of difference between men and women, and he places his actors so as to emphasize this, almost playing out the sex warfare of a Mailer or a Cleaver. His women are obsessed with childbirth, his men with dread/attraction toward homosexuality. Equally, however, Schechner's theater suggests the new fluidity and ease of sex roles, and there is in his productions considerable touching, hugging, kissing, embracing (of both cast and audience) that transcends homo/hetero, female/male lines. This fluidity becomes more explicit in much of the lesser-known experimental theater groups like the Theatre of the Ridiculous. Experimental theater, far less known than either music or film—and less touched by commercialism for that reason— has become an arena where society can rehearse for new roles and new relationships.

The counterculture is, of course, associated with the widespread use of drugs, though not, I would argue, to the extent that this association is usually made in the press. Similarly, while there has been much speculation about the link between drug taking and homosexuality, there has been some ambivalence toward homosexuality in the attitudes of the more fervent ideologues of turning-on. In a *Playboy* interview in 1966, Dr. Timothy Leary talked of homosexuality as a "perversion" and a "symbolic screw-up," and proclaimed LSD as a "cure" for homosexuality. (Drs. Reuben and Socraides please note.) This was in reply to a question as to whether LSD could trigger the acting-out of latent homosexual feelings.

In my opinion there is probably truth in both question and answer. Under the influence of any hallucinogen, repressed feelings are likely to emerge, so that both exclusive heterosexuals and homosexuals may discover and display the concealed part of their being. This would seem to me healthy, and only Leary's ideological view makes him talk of "cures," At the same time, my experience with acid heads is that they are likely to be frightened and often very hostile when these new feelings emerge. As James Baldwin once said, "American males are the only people I've ever encountered in the world who are willing to go on the needle before they'll go to bed with each other."

Countercultural "Gurus" and Gay Liberation

Joseph Epstein, in his article in *Harper's,* remarked on how "fascinating" it is that "many principal publicists and polemicists for youth culture are homosexuals." Yet it is a recent development to see homosexuals as ideologues of social radicalism. Writing in 1968, D. J. West commented that homosexuals, like most people who are stigmatized, "strive to avoid all taint of unorthodoxy in opinions and behavior. Few famous homosexuals have been radical reformers." Despite Lewis Feuer's attempt in *The Conflict of Generations* to suggest some connection between homosexuality and support for alienated and anarchist movements—the only evidence he suggests being the very different careers of Plato, Bakunin, and Paul Goodman—West is probably right. The social alienation of homosexuals has found expression in cultural rather than political activity, and only where these two become synonymous, as in *fin-de-siècle* Europe or contemporary America, are there likely to be prominent homosexual radicals.

At a time when the underlying cultural assumptions of American liberalism are being undermined, it is not surprising that homosexuals seem so prominent in cultural life. Their influence, indeed, extends far beyond the youth culture and into those very areas of violence and pessimism which as I have already noted, Reich ignores (and Roszak in part avoids). For there is within the counterculture a nihilistic strain, as for example among the kids—and there are numbers of them—who take drugs heavily in the full knowledge that they are likely to kill themselves. There is a grimness, a bitterness, a dark fear to the new consciousness, and its casualties are increasingly visible, not only Hendrix and Joplin, or for that matter the dead students at Kent State and Jackson State, but also the anonymous victims of drugs and urban violence.

The apocalyptic mood of much of the current American scene and the rejection of the liberal tradition of buoyant optimism owe much to homosexual writers, who have charted the dark side of the American dream. The two key figures here are William Burroughs and Jean Genet, for though Genet is a Frenchman his influence has been profound in America. Like many other homosexual writers, Burroughs and Genet are concerned with man's loneliness and his attempt to overcome it through physical experience, either externally induced (by drugs) or through continuous sexual experience—homosexuality is portrayed, ultimately, in completely asocial terms—and there is in their works a contempt for the individual which leads to the power plays of Genet and the sadomasochistic fantasies of Burroughs. *Naked Lunch,* in particular, is the ultimate extension of alienation in which life becomes totally nauseous and sexuality both obsessive and destructive or, as Ginsberg said of Burroughs' vision in *Naked Lunch,* an addiction. See, for example, the section "A.J.'s Annual Party," where sex between John/Mary/Mark ends with one of the boys being hanged and the literal disintegration of the others' bodies. Of such writers, the critic William Phillips observed:

In Burroughs we actually get a kind of sexual cannibalism, that doubles as a homosexual and a social symbol. In this sort of free-for-all, the family naturally disappears, too. In fact, the only place I know where Marx's prediction of the breakdown of the family is actually fulfilled is in the novels of Burroughs and Genet. Generally in the fluid world of the anti-world, in which there are no recognizable boundaries, all the people act like orphans, as well as drifters. As I recall, there are no sons or fathers in Burroughs, only spacemen on leave from reality. Hence all relations are incestuous and patricidal and all distinctions of age or authority tend to disappear. Selby's tough adolescents, too [Hubert Selby, *Last Exit to Brooklyn*], though always in motion, do not seem to be coming from or going anywhere.

Now Burroughs' writing seems to me an influence on the counterculture indirectly, and primarily through his association with Allen Ginsberg, with whom he has had a long and close relationship (see, for example, their jointly authored *The Yage Letters*) and who helped launch Burroughs' first book, *Junkie*. The image of Moloch in "Howl," and Ginsberg's attempt to develop a new consciousness through the use of drugs, both bear some mark of Burroughs' influence, though Ginsberg's vision of life is far less horrendous than Burroughs'. Ginsberg and Paul Goodman are, in fact, the two names specifically instanced by Epstein, and I would agree with him that they are considerable figures both for any evaluation of the counterculture and of the "new homosexual." To the best of my knowledge neither has really been considered in this way, and hence it would seem useful to examine them from a specifically gay point of view.

They are, of course, very different sorts of men; toward the end of his life Goodman became hostile to many of the features of the counterculture with which Ginsberg is associated. Yet both were important influences on the emerging counterculture in the early sixties—Ginsberg's "Howl," written in 1956, became the best-known product of the "beat" movement and is the first document Paul Jacobs and Saul Landau quote in their book *The New Radicals*, while Goodman's social criticism, and especially his *Growing Up*

Absurd, was probably second only to the writings of C. Wright Mills as a primary influence on the early theories of the New Left.

Roszak's book devotes some considerable space to both of these men, along with Marcuse, Norman O. Brown, and Alan Watts, and it is not my concern to duplicate his general discussion of their work. Rather I am concerned with just that part of Ginsberg and Goodman that Roszak omits, their extremely open and public homosexuality. While Capote, Vidal, Tennessee Williams, and Baldwin had all written of homosexuality in the postwar period, none sought to live public lives as homosexuals. (Truman Capote, for example, talked openly about his homosexuality for the first time only in 1969 in a Dutch magazine interview.) Ginsberg and Goodman did lead such lives, and their dual roles, as influences upon the emergent youth culture and as open homosexuals, give them some claim to be regarded as founding fathers of the gay liberation movement. To Roszak, Ginsberg's homosexuality is not worth comment and Goodman's is glossed over. It is true that Goodman thinks highly of Wilhelm Reich, and indeed wrote the introduction to the biography of Reich by his widow, but to talk of Reichian sexuality "as part of 'the essential Goodman'" without pointing to Goodman's total rejection of Reich's theory of male-female genital sex as the sine qua non of sexual liberation seems at best sloppy and at worst dishonest.

But then, perhaps, this reflects some ambivalence in Goodman himself. *Gestalt Therapy,* which he wrote in 1951 in collaboration with Frederick Perls and Ralph Hefferline, is partly influenced by Reich, yet nowhere in the parts of the book for which Goodman was primarily responsible does he take issue with Reich for his antihomosexual views. (It might be noted, however, that this book is enjoying a new popularity and has helped influence the current vogue for encounter and consciousness-raising groups, among them those of gay liberation.) Yet at the same time as writing *Gestalt Therapy,* Goodman was writing poetry and short stories (most of the latter are collected in *Adam and His Works*) that deal with his homosexuality. Indeed, there appears a disjunction between Good-man as poet and novelist on the one hand and Goodman as social critic on the other—although Goodman himself denied this.

Yet Goodman was always open about his homosexuality and was in fact fired from three colleges as a result. (It is strange, Good-man has remarked, that he was penalized for his homosexuality by radical institutions far more than by square ones.) When Goodman did talk about sex it was with an assured acceptance of the equal validity of homo- and heterosexuality that infuriated his opponents. The feud between Mailer and Goodman, of which Mailer writes in *Armies of the Night,* illustrates this perfectly. (It also illustrates Mailer's own sexual theories, summed up in the phrase "without guilt, sex was meaningless.")

Mailer is not only a neo-Victorian, he also misunderstood Good-man's position. Goodman would not regard masturbation as being "as good as" sex with another person—though he hardly shared Mailer's metaphysical guilt about it—and as I have already quoted, he found its very "dirtiness" one of the advantages of homosexual sex. At the least, Mailer's attribution to Goodman of the concept of "super-hygiene" suggests that he has never read the accounts of transitory, hurried sex on the waterfront charted in *Five Years.* The more fundamental criticism from Mailer's perspective, it seems to me, is that Goodman represents the very rational, logical, linear mind that Mailer, with his cult of "the hipster," is in some ways rejecting, and hence their mutual misunderstanding. For though each man has referred to himself as "conservative," they each speak from a different tradition, of which their differing views on sex are only a part.

In many ways Goodman represented the best of Consciousness I and II rather than the ethos of Consciousness III; there is, in his *New Reformation,* great stress on the need for earnest professionals. In the introduction to this book, Goodman talks of the need to "purge . . . the triumph of the Protestant Reformation." Yet he him-self subscribed to most of its tenets, with the great exception of its restrictive attitudes toward sexuality. It is a sad commentary on American liberalism that one of its best minds was forced so often into opposition to the liberal establishment, for Goodman represented a belief in rational thought that the young are repudiating because it seems to have led to the horrors of MyLai and Kent State. Mailer, too, rejects the purely logical and rational thought of a Goodman, although in favor of a metaphysic of constant struggle and guilt rather than the countercultural one of hedonism and doing your own thing.

Yet if Goodman has come to stand as a symbol of a guiltless and bisexual sexuality, he was in some ways a pseudo-bisexual, one who extolled bisexuality as an ideology without, in fact, appearing to fully live it. In the poems he wrote to his lovers in the pages of the *New York Review of Books,* Goodman upheld some kind of return to the Greek model, where he could be both paterfamilias and lover of young boys at the same time. In his autobiographical writings (e.g., the novel *Making Do*), wife and children hover uneasily as backdrops to his current affairs and pickups; they are there, one suspects, to provide security when his lovers move on. In his poem "June and July," written when Goodman was "pushing sixty" and miserable, ("Americans after their love affair hate me again and nobody will read my next book that I don't intend to write,") he says:

> I ought like a father to him
> Because I love him a lot
> To bring him home and let him alone
> But I'd never be content with that,
> And my wife wouldn't care for that.

Goodman always insisted that he was primarily a poet and novelist, and that his novel *The Empire City* is worthy of far greater critical consideration than it has received. As he has received virtually no attention from literary critics one is inclined to agree with him; as a novelist he was undoubtedly far more interesting than many more celebrated minor figures, although his style, admirably direct in social criticism, was less effective in more personal writings. Still *The Empire City* is a book worthy of inclusion amidst the important works of contemporary American writing, and if I neglect it, it is mainly for lack of space to do it full credit. Critics are, I imagine, irritated by Goodman's combination of humility and arrogance, for he was, as he wrote on his forty-third birthday:

> ...not a lonesome man, I need
> a sociable occasion and applause,
> otherwise I despond, my aim holds true
> but I lose fire power...

Above all, Goodman's very directness about his homosexuality may help explain his neglect by the critics, for he refused to be coy about it and deal with it in the symbolic and guilt-ridden fashion of writers like (the early) Truman Capote or James Purdy. Which is not to attack these writers, but merely to suggest that straight readers are made squeamish by Goodman's utter directness. As Goodman himself wrote in his essay "Underground Writing 1960": "It is as if people cannot feel they exist except by affirming, with a shudder, that they are different from something that they are against. But to be rid of it, we must indeed do without the boundaries." It is just this matter-of-fact attitude—and Goodman instances a splendid teacher "naturally queer" for his students—"that is shocking to the audience and unacceptable to the publishers, whereas any kind of 'underground' writing has become perfectly acceptable." Mailer is right that Goodman would dispense with guilt, and it is this that makes him important for the new culture.

"My one literary theme," wrote Goodman, "has been the Community, as in *Parents Day or Break-Up;* in *The Empire City* it is the band that acts as if it were the community and as if the others, who don't make sense, didn't exist." In *Making Do* the whole problem of a would-be community across the river from Manhattan is explored, along with Goodman's affair with a young kid (in some ways—this was written in 1963—a precursor of today's dropouts), whom Goodman loves but cannot like. Community, too, is a preoccupation of his social criticism, and according to Roszak is his most important contribution to the New Left. Yet in this discussion of community Goodman seems never to have fully considered the place of the homosexual, although as he wrote in 1969, in "Memoirs of an Ancient Activist": "I am all for community because it is a human thing, only I seem doomed to be left out."

It is a pity that Goodman has dealt only peripherally with homosexuality in his social criticism, for it is this social criticism which has been most influential. When I first heard of Goodman, in college days in the mid-sixties, it was as a man of supreme common sense, a radical in the true sense, that is, someone who looked to the roots of problems, and a man with unparalleled ability to see below the mystification of Cold War and technetronic ideology. I did not know of Goodman as a man with something particular to say about my own personal problems. Yet in the same year as I heard him speak at Cornell, he addressed an East Coast Homophile Organization conference, and talked of the need for a "decent" society, one in which "I don't think the word homosexual would be used." On the other hand, Goodman seems at times to underestimate the extent to which homosexuals are oppressed, a point Dick Leitsch made to him in a *Playboy* panel on homosexuality. (That panel, published in April 1971, was a perfect example of the majority culture's failure to come to terms with the new: of the eleven panelists—nine of them men, all white, average age 52—all but three were heterosexual, and none were associated with the new gay radicalism.)

In any case, to evaluate Goodman's influence on the "new" homosexual and society's attitude to him (for Goodman seems concerned exclusively with male homosexuality) is thus made difficult by the fact that he is not widely known for the writings in which he is most personal. Most bookshops that stock *Growing Up Ab-*

surd or *Utopian Essays and Practical Proposals* just do not have *The Empire City* or *Making Do*. Perhaps only with his article, "Memoirs...," published in *Liberation,* in 1969, did Goodman's homosexuality really make a large impact. This article is a remarkable affirmation of homosexuality, particularly when compared with the guilt of Dave McReynold's confessional in the same issue. Yet by the time of its appearance, one suspects, members of the counterculture were no longer reading Goodman, whose matter of factness and insistence on rationality irritated them. Despite this, Goodman both as a writer and a person had considerable influence in leading others to an acceptance of homosexuality, and was an important intellectual influence on the gay liberation movement.

The same comment can be made even more strongly of Ginsberg, for his homosexuality is an integral part of everything he writes, and Ginsberg is possibly more influential in breaking down attitudes of sexual repression than any other single contemporary writer. It is obviously impossible to ignore Ginsberg's homosexuality—one does not have to read much of "Howl" to find the lines:

> Who let themselves be fucked in the arse by saintly
>   motorcyclists, and screamed with joy,
> Who blew and were blown by those human
>   seraphim, the sailors, caresses of Atlantic and
>   Caribbean love,
> Who balled in the morning in the evenings in
>   rosegardens and the grass of public parks and
>   cemeteries scattering their semen freely to
>   whomever come who may,
> Who hiccupped endlessly trying to giggle but
>   wound up with a sob behind a partition in a
>   Turkish Bath when the blonde and naked
>   angel came to pierce them with a sword,

—although these lines are usually reprinted with asterisks replacing the word "fucked," and this is not the section excerpted by Jacobs and Landau in their anthology of the "new radicals."

Even with Ginsberg, however, the critics are squeamish, and Jane Kramer's book *Allen Ginsberg in America* first introduces Peter Orlovsky as his "room-mate of the past 13 years." Orlovsky, in fact, has been his lover, and this is one of the best-known facts about Ginsberg; Goodman may have got off with various students on his speaking tours, as he is fond of telling us, but Ginsberg appeared with Orlovsky and simply expected acceptance. Ginsberg and Orlovsky became for the counterculture what Gertrude Stein and Alice Toklas had been for the avant-garde in the twenties, a public homosexual couple—and Ginsberg's writings, unlike Stein's, are, of course, completely explicit about their bed relationship.

More than any other cultural figure of contemporary America, and unlike most others of the Beat generation, Ginsberg brings a full sense of sexual liberation into his vision. His view of the world is both apocalyptic and utopian, anguished and ecstatic. There is often a sense of lost loneliness in Ginsberg that runs beside the erotic and joyful—"I never wanted to be a 'human' being and this is what I got . . ." he wrote in his poem "Ankor Wat" written during a visit through the East in the early sixties. In our perspective, Ginsberg can be seen as the first of the "new" homosexuals. In his poem "In Society," written in 1947, he writes of a dream:

> I walked into a cocktail party
> room and found 3 or 4 queers
> talking together in queer talk.
> I tried to be friendly but heard
> myself talking to one in hiptalk . . .

There is the essence of the new countercultural homosexual, only twenty-two years before gay liberation.

Ginsberg, like Goodman, is an exponent of bisexuality, though there is more joy and less earnestness about him. Like the women and men of gay liberation he extols the need for sexual freedom, and he commented to Jane Kramer that he saw "the sexual commune as an intelligent, spiritual way of life as against a kind of dinosaur socialism run by a bunch of sexually and spiritually per- verted Marxists." Goodman would certainly agree, but Goodman would be less likely to talk of the need to change consciousness. "The Civil Rights Movement," Ginsberg told Jane Kramer, "hasn't succeeded in altering the fear-consciousness of the white Southern middle-class, but the hippies might." (Leslie Fiedler claims that Ginsberg was responsible for "the invention . . . of the theory of the alteration of consciousness itself," which seems to me something of an exaggeration.)

At the 1969 trial for alleged conspiracy which followed massive demonstrations at the 1968 Democratic Convention in Chicago, Ginsberg testified for the defense, and was cross-examined by the government counsel on his homosexual poetry. The poem most central to the prosecution's attack was one called "Love Poem on Theme by Whitman," which enabled Ginsberg to call on Whitman's romantic notion of tenderness between the citizens, known as "ad- hesiveness." While it was the intention of the prosecution to destroy Ginsberg's credibility, they in fact provided him with an opportunity to declare his sexual attitudes to a very large forum. If anything, Ginsberg won that cross-examination. It is interesting to remember that in the early sixties Goodman felt unable to appear as a character witness in court because of his unorthodoxy—the incident is de- scribed in *Making Do*. We have progressed a long way in one decade.

Ginsberg's belief that a broadened sense of erotic love is possible and necessary has had a major influence upon the counterculture. He has become in some ways its central, most visible guru, as much an influence through his life-style as through his writings. Unlike Marcuse and Norman Brown, Ginsberg is what he teaches; it is hardly surprising that one of the early signs of Czech revolt was the choice of Ginsberg in 1965 by Prague students to be King of the May: "And I am the King of the May," wrote Ginsberg in the poem "Kral Majales," "which is the power of sexual youth . . ."

Ginsberg was subsequently expelled from Prague, for acting on this principle.

Ginsberg's main significance is that he totally rejects all hypocrisy and pretense: he writes as he lives, and for Ginsberg there is no difference between art and life. "The problem," he said in an interview in *Paris Review,* "is to break down that distinction: when you approach the Muse to talk as frankly as you would talk with yourself or your friends." Ginsberg's whole merging of art and life has had an enormous influence on the way in which the Yippies—an important development of the counterculture—developed their theater of revolt. In a broader sense he exemplifies one of the major themes of the counterculture, its large-scale rejection of hypocrisy and guilt.

Speaking of the French Revolution, Hannah Arendt wrote: "after hypocrisy had been unmasked and suffering been exposed, it was rage and not virtue that appeared—the rage of corruption unveiled on one side, the rage of misfortune on the other." In many ways, "hypocrisy unmasked" explains much of the anger and alienation of so many young Americans.

Again this is a point that has been made at length by others. Especially under the traumatic impact of the black uprising and Vietnam, a much larger proportion of youth than ever before perceives the ways in which American society rests on pretense and hypocrisy. This is a particularly indefensible charge in a society based on grand premises—"life, liberty and the pursuit of happiness" are, after all, the essence of the American creed, and of the three, the last most of all—and the refusal of youth to regard these premises as rhetoric only is their greatest single revolutionary act. The declining tolerance of hypocrisy is one of the most common features of the new consciousness.

Western societies rely on very considerable hypocrisy about sexual behavior, preferring epidemics of venereal disease and crippling backyard abortions to any honest acceptance of the realities of sexual life. Nowhere is this more obvious than in the case of homosexuality, and both gays and straights have been caught up in a gigantic game of pretending that it in fact does not exist. In the new mood of the counterculture, it is not surprising that such pretense is rejected; to be told not to come out publicly because of social consequences becomes merely a reason to be more blatant. When gay liberationists proclaim "We are going to be who we are," they are echoing the mood of the broader counterculture. The very directness of the counterculture's language, its rejection of euphemisms, which distinguishes both the gay and the straight radicals from more traditional groups, is in part rejection of hypocrisy, although there is also a desire to assault the old consciousness by shock tactics and to find phrases that cannot easily be co-opted by the mass media.

Hypocrisy, said La Rochefoucauld, is the homage paid by vice to virtue, but if "doing one's thing" is no longer seen as a vice, then both hypocrisy and guilt disappear. Not only in their attitudes to society but in their private lives, the youth of the counterculture have rejected externally imposed standards and pretense. Now this, as I have already suggested, is an argument that can be overdone; one does not, in one fell swoop, abolish existing standards. It is a mistake, and one that Charles Reich in particular seems prone to make, to extol the counterculture/Consciousness III without recognizing how far it bears the mark of the old. Reich's book is remarkably squeamish about sex, and as far as I can see never descends from generalities about liberation to consider the homosexual at all. Nonetheless Reich is undoubtedly right when he says there is about Consciousness III "less guilt, less anxiety, less self-hatred."

In an article in *Esquire* in December 1969, Tom Burke made the first explicit link between the homosexual and the new culture. "Pity," begins the article, "just when Middle America finally discovered the homosexual, he died." Like all the best of *Esquire*, this is something of an exaggeration. *Boys in the Band* still describes a good part of the gayworld—did Burke visit Fire Island that summer?—nor is the swinging, drug-taking, bisexual that Burke presents less of a caricature than Crowley's characters. Yet he captures something of a real change, as in the words of one "red-blooded, with-it, all-American faggot": "*That's* what has died: this homosexual feeling of being isolated from the straight world by guilt. The whole country has divided into two groups: those who care about what people do in bed and those who don't. The guilty and the guiltless. The old queens are in the first category, the kids are in the second. That's why this camp business means nothing to them. I think camp was a way for queens to distract themselves from their guilt, and to-day, who needs it?"

It was out of this sort of mood that gay liberation emerged. The counterculture may not have fully embraced homosexuality, but it went far enough in the direction of undermining guilt, hypocrisy, and extreme sexual repression to make for a new type of homosexual. To these, the separate gayworld with its furtiveness, its campness, its preoccupations with elegance, Judy Garland, and the latest clothes was boring and unnecessary; the new youth culture, with its drugs, its music, its casualness about roles and relationships was much more attractive. The homosexual world shared much of the generation gap of the straight, and for homosexuals, at least for the younger ones, the counterculture offered a new alternative life-style which removed the feeling that existed prior to the mid-sixties that one had to choose either suburban straight America or the traditional gayworld with its bars, beats, and bitchinesses.

There were of course gay hippies; an article in a newsletter of the Chicago Gay Activists Alliance claimed that there were quite a number of homosexuals "on the scene" at the time when Haight-Ashbury (that part of San Francisco where hippy culture flourished) seemed to offer a new pattern for social community. The new sense of community that I have discussed in relation to gay liberation bears obvious marks of the counterculture, and in many cases that culture has proved sufficiently responsive to the challenge of gay liberation to allow for a considerable breakdown in the barriers between gay and straight. In the summer of 1970 I attended a dance sponsored jointly by the San Francisco Gay Liberation Front and the League for Sexual Freedom, a nude-rock dance where women danced with women and men with men or in combinations of three or four.

On the American West Coast particularly, gay liberationists tend to see themselves as very much a part of the counterculture. Thus one of the founders of the Los Angeles Gay Liberation Front, Don Jackson, wrote in an early issue of the San Francisco *Free Press*:

> Gay Liberation is a social and cultural revolution, a part of the general movement of young people in America. It is not political. A handful of dissidents are trying to turn the Gay revolution into a violent Marxist political revolution by allying it with the Old Left and para-military groups. As an outgrowth of the hippy movement, Gay Liberation is based on love, peace and freedom. It has nothing in common with these advocates of violence, hatred and tyranny. Gay Liberation does not need the support of these small noisy groups and violent agitators. The Old Left has fallen into disrepute. Gay liberation needs nothing from these elderly gentlemen who are desperately attempting to find some young converts for their dated gospel of hate and violence before they take their philosophy with them to their final rest at Forest Lawn Memorial Park.

The tone of hostility to the Left has become more muted within gay liberation, but the sense of being part of the larger counter-culture is found in most gay liberation groups, and is often referred to by activists as setting them apart from the more traditional groups such as SIR, CHE or CAMP. There seems to be a growing reciprocal influence between the gay movement and the cultural radicals, ex-pressed in publications like *Oz* in England or the *Digger* in Aus-tralia. (This has not meant of course an end to the old hang-ups; a countercultural variation of repressive tolerance toward homo-sexuals is often encountered.)

Because gay liberation opposes so many of the basic assumptions around which society is organized, because it repudiates both the expectations of the straight world and the guilts and hostilities that these have produced in the gay, it could only emerge amidst conditions of flux and considerable uncertainty about traditional moral values, of which conditions the counterculture is both cause and effect. Thus it is no accident that gay liberation emerged as a large-scale movement in the wake of black, youth, and women's protest, nor that it bears the mark of all three. These interrelations will be explored in the next chapter.

If the counterculture helped undermine the dominant cultural hegemony of white, middle-class, middle-age America, the women's and gay movements have carried the undermining one stage further, and together represent the next and vital step toward the creation of a genuinely new consciousness. This is a consciousness that need not necessarily bear the superficial hallmarks of "dropping out." American society can maintain a certain number of dropouts, and the kids who panhandle for a living along Sunset Strip or in the East Village are merely recognizing this fact. It is rather one that postulates an alternative mode of life to that of contemporary Protestant, capitalist (whether private or state), and exploitative societies.

The critique of American society that gay liberation has adopted bears the marks of a decade of rising expectations and rising frustrations. Just as the black movement has revealed how far the society rests on racism, so the youth revolt, fueled by the war in Vietnam, has been struck by the extent to which the American dream is an illusion based on extreme competitiveness and inequality, and on American domination abroad. Women and homosexuals have introduced new and critical concepts of "sexism" and "heterosexual chauvinism" in demonstrating that the very bulwark and centre of the dream, its faith in home and family, often disguised oppression and crude power relationships.

If the essence of gay liberation, as I have already asserted, is self-affirmation, then "Out of the closets and into the streets" is a revolutionary slogan, no less for the fact that one comes on to the streets to embrace rather than to trash buildings. It is precisely in its attack on the dominant cultural assumptions about woman/man, homo/hetero that gay liberation is revolutionary. For homosexuals who had involved themselves in the larger movement, it took a long process of struggle to reach the point where we could identify with our own oppression. Sidney Abbott, a member of Radicalesbians, speaking at a Columbia University forum, talked of how she came into gay liberation after first being involved in the civil rights and then the women's movements. In my own political development I recognize the same process. Someone who has grown up in a society that defines heterosexuality as the norm and homosexuality as a perversion, that offers only a furtive underworld to identify with, and places a high premium on hypocrisy and secrecy, is not likely to suddenly discover the extent of his or her oppression, for in such a society, as I have already discussed, the oppression is largely internalized. Without the example provided by the blacks, the young radicals, and the women's movement, gay liberation could not have been born.

In turn, as has happened with most of the American counterculture, gay liberation provided a model to be emulated in other countries of a similar level of socioeconomic development. In Britain, Canada, Australia, and New Zealand the American movement was a direct inspiration for the formation of groups which, while adapting to the particular circumstances of those societies, borrowed heavily from American analysis and practice. In the Netherlands, Germany, and Denmark, where homosexual organizations have a substantial history, and where legal and social pressures are less oppressive than in the United States, the American influence has nonetheless contributed to growing militancy among younger gays. As with the counterculture itself, changes in the consciousness of Americans over the past ten years are having an impact on the whole Western world. At a time when the American government appears increasingly reactionary, its insurgents seem far more successful than its counterinsurgents in influencing others.

6. The Impact of Gay Liberation

If gay liberation is in large part a product of the counterculture, it has begun, in turn, to influence that culture, and the various groups that make up what is loosely called "the movement." In the process of developing a new consciousness—a process that links cultural and political revolutionaries, hippies, and anarchists—each section of the movement influences the others, and a dialectic relationship is established. Ultimately the major impact of gay liberation, other than its role in developing the self-affirmation of homosexuals, seems to me to lie in the response of the movement, for if a new consciousness is coming into being it will be its capacity to incorporate a vision of sexual liberation which includes homosexuals that will ultimately determine our full acceptance into society.

The impact of gay liberation is not of course restricted to the movement. A general breakdown of the extreme stigma of homosexuals seems part of our current era, and the reasons for this go far beyond the pressures of the gay movement. Yet in choosing to go outside the bounds of liberalism, in demanding a revision of society rather than incorporation into it, gay liberation has intentionally limited its appeal. Unlike the old-line homophile groups, gay liberation sees part of its role as radicalizing homosexuals and winning a place for homosexuals in the movement through the assertion of their radical credentials. The language of the gay liberation press ensures that it is likely to be more acceptable to the straight underground than to the square gayworld.

Before moving to a general discussion of the impact of gay liberation on the movement, I want to consider its particular relationship with two major groups that also exist outside the dominant hegemony; blacks and women. Among both groups, but especially the latter, only a minority have begun to reject the dominant values of white, middle-class, male society. Both, but particularly the former, have tended to echo that society's denunciation of homosexuals. Yet the gay movement has been strongly influenced by both the analysis and practice of the radical black and women's groups, and the possibility of creating alliances around what is perceived as a common oppression is a major concern of many in the gay movement. Both the radical black and radical women's movements include, of course, homosexuals, many of whom feel pressures on them to choose with which group—black, women's, or gay—they should primarily identify. Yet the oppression each group faces seems to me different in kind, and these differences will necessarily influence the relationship between the three movements.

Cigarette packets bear the warning: "This may be hazardous to your health." This chapter should bear the warning that it is written by a white male, whose perspective is inevitably distorted by both characteristics. The chapter has been the most difficult to write, for it demands empathy with those whose experience is not, and never can be, mine. Yet in a way it is this very effort that makes the chapter important, for there is a danger that in the current enthusiasm for experiential politics we shall lose sight of the need to deal with those whose experience is different from our own. Consciousness III is in many ways a "honky" concept; the sexual liberation movements, for their part, too often verge on forgetting the basic racial and class inequalities of America.

The great dilemma that faces the movement is the difficulty of reconciling the individual development of a consciousness among oppressed groups with the task of building a coalition between them. The first, by highlighting the sense of anger and of separateness of a particular group, tends to make the second that much more difficult to accomplish, as the experience of black-white relations over the past few years has clearly demonstrated. The danger in what is now going on is that the desire to define the identity of particular groups will lead to the total estrangement of each from all others; the work of "divide and rule" is thus done for the establishment by the movement itself. With regard to gay liberation, this estrangement shows itself most clearly in two areas: the relations between women and men, and those between gay liberation and radical blacks, most particularly, in the United States, the Panthers.

Gay Liberation and Black Liberation:
The Faggot as Nigger

"The faggot as nigger" is an attractive figure of speech, and one that I have myself used in this book, for it highlights the extent to which there are common features to the oppression of blacks and homosexuals. It is not surprising that both black analysis and black political experience have had a considerable impact upon the gay movement, nor that in seeing the oppression of blacks and homosexuals as interrelated there has been a strong tendency to argue that the movements should also be interrelated. The reality is, as I have already suggested, less simple. The oppression of blacks is far more closely connected with the socioeconomic structure of society than is that of homosexuals; few blacks have the option of passing as white and are thus not faced with the dilemma of how to manage their stigma in the same way as are gays; most important, the knowledge of being black is not a realization that separates someone from her or his family.

It is true that both groups show similar marks of oppression. The parallel is most obvious on the psychological level, at that point, most destructive of all, where oppression is internalized. Whitney Young once wrote (in an *Esquire* symposium) of his "embarrassment and shame and bitterness" when he first realized he was a "nigger." Black literature—note the common theme behind titles such as Ralph Ellison's *Invisible Man,* James Baldwin's *Nobody Knows My Name,* John Williams' *The Man Who Cried I Am*— suggests the same search for identity, the same need for affirmation as one finds among homosexuals. Yet because blacks and homosexuals are stigmatized in similar ways and by similar mechanisms, often indeed by the same people (the motto of the KKK: "Don't be half a man, join the Klan"), this does not make their oppression identical. Nor, and this is the crucial point, does it prevent strong feelings of racism among homosexuals or male/heterosexual chauvinism among blacks. Indeed, as we shall see, the very similarity may reinforce such feelings.

The way in which blacks and homosexual radicals will respond to each other is in large part determined by the way in which racism is an attitude deeply ingrained in whites in most societies. There is no evidence of which I am aware which suggests that white homosexuals are less affected by racism than are white heterosexuals: the experience of persecution is no guarantee that one will not in turn persecute. This is most obvious in the United States; it is increasingly true of countries like Britain and Australia, where non-white minorities are beginning to confront institutionalized racism. If it is true that ultimately all American culture and politics are influenced by the fact, so long avoided by Hollywood, that America is not a white country, white homosexuals are as likely to exhibit the whole spectrum of fear/hate/guilt/attraction vis-à-vis nonwhites as anyone else.

White homosexuals *are* more likely, however, to mix with blacks than are their heterosexual peers. Because of social pressures against integration in America, only among otherwise stigmatized groups have blacks and whites mingled much. At least to a greater extent than is true of America as a whole, the gayworld is an integrated one. Among both black and white homosexuals, there is strong crossracial sexual attraction; the same attraction, with the same intensity, exists among heterosexuals, but they are more likely to be restrained by social barriers, except perhaps in contact with prostitutes. Nor is this crossracial attraction confined to America—in Britain the expression "dinge queen" is used to refer to someone who is sexually obsessed by blacks. No other society, however, is as hung-up over race and sex and the complex relations between the two as America.

The very furtiveness and outlaw status of the gayworld has led to its greater integration across color lines. The experiences of Charles Wright's hustler-hero in *The Messenger,* a black from Missouri, are the experiences of John Rechy in *City of Night,* a white from Texas. (Though among hustlers color takes on a commercial value: "You'd be surprised," says Wright's hero, "how my color helps business. Though I've missed out several times because, of course, I just wasn't dark enough.") The neon-spotted, drab, dirty streets on the west side of Manhattan around 42nd Street, with their all-night movies and greasy hamburger joints, are, along with the pseudo-bohemian, fluidly sexual worlds of Greenwich Village, the point in New York where black and white meet most easily. The New York street transvestites of whom I have already spoken include blacks, whites, and Puerto Ricans, united by a common bond of outlawry. Even the language of the gayworld, with its very physicality, has taken over more black idiom than that of the straight.

But this very integration is one of the difficulties that stands against a black-gay coalition. For the black does not come into the homosexual world as an equal, nor does he shed his color and the attached stigma by entering it. For if white middle-class homosexuals are marginally more willing to accept individual blacks than are their straight peers—and the interchange in Crowley's *Boys in the Band* between the black, Bernard, and the super-fag, Emory, is one of the more real and moving parts of that play—this does not mean that they regard blacks as equals nor that they are aware of the extent to which racism penetrates American society. Indeed in the eyes of many blacks, both gay and straight, homosexuality seems to be bound up with the whole oppression of blacks in the United States. Among homosexuals as much as heterosexuals, race affects sexual behavior. There are white homosexuals who seek out black partners because of their own self-disgust and loathing (at being homosexual), just as there are black homosexuals who seek to expiate their self-hate (at being black) by seeking out whites.

There has tended to be considerable squeamishness in dealing with the whole question of homosexuality among non-white Americans. Kinsey's study dealt only with white males; Hoffman's *The Gay World* is very guarded about Negro homosexuality; Calvin Hernton's book, *Sex and Racism,* barely mentions homosexuality.[1] I suspect, however—and this can be no more than a suspicion for the moment—that proportionately, significantly more blacks than whites are either homosexual or, more probably, bisexual, and certainly that more are aware of the gayworld and have mixed in it. At any rate what does seem true is that blacks in general do appear at one and the same time both more accepting of and more hostile toward homosexuality, and any discussion of the two movements must find a way to reckon with this.

It might be argued that this is merely a product of class differ-

1. I shall deal only in passing with other nonwhite homosexuals—brown, red, yellow—yet much of what I have to say about the complex relationship between blacks and homosexuals would apply to them as well. The problems of Spanish-American homosexuals are in some ways analogous to those of black, though the hostility they meet in their community is enhanced by the strong sexual repression imposed by the church on both Mexicans and Puerto Ricans—not always, of course, successfully—and the cult of "machismo" that accompanies this. Within the gay movement, the device of a Third World caucus has been used to link all nonwhite gays, but it is interesting that in Los Angeles a specifically Mexican-American gay group has already been organized.

ences, a reflection of the fact that proportionately more whites than blacks are middle-class, and hence likely to tolerate, rather than either persecute or accept homosexuality. Yet to argue this is to ignore the extent to which blacks have been feared, lusted after, and used by whites sexually, and the effect that this has had on both black and white attitudes to sex. There is considerable danger in the view that sees all blacks as less repressed, more sexually free than whites, a belief that enjoys considerable vogue at the moment. Equally it seems to me wrong to dismiss the possibility that blacks are more likely, because of the nature of their history in America, to stress the significance of their sexuality than are whites. Some blacks have suggested to me that because of this, homosexuality is more accepted in black communities than it is in white. As Julian Mayfield wrote in *The Grand Parade* of a black woman: "People said she was either sexless or a lesbian, and they would have preferred to discover she belonged to the latter category." Or as one black student put it: "Man, we have more to worry about than fags."

Yet against the claim that blacks are more accepting of homosexuality we need to place evidence of considerable hostility toward homosexuality. Eldridge Cleaver has written of "punk-hunting," and compares it to ritualistic lynchings of blacks by southern whites—that is, a psychological way of expressing anger and hostility by selecting a group even weaker than oneself. Similar attacks on homosexuals are of course not restricted to blacks or even America—the British go in for "queer bashing," the Australians for "beating up poofters"—nor is it difficult to see the guilt about one's own feelings that this activity disguises. The narrator of LeRoi Jones' quasi-autobiographical novel *The System of Dante's Hell* is constantly acting out a hostility to the "queers," one of whom he is in part: "We tell lies to keep from getting belted and watch a faggot take a beating in the snow from our lie. Our fear."

Ultimately blacks in America are prisoners of the American sexual mystique, and their escape from its repressions and its stereotypes can only be partial. This mystique teaches that homosexuality is a sign of weakness and emasculation. Little wonder that many black men, conscious of their oppression and frightened of emasculation, are particularly hostile to homosexuality, or that some blacks ascribe their own homosexuality to white racism. "I was a fresh black boy in Dixie," says the black poet in Edward Wallant's *Tenants of Moonbloom,* "and they took it out of me the only way they could—invisible castration. Now I know, but of course I can't put back that invisible dingus, can I? So I mess around with boys just to keep my prostate active." One finds similar reactions in some of the writings of Baldwin: "If you're a black boy," Fern Maya Eckman quotes him as saying, "you wouldn't be-*lieve* the holocaust that opens over your head with all those despicable—*males*—looking for someone to act out their fantasies on. And it happens in this case—if you're sixteen years old—to be you!" One might further note that for many blacks homosexuality is associated with either prostitution or jail, for in a society that imprisons vastly more nonwhites than whites it is not surprising that many more learn about faggotry the hard way. That prison experiences reinforce hostility toward homosexuality is suggested both in Cleaver's *Soul on Ice* and in George Jackson's *Soledad Brother.*

It is not difficult to find examples of extreme hostility to the gay movement among blacks. During the conflict at New York University discussed earlier, the former head of the Black Allied Student Alliance wrote to the student paper threatening to use force to remove the occupying homosexuals from the residence hall if the university would not. The following letter to *Gay* (September 1970) reflects the connection that some blacks at least make between homosexuality and white oppression:

Dear Gay,
    As a black person I would like to tell your publication that the constant referral of the Black or minority oppression as similar to the oppression of you white Homosexuals is an affront and is offensive to Black people. Those few who are crazy enough to buy your publication see nothing but the work of spoiled white cissies who've had their fill of men to the

point where they don't know what they want anymore. You white Homos have been catered to for years; Had a phony glorification even as (Homosexuals)!!! via physique Mags which nowadays come right out with puny white bitches on the front covers. But that's not enough now. You want the whole world to love you. Well, as far as I'm concerned, you racist cocksuckers can go on getting killed and go straight to Hell. You've got your nerve to use the struggles of Black people to further your selfish and sickening cause when very few if any can even relate to Blacks or give a damn about them. I don't care what the Hell you Queers do, but I'm warning you now that you'd better keep Black people out of it.

M. P. J.

Kill all white Homos! I hate whites!
Kill! Kill! Kill! Whitey!
P.S. I see why white girls are preferring Blacks, at least they're *Men!* Real *men*!

In slightly less virulent tones I have encountered the same reaction among urbanized Australian blacks.

Given the importance of questions of "manhood" and "emasculation" in much radical black thought, it is not surprising that homosexuality is a recurring theme for a number of contemporary black writers, nor that two of the most significant black cultural and political figures, James Baldwin and Eldridge Cleaver, divide sharply in their attitudes toward homosexuality. Baldwin writes most powerfully at the margin where sex and race coincide—though it is also here that he is most likely to overplay his hand, as in *Tell Me How Long the Train's Been Gone*—and his vision of America is one that sees her as doubly cursed through her inability to come to terms with either. It may be in part Baldwin's insistence on confronting homosexuality as much as racism that has led to his being played down as a writer; it is not uncommon to see discussions of Baldwin's works which ignore the fact that he wrote *Giovanni's Room* or mention it only in passing, as do the contributors in Herbert Hill's anthology *Anger and Beyond: The Negro Writer in the United States,* as an example of a novel that deals only with whites.

Giovanni's Room, as I have already suggested, is a weak book, one that is too pat in its melodrama, unlike *Another Country* where melodrama becomes both believable and necessary. The latter is the most powerful statement yet of Baldwin's belief that the black must free the white as well as himself, and that this demands overcoming America's fear and repression of sexuality. Here Baldwin and Cleaver are at one in seeing blacks as less oppressed by puritanism than whites. "Maybe we're worse off than you," says Cass, the white woman in *Another Country.* To which Ida, the black girl and sister of Rufus Scott around whom the book revolves, replies: "Oh you are. There's no doubt about it." What Cass says of America reflects Baldwin's underlying pessimism, his love-hate relationship with white America: "It's not a country at all, it's a collection of football players and Eagle Scouts. Cowards. We think we're happy, we're not. We're doomed." Baldwin was one of the early black intellectuals to proclaim that integration into *that* was hardly worth attaining.

While white and black liberals still saw salvation as lying in the civil rights movement and integration, Baldwin perceived the extent to which oppression was ingrained in the very marrow of American society. In an interview in 1963 he suggested how far fear of the black was intertwined with the fear of sexuality he sees as predominant in America. "If you fall in love with a boy," he said, "you fall in love with a boy. The fact that Americans consider it a disease says more about them than it says about homosexuality."

In the linking of sex and race, Cleaver owes much to Baldwin, whom he has bitterly denounced much as Baldwin had earlier renounced his mentor Richard Wright. Cleaver's "Notes on a Native Son" (in *Soul on Ice*) condemns Baldwin bitterly for "the most grueling, agonizing, total hatred of the blacks, particularly of himself, and the most shameful, fanatical, fawning, sycophantic love of the whites that one can find in the writings of any black American of note in our time." There seem to be two aspects of Baldwin that have led to this attack. The first is that Baldwin, recognizing how far blacks have been taught to despise themselves, is honest enough to admit that however hard he struggles he can never totally escape this self-hatred himself. The second, and for Cleaver the more important, I believe, is Baldwin's homosexuality.

In "An Open Letter to My Sister, Miss Angela Davis," published in the *New York Review* (January 1971), Baldwin makes the first point explicit. "The American triumph," he writes, "in which the American tragedy has always been implicit—was to make black people despise themselves. When I was little I despised myself, I did not know any better. And this meant, albeit unconsciously, or against my will, or in great pain, that I also despised my father. *And* my mother. *And* my brothers. *And* my sisters. Black people were killing each other every Saturday night out on Lennox Avenue when I was growing up; and no one explained to them, or to me, that it was *intended* that they should; that they were penned where they were like animals. Everything supported this sense of reality, nothing denied it: and so one was ready when it came time to go to work to be treated as a slave." That today's generation of blacks has begun the final escape gives Baldwin great hope. "You," he says to Angela Davis, "do not appear to be your father's daughter in the way that I am my father's son." In *Tell Me . . .* , he expressed the same admiration for Christopher, the young black militant and lover of the actor Leo Proudhammer. In addition, Baldwin himself, one of the first blacks to express to whites the undisguised anger of his people, and for this reason a political as well as a literary figure, has spoken out in passionate defence of the Panthers.

It is hard to reconcile this Baldwin with the Baldwin of Cleaver's denunciation. It is much easier to see what lies behind that denunciation when one confronts its real core, Baldwin's refusal to accept the conventional definition of masculinity. Cleaver, like Mailer,

whom he quotes approvingly, sees masculinity as demanding a renunciation of one's homosexuality, which he sees as part of a "racial
death wish":

> The case of James Baldwin aside for a moment, it seems that many
> Negro homosexuals, acquiescing in this racial death wish, are outraged
> and frustrated because in their sickness they are unable to have a baby by
> a white man. The cross they have to bear is that, already bending over and
> touching their toes for the white man, the fruit of their miscegenation is
> not the little half-white offspring of their dreams but an increase in the
> unwinding of their nerves—though they redouble their efforts and intake
> of the white man's sperm.

Shorn of the literary allusions, Cleaver hates, fears, and despises
Baldwin because he is homosexual, and "homosexuality is a sick-
ness just as are rape or wanting to become the head of General
Motors." Beyond this, his attack on Baldwin is inaccurate, emotionalism carried to a point where it no longer relates to what
Baldwin is in fact saying. When Baldwin talks of the need for blacks
to save whites, it is hardly a "self-effacing love"; Baldwin, for his
part, knows well enough that love between black and white is near-
impossible in America. "Somewhere in his heart," he wrote in *Another Country,* "the black boy hated the white boy. Somewhere in
his heart Vivaldo had feared and hated Rufus because he was
black." But Baldwin also knows that liberation demands that this
gulf be overcome, else we shall all, black and white alike, be
doomed.

Which, disregarding the rhetoric and the emotionalism, is basically Cleaver's position too. *Soul on Ice,* like *The Autobiography
of Malcolm X* before it, is remarkable because it represents the
struggle of a strong and angry black to overcome his hatred of
whites and move toward the very love, transcending racial difference, that Baldwin seeks. "There is in America to-day a generation
of white youth that is truly worthy of a black man's respect,"
Cleaver wrote in "The White Race and its Heroes," "and this is a

rare event in the foul annals of American history." What Cleaver cannot forgive is Baldwin's acceptance of the possibility that comradeship may become sexual, his belief that manhood is enhanced, not compromised, by tenderness toward other men. Cleaver's machismo, I would maintain, is the scar that a racist and sexist society has left upon him.

There is a further implication in Cleaver's argument which is important for an understanding of black ambiguity toward homosexuality. In the eyes of many blacks to be a fag is to opt out of being black, to quite deliberately move into the white world, as, in effect, Baldwin did in writing *Giovanni's Room*. Now it must be remembered that there is in fact a black gayworld with its own bars and parties; not all black homosexuals live in an integrated homosexual culture. (Even at bars frequented by both white and black gays, there is often considerable racial separateness.) More gay than straight blacks do live in an integrated society, however, and this in itself may seem a threat to the creation of a black solidarity in the same way that gays often feel threatened by bisexuals.

Before Cleaver emerged from obscurity with the publication of *Soul on Ice* in 1968, LeRoi Jones had been obliquely hitting at Baldwin for the same reasons that Cleaver was to express. Jones too is haunted by homosexuality—"faggot" is a term of abuse running through his works, the taunt of the black man to the white, as in Jones' play, *The Slave*—and, like Cleaver, he sees it as the peculiar curse the white man has imposed on the black. (Oddly enough, at one point, in an essay written in 1964, he identifies himself with Rimbaud and Ginsberg, both well known as homosexuals). Cleaver's hostility to Baldwin is foreshadowed, albeit somewhat vaguely, in Jones' 1963 essay "Brief Reflections on 2 Hot Shots" (Baldwin and the South African Peter Abrahams), where he says: "FACT: 'People should love each other' sounds like Riis Park at sundown. It has very little meaning to the world at large." (Riis Park is a beach in New York frequented by homosexuals.)

Two years later Jones wrote an essay, "American Sexual Reference: Black Male," which sounds very similar to Cleaver's "White Woman, Black Man." "Most American white men," begins Jones, "are trained to be fags." Here appear in embryo the characters of Cleaver's medieval allegory play, the weak effeminate white Omnipotent Administrator, the strong virile black Supermasculine Medial, the frigid pedestal'd white Ultrafeminine, the strong warm black Amazon. For both Cleaver and Jones, homosexuality is the ultimate degeneracy of the white's divorce between mind and body. Jones: "It is in the 'individualistic' ego-oriented society that homosexuality flourishes most since the Responsibility of bearing one's generations is not present among the kind of decadent middle-class such a society produces." Cleaver: "If a (white) lesbian is anything she is a frigid woman, a frozen cunt with a warp and a crack in the wall of her ice."

Despite the extravagant imagery of Cleaver's statement, the lesbian appears to be as invisible to blacks as to whites, if not more so. The only black lesbians in American literature are there as exotic background; virtually nothing has been written about them, and even to hypothesize is risky. It is not difficult to imagine that the extreme sexual objectification to which black women are subject from men both black and white may tend to drive them into choosing a homosexual life. It does seem true that, as among gay men, the lesbian world is more integrated than the straight, and Calvin Hernton's sole mentions of homosexuality stress how racial differences enhance mutual attraction between women. It is also probable that homosexual more than heterosexual black women are likely to identify with the women's movement. Which probably reinforces the straight black women's hostility toward women's liberation, a hostility born of the complex impact of racism on both black and white women.

Perhaps because Cleaver was a black revolutionary, the reviews that lauded *Soul on Ice* tended to ignore the crass rubbish of the last part of the book, with its talk of "transcending the Primeval

Mitosis" and "achieving supreme identity in the Apocalyptic Fusion." Or perhaps, nearly all critics being white, they suffered too much from awe before the black stud to argue with Cleaver's theories of sexuality. For where Baldwin, Cleaver, and Jones are all agreed is that the black represents in a peculiar way the repressed sexuality that so threatens America. For both gays and straights, the black is a symbol of sex, to be feared and lusted after at the same time.

The sexual fears and stereotypes of both blacks and whites will obviously affect relations between gay and black militants, and against the background of Cleaver's metaphysics, the statement by Huey Newton in August 1970 about gay and women's liberation takes on considerable significance. Newton, joint founder and supreme commander of the Black Panther party, of which Cleaver became minister for information and later representative-in-exile in Algiers, not only welcomed the women's and gay movements into the revolutionary ranks—and in so doing began the break with Cleaver that culminated in the counteraccusations and attempts to purge each other in early 1971—he also sought to come to terms with their position: "Whatever your personal opinions and your insecurities about homosexuality and the various liberation movements among homosexuals and women (and I speak of the homosexuals and women as oppressed groups), we should try to unite with them in a revolutionary fashion. I say 'whatever your insecurities are' because as we very well know sometimes our first instinct is to want to hit a homosexual in the mouth because we're afraid we might be homosexual; and we want to hit the woman or shut her up because we're afraid that she might castrate us, or take the nuts that we might not have to start with." And more specifically on homosexuality: " . . . there's nothing to say that a homosexual cannot be a revolutionary. And maybe I'm now injecting some of my prejudices by saying that 'even a homosexual can be a revolutionary.' Quite on the contrary, maybe a homosexual could be the most revolutionary."

Just why this statement was made by Newton is hard to say, and there is little doubt that it created considerable hostility and unrest within the party. Not surprisingly it was received ecstatically by the revolutionary wing of gay liberation, who had already sought to ally themselves with the Panthers as "the vanguard" of the revolutionary movement within America. Yet there was no indication that Newton's statement led Cleaver in any way to modify his attitude, and the film of Cleaver in Algiers showed a man with strong hostility to fags and little understanding of the position of women. Although Newton and Cleaver did not refer directly to their different attitudes toward the sexual liberation movements, it was an undertone to their feud and subsequent splits in the Panther party.

Following Newton's statement, members of various Gay Liberation Fronts attended the Panther-sponsored Revolutionary People's Constitutional Convention in Philadelphia (September 1970) and in Washington (November 1970). Neither meeting was a particular triumph for gay-black cooperation. At Philadelphia the gay women in particular objected to what they claimed was manipulation of workshop meetings and an inability of the Panthers to really recognize the extent of women's and gay oppression; most of the women walked out of the meeting. The subtlety of the problem was caught in a sympathetic comment Lois Hart made about Panther David Hilliard in her article for *Come Out:*

The bombastic Panther-in-public gave way to a black man caught in the contradictions of these times. Rising out of his incredible oppression the assertion of his humanity takes the form of "Being-a-Man" and that is what he has become. Now he is being told that this too is oppression and has to go. Perhaps through the discipline of the party and because of his own oppression he is open to this new struggle. I think perhaps I can be part of that struggle. Certainly in some way I felt that the people present had been affected by us; or would be. I know that I was touched and affected by them.

The November Conference in Washington was even less successful. Organizationally the conference never really took place;
inability to find a site prevented any gathering of the delegates other
than a couple of Panther-dominated rallies. Amidst the confusion
of several thousand delegates homeless in Washington over Thanks-
giving weekend, the gay and women delegates met in separate caucuses, only marginally connected with the Convention. Most of the
gay women chose to identify primarily with the women's caucus;
neither they, nor the gay men, made much impact in the total
confusion.

Yet if the gay caucus was shunned by most of the gay women,
it did retain a comparatively large number of nonwhites, an expression of the fact that gay liberation is one of the very few sections
of the movement that is in any real way racially integrated. At a
time of increasing separatism this seems to me a very important
achievement. While they represent only a small number over all,
the nonwhite members of gay liberation occupy a crucial role in
the development of the movement. It is easy to find examples of
racism among white homosexuals, or extreme heterosexual male
chauvinism among blacks. Whether the gap between the two groups
can begin to be closed, as Newton has sought, depends considerably
on nonwhite homosexuals.

Not all of those whites who identify with gay liberation are
particularly sympathetic to the Panthers, nor concerned to build
alliances with them. This was one of the factors making for the
split in New York's Gay Liberation Front, leading to the emergence
of the Gay Activists Alliance, and similar splits elsewhere. There is
an element of reverse racism in the attitudes of some gay liberationists toward nonwhites that reflects the guilt and fear felt by so
many Americans vis-à-vis blacks. At meetings, the attitude comes
out in the over-obsequious reception of black speakers, and it is
not difficult to see in the attitudes of many of the whites in gay
liberation the revised stereotyping of the sixties in which the black,
to Northerners now as much a symbol of liberated sexuality and

potential violence as he was to Southern whites, is lusted after and emulated instead of being suppressed. The white segregationist and the white radical share a fear and envy of the black, and for male homosexuals, confused as they often are by tension between the social images of masculinity and effeminacy, the Black Panther with his whole "macho" exterior is particularly attractive. It takes little imagination to perceive the sexual dimension of Genet's support for the Panthers.

Yet it is too easy to point either to white neuroses or black hostility as an argument against cooperation and support. A more convincing argument would be one that points out that the Panthers in fact represent only a very small part of the black community, that in their zeal to become the "vanguard" of the revolution they have neglected their own community. The Panthers have become, however, a symbol of black assertion—with more than a little help from their enemies—and the link with them is also mainly symbolic. In seeking it the gay movement has embarked upon a risky course, but it is hard to see what else would be consistent with a full analysis of oppression and liberation.

Still, only a small number of even activist homosexuals have adopted this position. Equally, the Panthers not only represent merely a small segment of American blacks, limited to lower-class urban radicals, but they also have been considerably discredited since the time when New York society attended their benefits, and the agitation over the trial of Panther Bobby Seale et al. threatened to paralyze Yale University. I suspect, and regret, that the CORE (Congress of Racial Equality) picketing of the Apollo Theater in Harlem for employing transvestites—"an attack on black man-hood"—is more representative of the emerging black consciousness than the uneasy coalitions at Philadelphia and Washington. Neither Cleaver nor Newton, but rather a sad mimicry of middle American respectability, still dominates much of the black movement.

Yet as *Gay Flames* claimed after Philadelphia, the Panthers were the first significant radical group to recognize gay liberation as a valid political movement. The importance of this recognition is twofold. First, it is likely to increase the awareness among at least the more radical white homosexuals of their own racism. And second, it strengthens the attitudes among the black community militating for acceptance rather than persecution of homosexuals. On these terms, Huey Newton, like James Baldwin, can claim to have made an important contribution to gay liberation's coming of age.

Gay Liberation and Women's Liberation: Joint Assault on the Throne Room

"A lesbian," begins a statement by New York's Radicalesbians,

is the rage of all women condensed to the point of explosion. She is the woman who, often beginning at an extremely early age, acts in accordance with her inner compulsion to be a more complete and freer human being than her society—perhaps then but certainly later—cares to allow her. These needs and actions over a period of years bring her into painful contact with people, situations, the accepted ways of thinking, feeling and behaving, until she is in a state of continual war with everything around her and usually with herself. She may not be fully conscious of the political implications of what for her began as personal necessity, but on some level she has not been able to accept the limitations and oppressions laid on her by the most basic role of her society—the female role. The turmoil she experiences tends to induce guilt proportional to the degree to which she feels she is not meeting social expectations and/or eventually drives her to question and analyze what the rest of her society more or less accepts. She is forced to evolve her own life pattern, often living much of her life alone, learning usually much earlier than her "straight" (heterosexual) sisters about the essential aloneness of life (which the myth of marriage obscures) and about the reality of illusions. To the extent that she cannot expel the heavy socialization that goes with being female she can never truly find peace with herself. For she is caught somewhere between accepting society's view of her—in which case she cannot accept herself—and coming to understand what this sexist society has done to her and why it is functional and necessary for it to do so. Those of us who work that through find ourselves on the other side of a tortuous journey through a night that may have been decades long. The perspective gained from that journey, the liberation of self, the inner peace, the real love of self and of all women is something to be shared with all women—because we are all women.

The lesbian is doubly oppressed, both as a homosexual and as a woman. For her, as for the nonwhite homosexual, there is the constant dilemma of dual allegiance and dual persecution. Gay women confront male prejudice within gay liberation and heterosexual fear within women's liberation. Such prejudice and fear poses problems for both movements, and yet, as I shall argue, the lesbian occupies a particularly important position, for in effect she provides a link between these movements which are in so many ways complementary.

Gay liberation began both in America and elsewhere as an organization that embraced men and women. This was different from the structure of old-line movements where, despite a few female members in groups such as the Society for Individual Rights, male and female homosexuals had remained apart in separate organizations, and read separate publications. (The commercial homosexual press has never really been aimed at lesbians.) As already mentioned, gay liberation was in part inspired by the women's movement, and the men who came into it were at least partially aware of the special problems facing women, if often less acquainted with the literature of sexism.

Because gay liberation was founded several years after the women's movement, and because of the direct influence of the women's movement, gay liberation was from its inception more radical and less concerned to excuse the reason for its existence. No one in gay liberation argued, for example, as Ellen Willis said of women's liberation before she changed her mind and helped form the Redstockings, that one of its main functions was to help recruit members for the Left. From women's liberation gays took the device of consciousness-raising and also the emphasis, forgotten by much of the straight (male) Left, on loose structures and personal involve-ment. Both groups stress the need to develop theory out of expe-rience, to break down the abstraction of ideologies that do not relate to the immediate existential knowledge of the group, to de-velop strong bonds of sister- and brotherhood. One hears from both activist women and gay men the same contempt for the "theo-rizers" of the (male) Left, who are regarded as divorcing personal, particularly emotional, experience from their political views. They retaliate by accusing the sexual liberation movements of overe-motionalism and failure to relate to the oppression of others.

Yet despite considerable goodwill, and the influence of women's liberation on the gay movement, it has not been that easy for gay men and women to get together. The traditional gayworld was, of course, highly segregated; those women who mixed with male ho-mosexuals were less likely to be lesbians than women who enjoy being with men more likely to regard them as social assets than as sexual objects. Gay liberation brought homosexual men and women together, often for the first time, but it also revealed that gay men were as sexist as straight if in somewhat different ways.

Just as the oppression of gays hardly guarantees them immunity from racism, so too gay men are likely to share socially approved attitudes toward women. Indeed some gay men go further and regard all women with considerable hostility, born partly of fear. I do not believe that this is true of all, or even most homosexuals (nor, of course, is it an attitude confined to homosexuals). Given that he is unlikely to be very interested in women sexually, the gay man has two options, either to ignore them or to treat them as people, and especially the more self-accepting will do the latter. Yet while many homosexuals claim to feel particularly comfortable with women—"some of my best friends . . . "—they are also likely to reflect straight attitudes, and may indeed compensate for their own stigma by behaving in a "macho" way toward women. "See," such men seem to be saying, "we're just as much men as you straights, and we'll prove it by being as tough to women as any of you."

It is my hope however that while gay men are at least as sexist as most straights, and possibly more, they will find this attitude easier to overcome once they become aware of it. Gay men, after all, have less personal stake in the subordination of women, and a greater possibility of appreciating their oppression. The gayworld has taught most male homosexuals the unpleasantness of sexual objectification; the male chauvinism that puts down women also puts down gays. As Carl Wittman wrote in "The Gay Manifesto," "chick equals nigger equals queer." Antihomosexuals such as Mailer and Cleaver also tend to epitomize male chauvinism, nor is it surprising that one magazine *(Harper's)* has published articles hostile to both movements. More important, the necessity to subordinate women is not as ingrained in the egos of male homosexuals; most of them accept that they have to do their own shit work. (Though homosexuals who marry to avoid this are not at all uncommon.) And homosexuals have repudiated the social norm that evaluates a man by the women he beds and teaches men to regard women as status symbols.

Yet even if all this were to be conceded, many lesbians question how far they can work together with male homosexuals. Male and female homosexuals have different life-styles and experiences; the very lack of a highly organized female gayworld comparable to that available to male homosexuals may make it easier for lesbians of very different age groups and cultural backgrounds to join together than is true for men. Equally this may reflect the fact that women—at least white women—in our society share more of a common culture than do men. At the Revolutionary People's Constitutional Conventions in both Philadelphia and Washington, a majority of lesbians felt their primary allegiance to be with other women rather than with gay men. Even among the old-line Daughters of Bilitis there has been a move away from working beside male-dominated gay groups toward closer alliance with the women's movement.

As the large Gay Liberation Fronts of 1969–70 have broken up, so too have the links between female and male homosexuals weakened. Nor is this true only of America. In London the women produced their own issue of *Come Together* which included an article entitled "Why I Cannot Work in the Gay Movement"— reprinted, interestingly enough, from an American publication. In Sydney gay women have in many cases found it easier to work within women's liberation rather than either CAMP or gay liberation. In Toronto *Body Politic* is produced by a virtually all-male collective. The promise of a genuinely nonsexist interaction of gay women and men that seemed to exist originally has been sorely battered.

Nor is such an attitude surprising. The lesbian is still in large part a product of social expectations about femininity, the male homosexual those of the male world. The problems and preoccupations of the two are different; women tend to be repelled by the heavy stress on cockmanship that is prevalent among (even) "liberated" gay men, men are unaware of the nature of the lesbian experience. The bitterness of Del Martin's renunciation of the male-dominated movement—she was both a founder of Daughters of Bilitis and an active member of SIR—is being echoed by other women: "I will not be your 'nigger' any longer. Nor was I ever your mother. Those were the stultifying roles you laid on me, and I shall no longer concern myself with your toilet training. You're in the big leagues now and we're both playing for big stakes. They didn't turn out to be the same." Because lesbians are likely to be particularly conscious of the oppression of women in our society—Simone de Beauvoir, indeed, has argued that it is to escape this oppression that some women chose homosexuality—they will feel it doubly difficult to accept the subordinate role that male homosexuals tend, often unconsciously, to demand of them.

There is a further problem facing the interrelationship of gay women and men. Just because society has for so long defined homosexuality as essentially a male phenomenon, with the lesbian added as an afterthought, it is very difficult for any integrated homosexual movement not to reflect this bias. More men seem to be overtly homosexual than women, and the position of men in our society makes it likely that proportionally more will attend, and be vocal at meetings. (Realization of this led some gay men to adopt the view that where gay liberation is represented, as at the Constitutional Conventions, there should be two women and two Third World people for every white male.) At the same time, open discrimination and persecution tend to be directed more against the male, partly because of the fact already suggested—male homosexuals threaten a male-dominated society more than do female homosexuals—and partly because male homosexuals are likely to be more obvious in their behavior than are lesbians. What, one wonders, must a female homosexual think when she is asked to devote her energies to worrying about men caught in baths and johns where she wouldn't go anyway. The male orientation of homosexual organizations is likely to be most obvious where law reform is involved, for lesbians are ignored in Anglo-Saxon legal practice, but the bias extends beyond this concern. The practice of defining "homosexual" as meaning male homosexual affects even gay women, who feel the lack of the considerable amount of literary, psychological, and sociological effort that has been expended on the man.

If gay women are relating increasingly to the women's rather than to a sexually integrated gay movement—while often retaining a separate identity, as in New York's Radicalesbians or London's Red Lesbians—this has not been achieved easily. Indeed antihomosexuality in the early days of the current women's movement was at least as great as any sexism encountered in the gay movement. The more conservative groups associated with women's liberation, in particular the National Organization of Women, tended to be very hostile toward lesbians, and "dyke" was the most hated and feared epithet that could be thrown at activist women, reducing a number to tears at the Atlantic City demonstration against the Miss America meat market. Some of the fellow travelers of women's liberation still echo this line. Thus as late as January 1971 Harriet van Horne, the New York *Post's* dispenser of liberal virtue, was proclaiming the need to exclude lesbians—who represent "a serious emotional aberration"—from the women's movement.

Luckily Ms. van Horne's influence is likely to be minimal. Early neglect by the women's movement of the lesbian—one searches in vain for comment about homosexuals in pre-1970 writings of the movement, although several lesbian organizations did attend a conference of Northeast feminists toward the end of 1969—has been replaced by concern and considerable self-analysis. In this development, Kate Millett played a special part. Her book *Sexual Politics* became a best-seller in mid-1970, and she emerged in the public view as one of the best-known exponents of the new feminism. Soon after, she "came out" publicly, with a speech to the New York Daughters of Bilitis, where she declared: "I'm very glad to be here. It's been kind of a long trip. . . . I've wanted to be here I suppose in a surreptitious way for a long time; but I was always too chicken. . . . Anyway I'm out of the closet! Here I am!"

Already in her book, Kate Millett foreshadowed her own coming out in her comments on Genet. Here she provides intellectual support for linking the oppression of women and homosexuals—although in her postscript, written, I assume, after the emergence of gay liberation, homosexuals are strangely absent from the coalition of "altered consciousness" she sees emerging. In the Millett version of Genet, the two oppressions of women and homosexuals fuse into one; "an insouciant queen in drag" challenges more than the taboo against homosexuality, for she has uncovered "the fact that sex role is sex rank." As Millett puts it: "Divorced from their usual justification in an assumed biological congruity masculine and feminine stand out as terms of praise and blame, authority and servitude, high and low, master and slave."

Less convincing is Millett's assertion that Genet moves from a position to rebellion to one of revolution, that is, toward "the creation of alternative values." Or rather, what she overlooks is that Genet's vision of such a transformation, a transformation she finds most clearly expressed in his play *The Screens,* omits the very group whose stigma he bears himself, the fags. Like others on the left, Genet finds it easier to identify with the oppression of others, in particular blacks (note again his support for the Panthers) and women ("Alone of our contemporary writers Genet has taken thought of women as an oppressed group and revolutionary force"—Millett), than with his own. Ironically, by coming out publicly, Millett lays *Sexual Politics* open to the same accusation, and to that extent her book has been superseded by its author's own life.

The lesbian makes one appearance in *Sexual Politics* and that is in a footnote that "whatever its potentiality in sexual politics, female homosexuality is currently so dead an issue that while male homosexuality gains a grudging tolerance, in women the event is observed in scorn or in silence." This is probably true. There is a great deal revealed in the fact that the two novels written by and about lesbians mentioned by Millett—*The Well of Loneliness* and Djuna Barnes' *Nightwood*—are both pre–World War II. Contemporary literature is remarkably bereft of lesbians. (There is also explicit lesbianism in some of the works of Gertrude Stein, notably *QED*, so that Stein is a strange omission from Millett's book, and strong lesbian overtones to Henry James' *The Bostonians*. In our time I can think only of Lakey in Mary McCarthy's *The Group*, but Lakey's coming out is achieved off-stage with the result that she appears less than almost any other character, of Nabakov's *Ada*, and in a different way of Monique Wittig's *The Guérillères*.)

This paucity of writings by and about lesbians underlies the extent to which they have been made invisible, and the need for female homosexuals to affirm themselves. Genet's homosexuals indeed reveal much about male chauvinism. But they tell us nothing about women, for Genet's world is generally as devoid of women as the current pop westerns that Betty Friedan deplores. (The women in *The Maids*, suggests Genet, should be played by men.) As more women come to terms with both their homosexuality and their subordination to men, one can hope for a resurgence of writing not only by women but about women relating with each other.

The reaction to Millett's public statement, in particular the snide comments of *Time* which had originally helped make her a national figure, brought together most of the women's movement in support of her and other homosexuals. (A notable absence from the statement issued by leading feminists was Betty Friedan.) Millett's coming out was the most publicized of a number of moves by lesbians to assert their place in the women's movement, and has influenced the considerable diminishment of hostility toward lesbianism and its growing acceptance and importance within women's liberation.

Just as the sort of man attracted to gay liberation, once confronted with his own sexism, can probably overcome it more easily than a straight, particularly because of his own consciousness of oppression, so too those in women's liberation are especially well placed to recognize both their own inherent homosexuality and the joint oppression of women and homosexuals. The exploration of sexuality involved in consciousness-raising has led many women to confront homosexuality directly, not as something "out there" to be feared, pitied, or mothered, but rather as something within, a part of every woman and man. Indeed some lesbians have come out through their participation in the women's movement. In "A Letter from Mary," an anonymous article in the women's journal *It Ain't Me Babe,* one wrote: "I probably would never have discovered my homosexuality without women's liberation. You have helped to create what you now despise and fear, the incarnation of the sisterhood which was to be a lovely ideal." It is not a far step to see lesbianism as a necessary part of full female liberation, to argue that sisterhood demands acceptance of sensual as much as spiritual love between women. As Jill Johnston has claimed, "the lesbian, however hated or oppressed, is the purest representative of the liberated ideal."

As sisterhood becomes more powerful—Robin Morgan ends her

introduction to the book *Sisterhood Is Powerful* with a letter to a sister underground that finishes:

> In sisterhood, in struggle,/
> and all that,/
> but mostly because/
> I think I love you—

it brings women together in a way that overrides the distinction between hetero- and homosexual. It is not that most of the women in women's liberation become men-haters, ideological lesbians who are seeking to cut themselves off from all men. More would accept that to love women may increase the possibility of loving men, and incorporate a belief in bisexuality into their vision of liberation.

Not all female—or, for that matter, male—homosexuals necessarily accept bisexuality as a desirable goal. There are also those who see, as Martha Shelley put it, lesbianism as "one road to freedom—freedom from oppression by men" and seem to be moving towards Ti-Grace Atkinson's position of total separatism. Those gay women who adopt such a position are likely to reject alliances not only with gay men but also with those in the women's movement who place high priority on cooperation with men. I have already referred to the reaction of some lesbians at the Constitutional Conventions.

One can understand why some women, and particularly gay women, brand men as the enemy. Not that to view all men as the enemy is a position particularly identified with lesbians—one of the strongest assertions of this position comes in the Manifesto of the New York Redstockings Group—nor have all gay women felt the need to repudiate cooperation with men. The response of a group of women to the lesbian walkout from Philadelphia becomes relevant:

> Is this revolution in which we, too, are implicated, nothing but an ego-tripping power struggle between one bunch of bad men and another bunch

of bad men? Do you really see *all* men as the enemy? Have none of us
known men who have led rotten lives, worked their asses off, and got
nothing for it except just enough to survive (and maybe just a little bit
more than that after 20 or 30 years)? Men who have been fucked from
head to toe, including their brains, and who have taken their misery and
frustrations out on women? Yes. They have and they do fuck us over badly.
But they get nothing from it. Not really. Nothing to make their conditions
better; nothing to change the indignities of their lives. Sure, we have to
take these men on too. Absolutely. Men do oppress us. But we know too
that one oppressor does not equal another oppressor does not equal pig.
(*Rat,* 17 November–16 December 1970)

At the moment gay women stand at the juncture of the two
movements, and the alliance between them rests largely in their
hands. The oppression of homosexuals and women has both common and separate qualities. While it is probably true to say that
they share a common oppressor (i.e. the macho straight male) they
do not thereby share a common oppression. It is futile to try to
measure one oppression against another; I vividly remember one
angry French Canadian maintaining that his people had been treated
far worse than the American Negro, which I think is nonsense. Yet
women, one must note, remain the one oppressed group which is
also honored; while one needs to recognize the underlying hostility
of the male mystique of women—the Southern white woman was
both a symbol to be revered and a person to be ignored—the hon-
oring of women at the very least complicates the picture (and helps
explain why black women, who never were so idealized, are often
hostile to women's liberation). Further, most lesbians apart, women
live enmeshed with their oppressors far more closely than blacks
or gays, and as a consequence of this relationship, their oppression
is far more interwoven with their class position than is that of the
homosexual (or the black). Because of these factors the oppression
of women as women tends to be more subtle than that of blacks
and gays. Even the best Uncle Tom blacks or Aunty Tom gays *know*
they are oppressed, however much this may be internalized; the
same is not true of women.

Moreover it should be recognized that the priorities of the homosexual and the women's movements must of necessity be different: women face more overtly economic problems than homosexuals, gays are faced with a much greater social stigma, and have more choice in coping with this. More fundamentally, women's liberation is primarily concerned with sex roles, gay liberation with sexuality, and though the two are interconnected they are not synonymous. Yet it is in fact the very interconnections between roles and sexual behavior that bring the two movements together, and it is on this level, on the level that separates the radical gay and women's movements from the old-line civil rights organizations, that they raise similar questions and approach them in a similar manner, making for almost instinctive sympathy between the two groups.

For gays and women are oppressed by similar conceptions of masculine and feminine roles, and by the assumption that the nuclear family is the ultimate form of achieving happiness. *That* is for both the ultimate oppression, and the alliance between gay and women's liberation thus becomes one that need be formulated in no treaties or coalitions, for it is embedded in both movements. Each can only benefit from the strength of the other, which is to say that both are concerned to break down the rigidity and narrowness into which sexuality and social roles have been channeled in our society. It is for this reason that Suzannah Lessard, writing in the *Washington Monthly* in December 1970, saw the two as linked in their opposition to the domination of the straight male. There is to Lessard's article a compassion and a sensitivity that is rare in the more strident tones of the movement: "And the culprit, the white male heterosexual king who sits in the throne room guarding his birthright, the recipient of all this wrath, what of him? Isn't the throne room as vicious a dungeon of his humanity as those in which he keeps his underlings?" It is in this attitude, as we shall see, that women's and gay liberation hold the greatest implications for straight men and, indeed, for full human liberation.

Gay Liberation and the Left: Toward Human Liberation

The traditional Marxist Left has been as contemptuous, as disregarding, as oppressive, once given the chance, of homosexuals as anyone else. Despite Lenin's moves toward sexual freedom in the Soviet Union, which included repeal of antihomosexual legislation, these laws were reintroduced in 1934, and prejudice against homosexuality as "a bourgeois degeneracy" became strongly imbued in Communist parties throughout the world. Few groups remain as uptight in their attitude toward gay liberation as the American Communist party, that sad little mirror-reflection of the FBI that keeps it alive. During a rally to "Free Angela Davis" in New York, Communist heavies threatened to call the police to remove some women holding a Gay Liberation Front banner.

In its earlier days the New Left tended to echo the Communist party's views. Homosexuality was pushed into the closet, and New Left groups resisted anyone who sought to open the door. In his "Gay Manifesto" Carl Wittman mentions the banning of homosexuality or man/man, woman/woman dancing in gay movement projects. Even the Yippies, with their stress on combining personal and social liberation and their admiration for Allen Ginsberg, tended to regard both women and homosexuals as inferior. There are antihomosexual remarks in Abbie Hoffman's *Revolution for the Hell of It* and Jerry Rubin's *Do It!*, and Rubin in particular is prone to attack his opponents as "fags." Tom Foran, the government prosecutor at the Chicago Conspiracy Trial, may have regarded Hoffman and Rubin as part of the "freaking fag revolution" but they were certainly not going to concede it.

Unlike the women's, the gay movement did not begin with caucuses within New Left groups; leftist homosexuals, unlike women, were able to hide their stigma. It took withdrawal from New Left organizations and the formation of their own before gays felt able to demand acceptance by fellow radicals, and a number of New

Leftists found themselves estranged from their former groups by coming out. When in the summer of 1970 a group of gay liberationists decided to go to Cuba on the Venceramos Brigade, a group of young American radicals who spend time working in Cuba, they encountered enormous hostility, but less from the Cubans—who have followed the orthodox Marxist line on homosexuality to the point of putting gays in concentration camps—than from fellow Americans in the Brigade. Those who were there as overt homosexuals were continually harassed, and none taunted them as much as those preoccupied with their own "masculinity." It might seem masochistic of gay liberationists to take part in the Brigade at all, given the attitudes of both straight radicals and the Cuban government. Those who did would claim that only through their participation could such attitudes be changed.

Nor is this search for left-wing acceptance confined to America. In 1971 the London Gay Liberation Front associated itself with protests against the Conservative government's Industrial Relations Bill—in Europe class issues bring out the same guilts and emotions as do racial ones in the United States—and joined a trade union protest march. The GLF contingent was relegated to the back of the march with other nonunion groups, although it is probably true that the organizers reacted with bewilderment more than hostility to the appearance of largely middle-class men and women bearing purple banners and chanting "Poof to the Bill."

It would be boring and a little pointless to discuss the relationship of the various New Left groups toward gay liberation. On the whole they have been less quick to respond than the women's movement, and those who have done so tend to come from the "soft" or less ideologically rigid Left. Thus *WIN Magazine,* published by the War Resisters' League, which is dedicated to "peace and freedom through nonviolent action," ran a special issue on homosexuality in November 1969—Paul Goodman and Dave McReynold's contributions have already been quoted—and their sister publication, *Liberation,* published Carl Wittman's "Gay Manifesto" the following February. Equally in England the semiunderground paper *Oz* was one of the first to discuss gay liberation. Since then the issue of gay liberation has begun to be discussed by both hard and soft left groups, and given increasing support. Despite this, much of the Left still ignores the homosexual, more markedly, I think in America than in Britain, Canada, or Australia where gay liberation has become in some quarters an example of radical chic. It is one of the ironies of the movement that mass publications like *Newsweek* and *Life* have given greater recognition to the gay movement in recent years than self-proclaimed radical publications such as the *New Statesman* or *New Republic*.

Experience with both Old and New Lefts have tended to make many gays feel they need to be anarchists; any regime, no matter what its ideology, will tend to persecute them. This position was expressed some time ago by Roger Peyrefitte in his novel *Diplomatic Diversions* where one of his characters states:

> Socratic love prefers anarchy to slavery. In any case it postulates liberty and that is why it is persecuted by dictatorships. Soviet Russia, which ought to have given it favorable treatment as a victim of bourgeois prejudices, insists on treating it as a bourgeois "vice." By so doing it neglects its duties as preached by nihilism from which Communism originated and which decreed the *abolition* of all morality. It lost the opportunity of attracting to itself a part—I make bold to say an eminent part—of the élite of the old world. Since so great a political, social, intellectual and religious revolution could take part without socratic love benefiting by it—and that in a country where it had long enjoyed toleration—we need never expect anything from any regime at all. And since no regime is *for* us it follows that we must be against all regimes.

With less snobbery about it, a similar position was strong in the early days of gay liberation particularly in California, and is still expressed in hostility to the policy of alliance with other revolutionary groups.

Yet the logic of its analysis leads gay liberation groups into seeking alliance with the Left; in California, for example, gay liberation has forged very close ties with the Peace and Freedom party, which has adopted a homosexual liberation plank, run gay liberationists as candidates for office, and in some areas seems very closely interwoven with gay organizations. The search for such alliances is consistent with gay liberation analysis, but it is one that bears a number of dangers. At times, the desire for acceptance by the Left becomes just another form of passing, of seeking to prove revolutionary respectability, rather as Mattachine once sought to prove straight respectability. Efforts to join the Left have often led to a neglect of the more conservative homosexuals, obviously the vast majority, for to identify oneself with gay liberation is to identify with the insurgent culture, and just as more radical gays were repelled by the uneasy combination of prurience and respectability that typifies the old-line groups, so more conservative homosexuals are frightened away by the revolutionary image of gay liberation.

There are problems, as well, in winning full acceptance from the Left. One of the first New Leftists to recognize the claims of the homosexual was Dotson Rader, whose book *I Ain't Marchin' Anymore,* written, unlike Rubin's, before the emergence of gay liberation, ends by talking of "the community of the victims.... We were apart.... We were the young and black and radical and disaffiliated and the homosexual and the head [freak]. We were the non-believers.... If Eldridge Cleaver was correct when he said that a civil war could be fought between one dissenter and his nation then a civil war was going on in America." *Newsweek,* according to the cover blurb on this book, referred to Rader as "the Cleaver of the white New Left." He isn't. But even more than Cleaver he is obsessed with homosexuality, and his writings—his second book *Government Inspected Meat* is an autobiography of a hustler written by someone Rader claims is not himself—suggest implicitly that sexual insecurity is as strong within the New as the Old Left.

In particular, as Kate Millett has warned, the Left is too prone to accept the old syndrome that violence-proves-masculinity, and the cult of violence that affects at least some of the Left seems born of sexual hang-ups. Rader himself recognizes this; like Mailer he sees the connection between violence and repressed homosexuality without even the "consolation" of being able to condemn homosexuality. Still, he cannot rid himself of his macho arrogance. It is sad that a man so conscious of what is wrong with America can be so uncaringly, carelessly sexist:

"I took a taxi down to the Village and went to two bars and finally picked up a piece in the Ninth Circle and took it home." "A piece." "It." Boy or girl?—it doesn't much matter, the macho arrogance is the same. There are too many Raders in the movement—on the one hand prepared to proclaim common cause with the homosexual, on the other still bearing all the traditional cultural attitudes of superiority—for one to feel fully at ease about those who would link us with the Left.

Political movements, all of them, attract people who are insecure, confused, sexually uncertain. There is also a tendency for political movements to be puritanical, and this tendency is particularly apparent on the American Left. "The radical woman, for very specific reasons, is probably more uptight about homosexuality than other women," wrote Judith Brown in *Voices from Women's Liberation*. So too the radical man. The very act of breaking from the mainstream politically seems to make them more afraid of breaking sexually, just as, conversely, many homosexuals will be extremely conservative in their politics. As one black told Laud Humphreys: "Look, I'm black and I'm gay! Isn't that asking for enough trouble without getting mixed up in this civil rights stuff too."

Moreover, as Rader's writings imply, movements (and not least, of course, the gay movement) become a way in which men often resolve doubts about their masculinity. The attraction the Panthers hold for so many on the Left is not unrelated to their machoism; one boy, ostensibly straight, spoke to me of their role as "the vanguard of the revolution," almost drooling over a cheesecake photo of Huey Newton. The same mood that leads some gay men into defiantly flaunting their homosexuality leads other in the movement into concealing their homosexual feelings behind a cult of virility not far removed from that of John Wayne.

On the other hand, and here we approach the guts of the problem, one cannot assume people are static. To expect nonhomosexuals to have had a "heightened consciousness" about us before we had developed our own is absurd. Rubin, at least in regard to women, claims that his views have changed; Leary has virtually repudiated his earlier hostility to homosexuality. Tom Hayden now claims gay liberation as an integral part of the movement. There are in the movement a number of straight men who are very seriously struggling to come to terms with the challenge posed by women's and gay liberation.

This is why the idea that men/straights/whites are "the enemy" is ultimately wrong. It may be necessary for the various culturally oppressed groups to organize themselves apart from the white straight male movement, for them (as movement people say) to "get their shit together" first. But homosexuals or women or blacks do not exist in a vacuum, and the real impact of "getting their shit together" involves changing the consciousness of others as well as of themselves. The logical place for gay liberation to start effecting changes in others is among those already disaffiliated from the mainstream of society. Which is why its impact on the rest of the movement becomes one of the key ways by which to evaluate it.

Some of this impact is already apparent. As gay and women's liberation movements have become more assertive they have affected the way in which straight males come to terms with their own sexuality. An important development has been the organization of men's liberation groups. Like women's and gay liberation they too seek to re-evaluate the roles and expectations of straight society. Here, as Suzannah Lessard argued, "gay is good for us all." Not all straight males welcome the role into which they have been cast; super-stud is often uneasy and unhappy about the image he has been taught to live up to. Just as coming to terms with oneself leads some gays to a recognition of their own potential bisexuality, so too some straight men are seeking to cope with this possibility.

Men's liberation as a movement seems strongest in California where the movement as a whole has always been more influenced than elsewhere in America by the counterculture, by religion, and by concepts of sexual freedom. Berkeley men's liberation has begun to produce a newspaper called *Brother,* which in its looseness, its stress on personal experience is very close to the papers of the women's and gay movements. Straight men are also involved in consciousness-raising groups, and as in the women's movement, this often brings together gays and straights, helping to dissolve the barriers between the two that we have erected in our consciousness. That the oppressor is also oppressed is the basic argument behind men's liberation; in an article in Berkeley's student paper, the *Daily Californian,* David Dubross, a member of men's liberation, wrote: "The guilt of finding yourself unknowingly exploitative of and sometimes rejected by women you love, the terror of our fears about gayness and proving masculinity, the horrible competitiveness that pits us against each other in ego power plays that inhibit expressions of vulnerability, weakness; all these things and many different motivations have turned each of us to other men to collectively struggle past our sexual identities."

To Lionel Tiger, men's liberation might well appear just another example of male bonding; "brotherhood is powerful" has been the slogan of cliques, gangs, and armies throughout history. That brotherhood may also be loving, warm, and noncompetitive is a less common concept, and here men's liberation becomes an important part of the overall struggle for liberation. For it too is part of the general movement to overcome sex roles and dichotomies, to create not just a new man but a new human, one who is no longer imprisoned by limitations on sexuality and compassion, who is both more autonomous and more communal in orientation than the human who at present exists.

Women's, gay, and now men's liberation are embarked on a revolution that is so unlike our traditional concept of revolution that we tend not to recognize it for what it is. It is hardly surprising that the Old, and large sections of the New Left, fail to relate to these developments. I quote from a mimeographed sheet distributed by a group called the International Socialists during the Washington Convention whose views are typical of many: "Newer movements like Women's Liberation and Gay Liberation are growing fast— but big sections of both are more and more into consciousness-raising. Nothing wrong with this in itself—but it isn't matched by a real growing *power* of these movements."

We are back then to the kernel of the problem. The movement, using that term in its broadest sense, is agreed on the need for massive change. It is agreed on little else. Already, I have argued, the cultural hegemony of the American elite is being undermined with little effect on its political and economic power. Yet to argue for a violent overthrow of that elite is to risk merely aping their oppression with another variety. (I leave aside for the moment the utter futility of such a course in today's Western industrialized societies where it is no longer clear which are the barriers that one would storm even if one wanted to.) Change will not come easily or smoothly or without casualties, even if we opt for a change in consciousness. Without such a change, however, it will come with greater casualties, and it is unlikely to take us any further toward human liberation which ultimately may mean human survival.

Thus the real impact of gay liberation cannot be measured by words such as power; it is far more meaningful to ask rather to what extent it and the other liberation movements have succeeded in breaking down the cultural and social structures that oppress us all, not least by a false division into homo- and heterosexuals. It may be that what is deplored by groups such as the International Socialists as being the present floundering and weakness of the movement disguises a real strength, a reevaluation of the very core assumptions about human beings and human nature by which we are all trapped.

Both Kate Millett and Germaine Greer conclude their books on women with somewhat similar hopes, although in the case of Greer the path toward a new female consciousness that she suggests seems limited by wealth and education, which is to say by class. Both are agreed on the need to escape preoccupation with power and violence, which they, like myself, see as closely interwoven with the cult of masculinity. I am less convinced that, as Greer states, "women must humanize the penis, take the steel out of it and make it flesh again." Women alone can hardly achieve this, and steel will not become flesh until men learn to relate to each other with the same love Greer would have them show for women. "No Revolution Without Us" proclaims one of the slogans of gay liberation. No real sexual, and hence no full human liberation is possible without embracing all the potential for human love, and Greer's book is weaker for not fully dealing with this.

In its rejection of the macho image of manhood consecrated by violence, gay liberation is affecting the self-definitions of many in the movement; it may succeed in turning the movement away from a glorification of violence that threatens to imbue it with the worst qualities of the society it is seeking to change. (One example: the fringe that praised the Manson murders as a revolutionary act.) Which is not to deny that there are situations where violence may be necessary, only to suggest that the choice to use violence is almost always a corrupting one, and that human liberation depends on the ability to control our aggression. I have already pointed to a minority of gay liberationists who are attracted to a glorification of violence. More significant are those gay liberationists who have begun to argue that gayness by its very nature rejects violence, and especially war. Thus Gay May Day Tribes took part in antiwar protests in the spring of 1971, and to quote from one of their broadsheets:

Wars are conceived and fought by men who are reared to play a "Macho" role and to feel guilty if this sexual role is not fulfilled.

As homosexuals it is especially ludicrous to ape this nonhomosexual role playing. As gay people and people who oppose sexism we can offer a truly permanent peace by offering a viable alternative.

Sexism is the most elemental form of politics. Indoctrination into the system begins at birth. Human interaction based on sexual roles conditions boys to be aggressive and to fight others, while it conditions females to submit to a lesser status in the hierarchy. This same system brands those outside these two stereotypes as "queer" or "foreign."

If the change in consciousness toward which the gay and women's movements are moving helps to break down the American preoccupation with violence (of which women, it should be added, often the most zealous spectators of male bloodsports, are as much the prisoners as men), this may be its greatest contribution to the movement for a new America, and elsewhere for a new world.

7. Conclusion: The End of the Homosexual?

Any movement has a double impact, both on those it represents and on society at large. This is particularly so of a movement like gay liberation which represents a process whereby homosexuals seek to come to terms with themselves and through self-affirmation start out on the path toward human liberation.

The essence of gay liberation is that it enables us to come out. "Out of the closets and into the streets" becomes a liberating process which if not sufficient to overcome oppression—in the short run it may indeed bring oppression more heavily to bear—is certainly a necessary first step. Those who are touched by the new affirmation discover a new perception of how they have been oppressed by society and social norms, and out of this realization comes peace with oneself and anger at the victimization that we and others have suffered. "I am," wrote Jill Johnston of her new gay consciousness "more in sympathy with the black cause than ever before, and in fact with all causes, for it has recently occurred to me that all causes are the same . . . and that what we're doing here then is educating all the members of ourselves to certain needs which have gone unheeded or unrecognized or worse damned and vilified and thrust underground so that we can all coexist more happily together . . . "

For the homosexual, the new affirmation involves breaking away from the gayworld as it has traditionally existed and transforming the pseudo-community of secrecy and sexual objectification into a genuine community of sister- and brotherhood. When a gay group was established at Sydney University where I teach I was surprised how strongly its members felt the need to be with other gay people where they could be friendly without this being taken as a prelude to "getting off." Gays are having to create for themselves the very basis of ordinary decent social relationships, for without these we cannot achieve the self-respect necessary to transcend the oppression we have internalized.

But one might argue that this merely reinforces separatism, exchanging, at best, one sort of gay ghetto for another. In part this is perfectly true: the price of solidarity, whether for blacks, women, or gays, is separation. But against this, my own experience has been that becoming more open about my gayness has enabled me to feel closer to both gays and straights. Friendship demands a reciprocity of confidence, and if one is constantly guarding against being "discovered"—which is a real agony for most homosexuals—one is forced into mixing only with others who bear the same stigma and the same need for camouflage.

In coming out, in seeking a gay community, in declaring ourselves as homosexuals, we are accused of homosexual chauvinism. This charge could mean either that we see homosexuality as inherently superior to heterosexuality, or that we perceive everything in terms of our homosexual status. The former I deny; the latter I admit. It seems a mark of our oppression that each assertion of the validity of homosexuality is regarded as an attack on heterosexuality, as when Mailer spoke in his "Homosexual Villain" of "many homosexuals [going] to the direction of assuming that there is something intrinsically superior in homosexuality . . . " Equally, many whites perceived Black Power as racism in reverse, when in fact it only appeared as such because the whole structure of our culture and our language is so weighted in favor of white supremacy that any attempt to rectify it is seen as a move to create a new dominance/subordination.

But yes, we homosexuals are coming to perceive everything in terms of our gayness because up to now society has structured everything according to a heterosexual norm and expected us to accept it. Such structuring extends from the whole image of the world as presented to us by the advertising agencies to the jokes of my colleagues, in which I am expected to join, about the potential sexual favors of our female students. That I, like the women around, may be repelled by this objectification—or more honestly wish to make the same jokes about our male students—is ignored. As one boy put it, accepting what people do in bed is the least problem. What straights find most difficult to accept is that when we walk down the street we look at others of the same sex.

Just as liberals would like to forget that blacks, because of the color of their skin, have quite different social experiences to whites, so liberals would prefer to regard homosexuals as people who happen to be attracted to others of the same sex, without recognizing how far that single fact becomes an essential part of their whole being. Now the vision of liberation that I hold is precisely one that would make the homo/hetero distinction irrelevant. For that to happen, however, we shall all have to recognize our bisexual potential, and until that is done homosexuality, like blackness, will remain a major category that defines our lives.

As homosexuals come to accept this, to see that society has so defined us that homosexuality becomes a constant part of us rather than a role we can take up and discard when convenient—most homosexuals still seek to do this, with the result that they lead quite remarkably schizophrenic lives—we come also to see that our oppression *has* made us different from other people and that this has its strengths as well as its weaknesses. "Being a nigger," wrote Goodman "seems to inspire me to want a more elementary humanity, wilder, less structured, more variegated and where people have some heart for one another and pay attention to distress. That is, my plight has given energy to my anarchism, utopianism and Gandhianism. There are blacks in this party too."

The homosexual writers with whom I have been predominantly concerned—Baldwin, Genet, Ginsberg, Isherwood, Millett, even John Rechy—would all I think belong to Goodman's party. (And one might add others, for example W. H. Auden and E. M. Forster.) This is not, emphatically, a claim for homosexual superiority; there are plenty of homosexual villains, real ones, nor are straights excluded from the broader humanity and diversity that Goodman suggests. It *is* to point out that our homosexuality is a crucial part of our identity, not because of anything intrinsic about it but because social oppression has made it so. On one level, to love someone of the same sex is remarkably inconsequential—after all, but for some anatomical differences, love of a man or a woman is hardly another order of things—yet society has made it something portentous, and we must expect homosexuals to accept this importance in stressing their identity.

The liberal hope that homosexuals will come to merge imperceptibly into society as we now know it (as one conservative homophile spokesman put it on British television, we should look forward to the time when straights will invite the homosexual couple next door in for dinner) seems as unlikely as the hope that integration of black and white could be achieved in America without major social change. There seem two reasons for this: the structure of our society which appears to produce an unquenchable need for minorities, and the new assertion of identity by homosexuals. Liberals who want to "accept" homosexuals want homosexuals who are exactly like them; they are not very likely to invite homosexuals who insist on, and act out, their homosexuality.

As long as society is based on competitiveness and sexual repression there will be a need to demarcate it into categories, to maintain socially induced repressions by stigmatizing heavily all those who fall outside the norm. For such purposes the homosexual will remain one of the more attractive minorities. "A minority," says George in Isherwood's *Single Man,* "is only thought of as a minority when it constitutes some kind of threat to the majority, real or imaginary. And no threat is ever *quite* imaginary." Which is echoed by Goodman (see his essay "Underground Writing 1960" in *Utopian Essays and Practical Proposals*) and Baldwin, who writing of Gide (in "The Male Prison," *Nobody Knows My Name*) doubts that "at least in the world we know" homosexuality can ever be accepted: "And one of the reasons for this is that it would rob the normal—who are simply the many—of their very necessary sense of security and order, of their sense perhaps, that the race is and should be devoted to outwitting oblivion—and will surely manage to do so."

Homosexuals can win acceptance as distinct from tolerance only by a transformation of society, one that is based on a "new human" who is able to accept the multifaceted and varied nature of his or her sexual identity. That such a society can be founded is the gamble upon which gay and women's liberation are based; like all radical movements they hold to an optimistic view of human nature, above all to its mutability.

Yet such a view becomes realistic precisely because of the impasse to which our present conception of human nature seems to have led. Only recently and through a long and painful process have we come to realize how much of what we consider normal, especially in family and sex relationships, is in fact learnt, and it is the contribution of the gay and women's movements to force a reassessment of what we have grown up believing was part of human nature. Technological change has provided both the means and the necessity for a large-scale reassessment of the way we order our lives; if, in Baldwin's words, we will "outwit oblivion"—and there is no guarantee of this—we need to unlearn much of what has hitherto been considered natural, including attitudes toward competition and aggression as much as toward sex.

Anthropological evidence suggests that homosexuality is neither alien nor perverse. But beyond this neither history nor anthropology offers much guide to the future, for our society is qualitatively different to any ever known, and its potential for transformation correspondingly greater. Under the joint impact of technology and the women's movement we are divorcing procreation from sex, and anatomy from role; the demand to recognize homosexuality as a valid form of human relationships seems a logical extension of this development.

There are of course many within and without the gay movement who question the assumption that the fate of the homosexual depends on revolutionary change and argue, as did the president of the Society for Individual Rights in his 1969 report, that: "SIR is a one-issue organization . . . its position has to be more like the A.C.L.U. than . . . a political club . . . " Tolerance, as I have already suggested, *can* be achieved by liberal means, and within the framework of existing liberal society, and for the achievement of certain very necessary legislative changes Tom Maurer's position makes sense. Acceptance, however, demands a major change in our social framework; only those who, as in the movement, are prepared to question the basis on which society is organized, are likely to fully accept homosexuality as a part of the human condition rather than a discrete and foreign phenomenon. It has been said that a liberal is someone who wants to help others; a radical is someone who knows that he or she needs help. The liberal sees homosexuals as a minority to be assisted into a full place in society. The radical sees homosexuality as a component of all people including her- or himself.

In several important ways the gay movement does, I believe, contribute to the development of a new woman/man, and gay is indeed good for us all. As homosexuals come out they lead heterosexuals into a greater acceptance of their own sexuality, in part perhaps because many homosexuals are more aware of sexuality than are straights. The other side to homosexual promiscuity—seen in its most extreme form when the hunt for sex becomes an obsession—is that sex per se tends to become less imminently important, while the nature of relationships, by contrast, is less taken for granted. It is true that homosexual couples of long standing are rare; this is in part because a bad homosexual "marriage" is likely to be dissolved far more easily than is a bad straight one. Homosexuals, and especially those not unduly worried by guilt and self-disgust, are often able to approach sex more casually than can heterosexuals, and to realize that fidelity and love depend on much more than with whom or how one beds. The real infidelity is an existential, not a physical one.

More than this, however, the gay contributes to the straight just because we are defined in exclusively sexual terms. Our sense of being different enables us to see the sexual component to much of life that is not immediately obvious, to escape to a limited degree the repressions upon our sexual and erotic impulses. To accept that part of ourselves which is sexual is a necessary stage toward overcoming the repressions and anxieties under which we all labor, which achievement probably means an increase in homosexuality, if not in exclusive homosexuality. As is already happening within the women's movement, homosexuality needs to come to be accepted by a greater number of people as a possibility *for them;* a development which is deplored by the custodians of the old values. In their book *Growing Up Straight,* the Wydens make exactly this point (though not, of course, as advocates): "The more acceptable the viewpoints of organized homosexuals become the more likely that we will see the growth of an ever less covert and more accepted Gay World." Gay liberation liberates straights as much as gays.

Homosexuals too come to see themselves as potential heterosexuals: but this is a lesser revelation. "I think all of us are authorities on the heterosexual problem," wrote Jill Johnston. "Knowledge on the subject is instantly available, in case you've missed out, in every daily newspaper with their front page accounts of the Wars. We are bored with the news from the heterosexual fronts." Exactly. We, even those of us who are behaviorally, on the Kinsey scale, totally homosexual (and how many in fact are?) know about heterosexuality. Few homosexuals will deny their straight component, and this is an important part of the gay's knowledge of the world under which he or she lives.

Seymour Krim in an *Evergreen* article hailed the blurring of both homo/hetero, female/male distinctions: "Heterosexual love emphasized basic differences, homosexual love emphasizes basic sameness . . . ," he wrote. As the difference dwindles he sees it easing relations between men and women, now "a nervous, cryptic, exasperating psychodrama that has ripped the guts out of practically all of us." I am less sure than he of the first point, for opposites attract within the gayworld as much as without, nor are heterosexual couples who mirror-reflect each other uncommon. But this latter point, is, I think, important. Warfare between the sexes is an unnecessary product of competitiveness, repression, and fear. If accepting homosexuality helps people move closer to an acceptance of their intrinsic erotic and polymorphous natures, it can only ease relations between men and women.

Gay liberation, then, is part of a much wider movement that is challenging the basic cultural norms of our advanced industrial, capitalist, and bureaucratic society and bringing about changes in individual consciousness and new identities and life-styles. It is a movement that is political, not in the traditional way that we have used that word, but because it challenges the very definitions and demarcations that society has created. In many ways the argument between the "political" and the "cultural" revolutionaries is a false one; gay liberation, like the other sexual liberation movements, is in the long tradition of romantics and existentialists in its insistence that politics and culture merge into one. Unlike liberalism "the Movement" in Western societies today recognizes no barriers between politics and culture, art and life, public and private. Gay liberation is both an affirmation of the right to live as we choose and an intent to extend that right to others.

In some ways gay liberation is an extension of the Yippie philosophy: "revolution for the hell of it." "What's a revolution if it isn't fun?" said Kate Millett, speaking of her gayness to the Daughters of Bilitis. One of the strengths of gay liberation is that because it is involved in an affirmation of sexuality it is also involved in an affirmation of eroticism and play, an important antidote to the humorlessness of much of our time. Unlike virtually all other movements, the gay does seem protected by its very being from an over-earnest puritanism.

Which is not to claim perfection for the gay movement, nor to deny the divisions which encumber it and which can be expected to increase as the movement itself increases. Like all movements it is prone to moments of hyperbole, hysteria, and childish feuding; like other groups on the left it tends to be extraordinarily uncritical of its heroes (e.g., the Panthers) while equally intolerant of those whose style is different (e.g., the older homophile groups). As it grows and embraces a wider range of members, it is likely to find greater difficulty in reconciling competing life-styles and interests. Already, I suspect, the gay movement, albeit smaller than the women's movement, embraces a wider range of persons across racial lines; in class terms too it is less irredeemably middle class than many women's groups tend to be, and the presence of street transvestites—for transvestites come disproportionately from lower-class backgrounds—is a welcome contrast to university students. As liberated homosexuals seek to construct an alternative to the gayworld it will be just as heterogeneous and varied, even if drugs pose more of a problem than alcohol, petty criminals more than blackmail or Mafia control.

In as far, however, as gay liberation involves the construction of a new consciousness, a heightened sense of awareness of our position in society and a comprehension that we are not so much fucked up as fucked over, it is an essential ingredient of the insurgent culture, and one that is likely to have considerable influence on its peers. There are those who would argue that society will be able in time to domesticate the angry gays, to offer them sufficient incorporation into the ongoing framework so as to destroy their radicalism. I doubt this, as Huey Newton seems to doubt it, because I question whether society as presently constituted could ever offer more than tolerance, and that, as I have sought to show, is not enough. Indeed homosexual assertion—"Blatant is beautiful!"—is likely to outrun society's ability to remove its stigma, at least for some time.

Ultimately, homosexuals are a minority quite unlike any other, for we are a part of all humans—not metaphorically, as the French students might proclaim "*nous sommes tous juifs allemands*"—but actually. Everyone is gay, everyone is straight. This is why the homosexual has been so severely oppressed, for social oppression becomes a means for individual repression, and only when the latter is no longer prescribed will the former be fully overcome. In the long run, then, gay liberation will succeed as its raison d'être disappears. We are, I believe, moving toward a far greater acceptance of human sexuality and with that toward both a decrease in the stigma attached to unorthodox sex and a corresponding increase in overt bisexuality. To see the total withering away of the distinction between homo- and heterosexual is to be utopian. I suspect however, it will come before the withering away of the state and may indeed be a necessary prelude to that.

Given that such changes are only embryonic for the moment it is not unreasonable to expect a considerable growth in the gay movement, both in America and in other highly developed Western societies. Indeed, the growing tolerance toward homosexuals by that well-known process of a revolution of rising expectations is likely to bring a sharp increase in those ready to come out and angry enough to identify with gay liberation. Here the peculiar stigma of homosexuality, its secrecy, becomes crucial. To join a gay group is an act of affirmation that is often cathartic in its effect. Whatever the possibilities for individual liberation without full social liberation, and the possibilities are I feel limited, the act of involvement with gay liberation brings with it a new perception of the world that is remarkably radicalized.

The dilemma remains: any vision of our full liberation involves at the same time an end to our special status and any claims that can be based upon it for an intrinsically gay culture. Those who most clearly perceive this are also likely to be those most involved with the present creation of a gay community; Dotson Rader in his article on gay liberation in *Evergreen* claimed that "homosexuals in the gay liberation movement are now beginning to suspect that in eliminating their status as outlaws they may be delimiting the consciousness (i.e. their position, as rebels) which animates both their extraordinary creativity and their role as a regenerative body." The price, one suspects, is greater for straights than for gays, given the human misery out of which much of this "extraordinary creativity" has sprung, but the dilemma is a real one. If we finally transcend the divide between hetero- and homosexual do we also lose our identity?

One hopes that the answer lies in the creation of a new human for whom such distinctions are no longer necessary for the establishment of identity. The creation of this new human demands the acceptance of new definitions of man- and womanhood, as are being urged by gay and women's liberation. Throughout this book I have been concerned with questions of identity and definition. Indeed the homosexual's very existence is an affront to the way in which society defines roles, sexuality, and achievement, and this fact is the essence of our oppression and of our revolutionary potential. Gay liberation affirms full eroticism and play, and rejects violence; it seeks human diversity and community and discards the narrow roles that "normality" has prescribed. If these affirmations and objectives can be achieved for us all, Gore Vidal's hope that "homosexual" will be used only as an adjective to describe behavior rather than as a noun to describe a person may be fulfilled, and the homosexual as we know him or her may indeed disappear.

In the attempt to realize this new human, gay liberation as a movement will exhibit all those excesses and mistakes that those who seek liberation are prone to. Gay liberation as a new consciousness, however, can only add to growth in the acceptance of human diversity, of the realization that we all possess far greater potential for love and human relationships than social and cultural structures have allowed us to reveal. "A man's reach should exceed his grasp, or what's a heaven for," wrote Browning. That a heaven can be attained on earth is implicit in the challenge of the sexual liberation movements. If man- and womankind reaches the point where it is able to dispense with the categories of homo- and heterosexuality the gain will be well worth the loss.

Afterword

Traditionally one's twenty-first birthday marked entrance into adulthood, so it is perhaps appropriate that *Homosexual* is being republished in 1993, just over twenty-one years since it was first issued in New York. *Homosexual*—the title was the choice of the publishers, not mine—was published in late 1971 by a small firm, Outerbridge and Dienstfrey, long since defunct.

The book appeared in November, but I was back in Sydney and there was little sign for some months that anyone had noticed it. The publishers could afford little in the way of promotion, but the book was saved by two reviews. It received guarded approbation in *Time* magazine, which guaranteed it was noticed, and Martin Duberman, in a long roundup of new gay writing for the *New York Times* the following year, wrote glowingly of it. Thanks in part to these two reviews a paperback sale was assured, and for a very small sum of money the rights were picked up at Avon, by Bob Wyatt, later to become known as one of the leading gay editors in the United States. In May 1972 I paid a quick visit to the United States and Canada, and spoke at a number of events organized by groups which were part of the now rapidly growing gay liberation movement.

That particular trip was a fairly traumatic one: I fell sick in

Madison, and dragged myself through the remainder of my engagements with all the enthusiasm of a losing candidate at the end
of the primary season. On my return the book was published in
my native Australia where I was then teaching politics at Sydney
University. Its publication coincided with a forty-minute interview
on national television in which I crossed swords with a conservative
politician and intellectual (not in this case a contradiction in terms)
and a well-meaning radio cleric. This was not the first time an open
homosexual had appeared on Australian television, but it was the
longest and most publicised interview to date.

Books are sold by television, and the book did well for the next
few months, aided by considerable media coverage and largely favorable reviews. Local reviewers, including Anne Summers (who
later moved to New York and became editor of *MS*) wrote nice
things about me; the managing editor of the *Sydney Morning Herald,* still a force for propriety, allegedly pulled a review from the
Saturday book pages. I received an embarrassing amount of mail,
virtually none of it hostile, and including a long series of gushy
letters written by a resident of a Catholic men's home. At least in
my own country the book had established me as "a public homosexual," and I am still occasionally approached by the media anxious
for "the gay spokesman" even where I am not a particularly appropriate choice.

I should note that the edition of the book you are now reading
is essentially the slightly revised text prepared for the Australian/
British paperback version published by Penguin in 1973. I have
used this text rather than the original because it incorporates a little
more material on the emerging movement outside the United States,
while retaining all the basic material of the original work. The
temptation to rewrite was considerable, but I have contented myself
with a few grammatical corrections and one or two clarifications.

I drifted into writing *Homosexual,* just as I drifted into the gay
movement. In late 1970 I went to New York on eight months' leave

from the University of Sydney, and briefly worked as a volunteer in Bella Abzug's campaign for the House of Representatives. After a series of slightly sordid encounters in search of housing I came to share a large apartment with a painter in the not-yet-fashionable East Village, where the collective of the early gay newspaper *Come Out!* used to hold meetings. With this introduction—and with the time provided by a university salary from home—I threw myself into the world of early New York City gay politics as described in the book.

"You should write a book about it," said several people to me, and gradually the possibility became an obsession. I walked past bookstores like Brentano's or Doubleday's and imagined my book piled in the shop window (something I was not to see until 1982 when *The Homosexualization of America* had a short life in a window front on the corner of Fourth Street and Sixth Avenue). I wrote proposals for junior editors, and carried my laboriously typed pages through windy fall New York streets, determined not to give up until I convinced someone that I could write a book—*the* book— about this new movement which would, we were sure, revolutionize the sexual mores and order of America.

It was Lillian Roxon who sent me to Harris Dienstfrey, and I owe a great deal to Lillian, a minor legend in her time. She was an Australian journalist, author of a well-known Rock Encyclopedia, and, as well as pushing me to write the book, she also took me to the first concert ever given by Elton John in New York (where he was a supporting act to Leon Russell). Lillian knew Harris, who was half of a new, small publisher, Outerbridge and Dienstfrey, and Harris—not, I should stress, a gay man— grasped the possible significance of the book much faster than most of the editors I had spoken to. (Years later I was consoled when a well-known publisher in New York told me he remembered me because he always remembered the people he had mistakenly rejected.) Harris was an intelligent and demanding editor, one of several I have worked with in the United States (I think, as well, of Michael Denneny at St. Martin's and Richard Goldstein at the *Village Voice*).

The book was begun in the United States, but written largely back in Australia in the early part of 1972. Much of the first chapter was in fact written in a decrepit motel on the beachfront at Santa Monica (a beach suburb of Los Angeles) where I spent the last part of 1971, waiting for my then lover, Reinhard Hassert (to whom the book was dedicated), to join me from Sydney. It was, I think, part of my enormous admiration for and indebtedness to Christopher Isherwood which led me to spend a week alone in Santa Monica; he and Don Bachardy lived up in the hilly part of the town, and I had first visited Santa Monica three years earlier to meet them.

I could not have written that book had I not immersed myself for six months in the new gay politics of New York, and come to know some of the early figures of the movement, such as Vito Russo and Martha Shelley and Arthur Bell. But other influences were at work as well: the most cited names in the index are James Baldwin, Norman O. Brown, Christopher Isherwood, Norman Mailer, Herbert Marcuse, Kate Millett, and Gore Vidal—all, but Kate, a generation older than me, and three of them (Baldwin, Isherwood, and Vidal) among the handful of authors who had openly addressed homosexual themes in their writings.

I am abashed looking back at how little I had read of lesbian writings at this time. This was particularly odd as one of the crucial influences on me was Kate Millett's *Sexual Politics*, which I had read on arrival in the States in August 1970, and which is one of two or three books in my life whose impact I still recall. I certainly had read *The Well of Loneliness* by this time, and a certain amount of early lesbian feminist literature (as shown in the bibliography), but while I tried very hard to include lesbians in the book it was without any great understanding of the difference between the male and female experience of homosexuality.

I was more aware of racial divisions; the early gay liberation movement was as much a product of the civil rights and antiwar movements as of the feminist, and I had attended a Black Panther event in Washington, D.C., as part of a largely unsuccessful attempt by gay radicals to associate themselves with what then seemed the cutting edge of black militancy. Homosexuality was a major issue for the radical black movement; as I explain, it was used to attack James Baldwin and later Huey Newton. One of my prize possessions is a letter from Newton, addressed to "Comrade Altman," and signed—ah, the innocence of those days—"all power to the people."

The biggest theoretical influence on me was the radical Freudianism of Marcuse and Brown, now largely forgotten, and never particularly popular in the gay movement. Without fully understanding what I was writing, I was in fact a social constructionist without knowing the term—the ideas which were to be developed over the next two decades by scholars such as Jeffrey Weeks, Michel Foucault, etc., about the ways in which a homosexual identity is a particular historical construction are present in a not very clearly formulated way in my book. I had already read the single article which more than any other piece has influenced modern scholarly conceptualizations of homosexuality, Mary McIntosh's "The Homosexual Role" (1968), and the final chapter of *Homosexual* has far more in common with the ideas of early constructionists than with the essentialist views of some sort of ahistorical inborn gay spirit which underlie much early gay liberation writing such as Jonathan Katz's pioneering history anthology. (Jonathan has subsequently made this very criticism of his own early work.)

"It was very brave of you to write that book" was a comment I have heard frequently over the years, but at the time bravery seemed irrelevant; I suspect my thirst for achievement as a writer blinded me to any unfortunate consequences publishing the book might have had. In fact, there were virtually none; twice universities have delayed promoting me because of doubts as to whether writing about the gay movement was "really" political science, but this has been a trivial blow to my ego compared with the satisfaction of becoming known as a theorist and writer as the movement has expanded throughout the world.

The career of "a public homosexual" has not always been an easy one. I found myself criticized for hogging the limelight—the media tended to turn to me too often—and just as often for refusing to support the movement if I refused to speak. Few of us respond well to instant notoriety, and I exhibited the same mixture of vanity and shyness which most people do in these situations. I wanted to be lionized and treated like everyone else at the same time, and not surprisingly others found this grating. Looking back I remind myself of those writers on book tours who leap up at every opportunity to proclaim how much they hate public attention.

But there were compensations: I met plenty of people and I traveled a lot, taking part in early gay movement activities in every state of Australia. In North America—and later that decade in Europe and Brazil—I found that *Homosexual* gave me an automatic introduction to the ever-expanding network of the gay movement. The generation of writers who were influenced by the upsurge of gay activism in the 1970s felt bonds which linked us across oceans and continents—bonds often cemented through early gay publications such as *Body Politic* (Toronto), *Christopher Street* (New York), and *Gay Left* (London)—and it has been a rich experience to be part of this world. And, yes, there was a certain thrill in seeing my book in shop windows and in its French and Italian editions (though I felt sorry for whoever purchased the plastic-wrapped copy which I saw on display in the window of a Canadian sex shop.)

I was also lucky in that I received considerable support from my colleagues at Sydney University, and, indeed, shared the corridors with two of the early presidents of Australia's first "out" lesbian/ gay organization, the Campaign Against Moral Persecution (named for its acronym, CAMP). This was a period in Australian history which the writer Donald Horne has termed "the time of hope":

my book was published there in the year which was to end with the election of a Federal Labor government for the first time in twenty-three years, and there was a feeling about that Australia was poised to become a considerably more tolerant and diverse society. I sent a copy of the book to Gough Whitlam who would soon be elected as Labor prime minister, and he wrote to me that: "My deep belief is that a change of government after so long will have a profoundly liberating effect on the whole community, and that, in such an atmosphere, the community will shake itself free of a great deal of the preoccupations and hang-ups which have led to so much persecution."

It was not surprising that I was also criticized in my own country as—I quote a phrase used by a leading right-wing polemicist—"an agent of American cultural imperialism." Shorn of the emotive language, he was, of course, right, for the growth of a new lesbian/gay community and movement in the United States was to influence the rest of the world, a theme I have dealt with in a number of pieces dealing with Australia, France, and Brazil which are included in my collection of essays *Coming Out in the Seventies* (Wild & Woolly 1979).

For the next two decades I was to repeat the pattern I had followed in writing *Homosexual,* spending considerable time in the United States, but then retreating back to Australia to write about my experiences. I wrote some of *The Homosexualization of America* (St. Martins 1981) and *AIDS in the Mind of America* (Doubleday, 1986) in this way, though the latter was written in a period of my life when I came close to settling permanently in the United States. In the end I decided I had little talent as an expatriate, and since 1985 I have been based in Melbourne. My contact and fascination with the United States persist, fed by the fact that I teach American politics to Australian students.

Re-reading this book today is like visiting another country, and it takes perserverance not to cringe. There are touches of both moralism and utopianism in *Homosexual* which I would eschew today, and which in some ways are contradicted by what I wrote a decade later in *The Homosexualization of America*. Books are very much products of their time and place, and whereas you can read *Homosexual* as a historical document, for me it is a reminder of a turning point in my life. Writing that book turned me into "a gay activist"— in those days we still used "gay" to mean both women and men— and set my career on a certain path which I still struggle to leave at times. My most recent book—published early in 1993—is a novel (*The Comfort of Men*) set in Australia during that "time of hope" of which I have spoken.

Homosexual has been out of print for a number of years, and it is difficult for me to be objective about its influence on the gay movement, although I know it has been widely read across most of the Western world. Increasingly I come across it as a source for theses and academic work, testimony to the relentless way in which activism becomes co-opted by academia. (I should also acknowledge that it appears largely unknown to the new generation of lesbian/gay scholars from cultural studies and literature who are currently refashioning "queer studies.") The book is eclectic, drawing on a wide range of sources, including literature, but when I wrote it I was still grappling to find the coherent philosophical framework one expects from good political theory.

Reading it now it seems to me that I both tried too hard to connect the gay movement to a general radicalism—and, at the same time, that this argument is an important one to which it is worth returning. I have written elsewhere of how a new generation, working through groups such as ACT UP and Queer Nation, have rediscovered some of the analyses and tactics of gay liberation.[1] To say this is not to denigrate people who are, after all, reacting to new crises within very different social and cultural situations, but

1. See, e.g., D. Altman, "AIDS and the Reconceptualization of Homosexuality," in Altman et al., *Homosexuality, Which Homosexuality?* (London: GMP, 1989).

it is not irrelevant to ask what can be learnt from the early history of gay liberation. The term itself now seems dated—the Sydney activist Craig Johnston once wrote of the disappearance of the terms *oppression* and *liberation* as the new gay world split along gender lines, and the male part, at least, became commercialized.[2]

Within that now largely abandoned concept of "liberation" lie some important questions, questions which the gay movement needs to re-address. In this sense the "radicalism" of *Homosexual* seems more up to date with the current mood of up-front activism and co-sexual explorations of sexual desires than with the mood of the late 1970s, when the movement seemed almost totally divided by gender, and dominated by respectable pressure group tactics.

Of course there's a lot in the book with which I might differ today: in this sense all writing is part of a work in progress, which continues until one stops writing altogether. At the risk of sounding cute, I think of books as like children: after they are published they need to live lives of their own, and they become increasingly distant from the author, who will have moved onto different, maybe contradictory preoccupations. I have spoken to enough people over twenty years to know that there are many versions of *Homosexual*, and that a number of people read the book—or gave it to parents and friends to read—as part of coming out. In so doing they have read a book which is in some ways very different from the book I thought I was writing, just as someone who was born in the years since the book was written and has come to adulthood in the period of AIDS and Reaganism will read it very differently.

Even so, the basic theme of *Homosexual* remains central today: how do we create out of our shared sexuality and experience of a heterosexist society a common community and a progressive movement? As long as this is the case it is worth reading the book again, if only to remind us of the (comparatively) short history of the

2. See Craig Johnston, "Radical Homosexual Politics: Into the Eighties," *Gay Information* (Sydney), no. 3 (Aug.–Sept. 1980), pp. 8–12.

movement which helped make today's lesbian and gay world possible. Re-reading the book I notice my own ambivalence about the growth of a new community: I both identified it as the central goal of the movement, and expressed concern that it could become a means of further exclusion and ghettoization. (Thus my doubts about the development of "homophile studies" are ones I continue to feel.[3]) This debate seems to me an important one to continue, even if history has not developed as we might have expected two decades ago.

Reading the book today it is interesting to note what has and has not changed over the past two decades. In the United States the basic legal prohibitions against (male) homosexuality still remain in a number of states, reinforced, of course, by the appalling decision of the Supreme Court (in the Hardwick case) not to extend the right of privacy to homosexual relations, even between consenting adults in their own homes. (Outside the United States the only jurisdiction in what we used to call "the free world" where such prohibitions remain is, I believe, the Australian state of Tasmania.) The attitudes of mainstream churches on homosexuals have, if anything, become more hostile with the politicization of evangelical Protestantism and the harsh moral tone of the current pope. The lesbian baiting of Kate Millett which I described was recently echoed in attacks on Patricia Ireland, president of NOW.

Yet other things have changed dramatically. In 1971 I wrote that: "We have not yet reached the point . . . where an overt homosexual could run for office and hope to win." That point has now been reached, not only in Massachusetts, California, and Minnesota, but also in Australia, Canada, Britain, Italy, and Norway (at least). The attempt to turn Alpine County, California, into one where there would be a lesbian/gay majority is a largely forgotten

---

3. See, e.g., D. Altman, "Gay Studies and the Quest for Academic Legitimacy," *The Advocate*, October 14, 1983.

precursor to the emergence of the City of West Hollywood in the 1980s.

Homosexual is a book written by a young man about a young movement. In the end, however, there is enough continuity between those early days of gay liberation and the present to make the book relevant to current debates.

Melbourne   DENNIS ALTMAN

Bibliography

(This revised bibliography includes works quoted in the text and others I have found particularly useful.)

Books and Articles Relating to Gay and Women's Liberation

Abbott, Sidney, and Love, Barbara. *Sappho Was a Right-on Woman*. Stein and Day, 1972.

Altman, Dennis. "Redefining Sexuality." *Arena*, Melbourne, no. 29, 1972.

Bentley, Eric. "Men's Liberation." In *Theatre of War*. Viking, 1972.

Burke, Tom. "The New Homosexuality." *Esquire*, December 1969.

Byron, Stuart. "Gay News and the Times: An Indelicate Balance." *Village Voice*, 1 April 1971.

Cory, Donald. *The Homosexual in America*. Greenberg, 1951 (Paperback Library, 1963).

de Beauvoir, Simone. *The Second Sex*. Penguin, 1972.

Durgin, Karen. "Women's Liberation." In Edward Rice and Jane Garmey, *The Prophetic Generation*. Renssalaerville, New York, The Catholic Art Association, 1970.

Epstein, Joseph. "Homo/Hetero: The Struggle for Sexual Identity." *Harper's Magazine*, September 1970.

Firestone, Shulamith. *Notes from the Second Year: Women's Liberation*. Morrow, 1970.

———. *The Dialectic of Sex: Case for Feminist Revolution*. Cape, 1971.

Friedan, Betty. *The Feminine Mystique*. Penguin, 1965.

261

Goodman, Paul. "Memoirs of an Ancient Activist." *WIN Magazine,* 15 November 1969.

Gornick, Vivian. "The Light of Liberation Can Be Blinding." *Village Voice,* 10 December 1970.

———. "In Any Terms She Shall Choose." *Village Voice,* 18 March 1971.

Greer, Germaine. *The Female Eunuch.* Paladin, 1971.

Harvey, Ian. "The Homosexuals' Plight." *New Statesman,* 9 April 1971.

Humphreys, Laud. "New Styles in Homosexual Manliness." *Transaction,* March/April 1971.

Johnston, Jill. "Lois Lane Is a Lesbian." *Village Voice,* 4, 11 & 25 March 1971.

Krim, Seymour. "Fonda My Buddy." *Evergreen,* February 1971.

La Rue, Linda J. M. "Black Liberation and Women's Lib." *Transaction,* vol. 8, nos. 1 & 2, November–December 1970.

Lessard, Suzannah. "Gay Is Good for Us All." *Washington Monthly,* December 1970.

Lyon, Phyllis, and Martin, Del. *Lesbian Women.* Bantam, 1972.

McReynolds, David. "Notes for a More Coherent Article." *WIN Magazine,* 15 November 1969.

Mailer, Norman. "The Prisoner of Sex." *Harper's Magazine,* March 1971.

Martin, Bob. "The New Homosexual and His Movement." *WIN Magazine,* 15 November 1969.

Miller, Merle. *On Being Different.* Random House, 1971.

Millett, Kate. *Sexual Politics.* Hart-Davis, 1971.

Mitchell, Juliet. *Woman's Estate.* Penguin, 1971.

Morgan, Robin, ed. *Sisterhood Is Powerful.* Random House, 1970.

Munaker, Sue; Goldfield, Evelyn; and Weisstein, Naomi. "A Woman Is a Sometime Thing." In Priscilla Long, ed., *The New Left.* Porter Sargent, 1969.

Nappey, Pierre-Claude. "An Open Letter on Homosexuality." *Cross-Currents,* vol. 20, no. 2, Spring 1970.

Piercy, Marge. "Women's Liberation: Nobody's Baby Now." *Defiance,* New York, no. 1, October 1970.

Rader, Dotson. "Gay Liberation: All the Sad Young Men." *Evergreen,* November 1970.

Roszak, Betty, and Roszak, Theodore, eds., *Masculine/Feminine: Readings in Sexual Mythology and the Liberation of Women.* Harper Colophon Books, 1969.

Sagarin, Edward. "Behind the Gay Liberation Front." *The Realist*, May–June 1970.

———. *Odd Man In*. Quadrangle, 1969.

Silverstein, Michael. "The Development of an Identity: Power and Sex Roles in Academie." *Journal of Applied Behavioral Science*, vol. 8, no. 5, 1972.

Tanner, Leslie, ed. *Voices from Women's Liberation*. Signet, 1970.

Teal, Donn. *The Gay Militants*. Stein and Day, 1971.

Tobin, Kay, and Wicker, Randy. *The Gay Crusaders*. New York Paperback Library, 1972.

Ware, Cellestine. *Woman Power: The Movement for Women's Liberation*. Tower, 1970.

Weltge, Ralph, ed. *The Same Sex: An Appraisal of Homosexuality*. United Church Press, 1969.

Wildeblood, Peter. *Against the Law*. Penguin, 1957.

Willis, Ellen. "See America First." *New York Review of Books*, 1 January 1970.

Wittman, Carl. "The Gay Manifesto." *Liberation*, February 1970.

Young, Allen. "A Gay Manifesto." *Ramparts*, November 1971.

Most useful, of course, are the publications of the movements themselves. In particular I have used the "Gay Liberation Packet," a series published by the Gay Flames Collective in New York; *Come Out!*, New York; *Gay Sunshine*, San Francisco; and *Body Politic*, Toronto.

Others referred to or used include *The Advocate*, Los Angeles; *Arena III*, London; *Brother*, Berkeley; *Camp Ink*, Sydney; *The Digger*, Sydney; *Gay*, New York; *Gay Flames*, New York; *Gay Liberator*, Detroit; *Gay News*, London; *Gay Youth's Gay Journal*, New York; *Los Angeles Free Press; Mattachine Times*, New York; *Mejane*, Sydney; *Oz*, London; *Rat*, New York; *San Francisco Free Press; Vector*, San Francisco.

Organizations and publications have, unfortunately, such an ephemeral life that it is pointless to try to provide addresses and publishing details. Local gay organizations can usually provide these.

Novels, Plays, Poetry, etc.

Ackerley, J. R. *My Father and Myself*. Bodley Head, 1968.

Albee, Edward. *Who's Afraid of Virginia Woolf?* Penguin, 1970.

Baldwin, James. *Another Country*. Corgi, 1970.

———. "Disturber of the Peace," an interview. *Mademoiselle,* May 1963.

———. *Giovanni's Room.* Corgi, 1969.

———. *Going to Meet the Man.* Corgi, 1970.

———. *Nobody Knows My Name.* Corgi, 1969.

———. *Notes of a Native Son.* Corgi, 1969.

———. "An Open Letter to My Sister, Miss Angela Davis." *New York Review of Books,* 7 January 1970.

———. *Tell Me How Long the Train's Been Gone.* Corgi, 1970.

Blechman, Burt. *Stations.* Random House, 1964.

Burroughs, William. *Naked Lunch.* Corgi, 1968.

Burroughs, William, and Ginsberg, Allen. *The Yage Letters.* City Lights, 1963.

Burroughs, William, and Odier, Daniel. *The Job: Interviews with William Burroughs.* Cape, 1970.

Capote, Truman. *In Cold Blood.* Penguin, 1970.

———. *Other Voices, Other Rooms.* Penguin, 1964.

Chester, Alfred. *Behold Goliath.* Sphere, 1971.

Cleaver, Eldridge. *Soul on Ice.* Panther, 1971.

Cleaver, Eldridge, and Lockwood, Lee. *Conversation with Eldridge Cleaver—Algiers.* Cape, 1971.

Crowley, Mart. *The Boys in the Band.* Penguin, 1970.

Dennis, Nigel. *Cards of Identity.* Weidenfeld & Nicolson, 1955.

Duffy, Maureen. *The Microcosm.* Hutchinson, 1966.

Forster, E. M. *Maurice.* Edward Arnold, 1971.

Friedman, Sanford. *Totempole.* Dutton, 1965.

Garland, Rodney. *The Heart in Exile.* W. H. Allen, 1953.

Genet, Jean. *The Blacks: A Clown Show.* Faber, 1967.

———. *Deathwatch.* Faber, 1963.

———. *Funeral Rites.* Faber, 1966.

———. *The Maids.* Faber, 1963.

———. *Our Lady of the Flowers.* Panther, 1966.

———. *The Screens.* Grove, 1962.

———. *The Thief's Journal.* Penguin, 1967.

Ginsberg, Allen. *Ankor Wat.* Fulcrum Books, 1968.

———. *Empty Mirror.* Corinth, 1961.

———. *Howl and Other Poems.* City Lights, 1956.

———. *Kaddish and Other Poems.* City Lights, 1961.

———. *Reality Sandwiches,* City Lights, 1963.

———. Several poems in Donald Allen and Robert Creeley, *The New Writing in the U.S.A.* Penguin, 1967.

————. "Allen Ginsberg", an interview with *Paris Review*. In Alfred Kazin, ed., *Writers at Work*. Viking, 1967.

The transcript of Ginsberg's testimony at the Chicago Conspiracy Trial is included in Jason Epstein's "The Chicago Conspiracy Trial: Allen Ginsberg on the Stand." *New York Review of Books,* 12 February 1970.

Gombrowicz, Witold. *Pornographia*. Calder and Boyars, 1966.

Goodman, Paul. *Adam and His Works*. Vintage, 1968.

————. *The Empire City*. Bobbs-Merrill, 1959.

————. *Five Years*. Brussel and Brussel, 1966.

————. "June and July." *New York Review of Books,* 8 October 1970.

————. *Making Do*. Macmillan, 1964.

————. *New Reformation: Notes of a Neolithic Conservative*. Random House, 1970.

————. *People or Personnel and Like a Conquered Province*. Vintage, 1968.

————. *Utopian Essays and Practical Proposals*. Vintage, 1962.

————. *The Well of Bethlehem*. New York, published by the author.

Goodman, Paul; Perls, Frederick; and Hefferline Ralph. *Gestalt Therapy*. Julian, 1951.

Gray, Simon. *Butley*. Methuen, 1971.

Hall, Radclyffe. *The Well of Loneliness*. Hammond, 1956.

Hellman, Lillian. *The Children's Hour*. Dramatists Play Service, New York, 1961.

Herbert, John. *Fortune and Men's Eyes*. Grove, 1967.

Herlihy, James. *Midnight Cowboy*. Panther, 1968.

Isherwood, Christopher. *Down There on a Visit*. Signet Books, 1968.

————. *Exhumations*. Penguin, 1969.

————. *Kathleen and Frank*. Methuen, 1971.

————. *A Meeting by the River*. Penguin, 1970.

————. *A Single Man*. Penguin, 1969.

————. *The World in the Evening*. Methuen, 1954.

Jones, LeRoi (Imamu Amiri Baraka). *Dutchman and the Slave*. Faber, 1965.

————. *Home: Social Essays*. Morrow, 1966.

————. *The System of Dante's Hell*. Grove, 1965.

Kirkwood, James. *Good Times/Bad Times*. André Deutsch, 1969.

Koch, Stephen. *Night Watch*. Calder, 1970.

Lambert, Gavin. *Norman's Letter*. Hamish Hamilton, 1966.

McCarthy, Mary. *The Group*. Penguin, 1970.

Mailer, Norman. *Advertisements for Myself*. Panther, 1970.

————. *An American Dream*. Panther, 1972.

————. *The Armies of the Night*. Penguin, 1970.

————. *Miami and the Siege of Chicago*. Penguin, 1971.

————. *The Presidential Papers*. Penguin, 1968.

————. *Why Are We in Vietnam?* Panther, 1970.

Malcolm X (with Alex Haley). *Autobiography*. Penguin, 1970.

Mayfield, Julian. *The Grand Parade*. Vanguard, 1961.

Mishima, Yukio. *Confessions of a Mask*. Peter Owen, 1960.

————. *Forbidden Colours*. Penguin, 1971.

Moorhouse, Frank. *The Americans, Baby*. Angus & Robertson, 1972.

Murdoch, Iris. *A Fairly Honourable Defeat*. Penguin, 1972.

Peyrefitte, Roger. *Diplomatic Diversions*. Secker & Warburg, 1953.

Purdy, James. *Eustace Chisholm and the Works*. Cape, 1968.

————. *Malcolm*. Cape, 1960.

Rader, Dotson. *Government Inspected Meat*. McKay, 1971.

————. *I Ain't Marchin' Anymore*. McKay, 1969.

Rechy, John. *City of Night*. Panther, 1965.

————. *Numbers*. Grove, 1967.

Roth, Phillip. *Portnoy's Complaint*. Corgi, 1971.

Salas, Floyd. *Tattoo the Wicked Cross*. Grove, 1967.

Schneebaum, Tobias. *Keep the River on Your Right*. Cape, 1970.

Selby, Hubert. *Last Exit to Brooklyn*. Corgi, 1970.

Vidal, Gore. *The City and the Pillar*. Heinemann, 1965.

————. *The City and the Pillar,* Revised. Dutton, 1965.

————. *Myra Breckinridge*. Panther, 1970.

————. *A Thirsty Evil*. Zero Press, 1956.

Wallant, Edward. *The Tenants of Moonbloom*. Gollancz, 1964.

Williams, Tennessee. *Hard Candy*. New Directions, 1959.

————. *A Streetcar Named Desire*. New Directions, 1947.

————. *Suddenly Last Summer*. New Directions, 1958.

White, Patrick. *The Vivisector*. Jonathan Cape, 1970.

Wilson, Angus. *Hemlock and After*. Penguin, 1956.

————. *No Laughing Matter*. Penguin, 1969.

Windham, Donald. *Two People*. Penguin, 1971.

Wittig, Monique. *The Guérillères*. Peter Owen, 1971.

Wright, Charles. *The Messenger*. Farrar, Straus & Giroux, 1963.

Books and Articles on Homosexuality and Sexual Behavior

Bailey, Derrick. *Homosexuality and the Western Christian Tradition*. Longmans, 1955.

Becker, Raymond de. *The Other Face of Love*. Sphere, 1969.

Bieber, Irving, et al. *Homosexuality: A Psychoanalytical View*. Basic Books, 1963.

Churchill, Wainwright. *Homosexual Behavior among Males*. Hawthorn Books, 1967.

Cory, Donald. *The Lesbian in America*. Citadel, 1964.

Davis, Kingsley. "Sexual Behaviour." In R. Merton and R. Nisbet, *Contemporary Social Problems*. Harcourt, Brace, 1966.

Deisher, Robert, et al. "The Young Male Prostitute." *Pediatrics,* vol. 43, no. 6., June 1969.

Ford, Stephen. "Homosexuals and the Law: Why the Status Quo?" *Californian Western Law Review,* Spring 1969.

Freedman, Mark. *Homosexuality and Psychological Functioning*. Wadsworth, 1971.

Freud, Sigmund. *Group Psychology and Ego*. International Psycho-Analytic Library, 1922.

———. *Three Essays on the Theory of Sexuality*. Translated and edited by James Strachey. Hogarth Press, 1962.

Hernton, Calvin. *Sex and Racism in America*. Grove, 1966.

Hoffman, Martin. *The Gay World*. Basic Books, 1968.

Hooker, Evelyn. "The Adjustment of the Male Overt Homosexual." *Journal of Projective Techniques,* vol. 21, 1957.

———. "Male Homosexuals and Their Worlds." In Judd Marmor, ed., *Sexual Inversion*. Basic Books, 1965.

Humphreys, Laud. *Tearoom Trade: Impersonal Sex in Public Places*. Aldine, 1970.

Hyde, H. Montgomery. *The Love That Dared Not Speak Its Name*, Little, Brown, 1970.

Karlen, Arno. *Sexuality and Homosexuality*. Norton, 1971.

Kinsey, Alfred; Pomeroy, Wardell; and Martin, Clyde. *Sexual Behavior in the Human Male*. W. B. Saunders, 1948.

Lindner, Robert. "Homosexuality and the Contemporary Scene." In *Must You Conform?* Holt, 1956.

McIntosh, Mary. "The Homosexual Role." *Social Problems,* vol. 16, no. 1, Summer 1968–69.

McLuhan, Marshall, and Leonard, George. "The Future of Sex." *Look,* vol. 31, 25 July 1967.

McPartland, John. *Sex in Our Changing World*. Rinehart, 1947.

Magee, Brian. *One in Twenty*, Secker & Warburg, 1966.

Masters, R. E. L. *The Homosexual Revolution*. Julian, 1962.

Pittman, David. "The Male House of Prostitution." *Trans-action*, March/
    April 1971.
Reich, Wilhelm. *The Sexual Revolution*. Farrar, Straus & Giroux, 1963.
Reiss, Ira. "How and Why America's Sex Standards Are Changing." *Trans-
    action*, March 1968.
Reuben, David. *Everything You Always Wanted to Know About Sex . . .
    But Were Afraid to Ask*. McKay, 1970; (reviewed by Gore Vidal, "Num-
    ber One" in *New York Review of Books*, 4 June 1970).
Ruitenbeek, Hendrick, ed. *The Problem of Homosexuality in Modern So-
    ciety*. Dutton, 1963.
———. *Sexuality and Identity*. Dell, 1970.
Simon, William, and Gagnon, John. "Homosexuality: The Formulation of
    a Sociological Perspective." *Journal of Health and Social Behaviour*,
    vol. 8, no. 3, September 1967.
Simon, William, and Gagnon, John, eds. *Sexual Deviance*. Harper and
    Row, 1967.
Slater, Philip, and Slater, Dori, "Some Social Psychological Characteristics
    of Warlike Cultures." Unpublished paper, Boston, n. d.
Stoller, Robert. *Sex and Gender*. Science House, 1968.
Szasz, Thomas. *The Manufacture of Madness*. Harper and Row, 1970.
Taylor, Rattray. *Sex in History*. Ballantine, 1954.
Weinberg, George. *Society and the Healthy Homosexual*, St. Martin's,
    1971.
Weinberg, Martin. "The Male Homosexual: Age-Related Variations in
    Social and Psychological Characteristics." *Social Problems*, vol. 18, no.
    1, Spring 1970.
West, Donald. *Homosexuality*. Penguin, 1968.
Williams, C., and Weinberg, M. "Being Discovered: A Study of Homo-
    sexuals in the Military." *Social Problems*, vol. 18, no. 2, Autumn 1970.
Wyden, Peter, and Wyden, Barbara. *Growing Up Straight*. Stein and Day,
    1968.

Literary Criticism

Bigsby, C. W. E., ed. *The Black American Writer*. Penguin, 1971.
de Mott, Benjamin. *Supergrow*. Gollancz, 1970.
Dickstein, Morris. "Allen Ginsberg and the Sixties." *Commentary*, January
    1970.
Eckman, Fern Maya. *The Furious Passage of James Baldwin*. Evans, 1966.
Fiedler, Leslie. *Love and Death in the American Novel*. Paladin, 1970.

———. *Waiting for the End.* Penguin, 1967.

Gilman, Richard. *Confusion of Realms.* Weidenfeld & Nicolson, 1970.

Hill, Herbert, ed. *Anger and Beyond: The Negro Writer in the United States.* Harper and Row, 1966.

Kazin, Alfred, ed. *Writers at Work.* The *Paris Review* Series, vol. 3, Secker & Warburg, 1968.

Kramer, Jane. *Allen Ginsberg in America.* Random House, 1969.

Moore, Harry, ed. *Contemporary American Novelists.* Southern Illinois University Press, 1964.

Phillips, William. "Notes on the New Style." *Nation,* vol. 201, 20 September 1965.

Sontag, Susan. *Against Interpretation.* Farrar, Straus & Giroux, 1966.

Other References

Arendt, Hannah. *On Revolution.* Faber, 1964.

———. *On Violence.* Allen Lane, 1970.

Berke, Jo, ed. *Counter-Culture.* Peter Owen, 1969.

Berman, Ronald. *America in the Sixties.* Free Press, 1968.

Breines, Paul. *Critical Interruptions: New Left Perspectives on Herbert Marcuse.* Herder and Herder, 1970.

Brown, Norman O. *Life against Death.* Sphere, 1970.

———. *Love's Body.* Random House, 1966.

Carmichael, Stokely, and Hamilton, Charles. *Black Power: The Politics of Liberation in America.* Penguin, 1969.

Conway, Ronald. *The Great Australian Stupor.* Sun, 1971.

Cooper, David, ed. *The Dialectics of Liberation.* Penguin, 1968.

Eisen, Jonathan *The Age of Rock,* vol. 2. Random House, 1970.

Feuer, Lewis. *The Conflict of Generations.* Heinemann Educational, 1969.

Friedrichs, Robert. "Interpretation of Black Aggression." *Yale Review,* Spring 1968.

Gillett, Charlie. *The Sound of the City.* Sphere, 1971.

Goodman, Mitchell, ed. *The Movement toward a New America.* Knopf, 1970.

Gramsci, Antonio. *The Modern Prince.* International Publishers, New York, 1957.

Grier, William, and Cobbs, Price. *Black Rage.* Cape, 1969.

Hacker, Andrew. *The End of the American Era.* Sidgwick and Jackson, 1971.

Hoffman, Abbie. *Revolution for the Hell of It.* Dial, 1968.

Horowitz, Irving, and Liebowitz, M. "Social Deviance and Political Marginality." *Social Problems*, vol. 15, no. 2, 1967.

Jacobs, Paul, and Landau, Saul. *The New Radicals*. Random House, 1966.

Laing, R. D. *The Politics of the Family*. Tavistock Publications, 1971.

Laing, R. D., and Cooper, David. *Reason and Violence*. Tavistock Publications, 1971.

Leary, Timothy. *The Politics of Ecstasy*. Paladin, 1970.

McLuhan, Marshall, *Understanding Media*, Sphere, 1970.

Marcuse, Herbert. *Eros and Civilization*. Allen Lane, 1969.

———. *An Essay on Liberation*. Penguin, 1972.

———. *Five Lectures*. Allen Lane, 1970.

———. *One Dimensional Man*. Routledge, 1964.

Mead, Margaret. *Culture and Commitment*. Bodley Head, 1970.

Neville, Richard. *Play Power*. Cape, 1970.

Paranti, Michael. "Ethnic Politics and the Persistance of Ethnic Identification." *American Political Science Review*, vol. 61. September 1967.

Polsky, Ned. *Hustlers, Beats and Others*. Penguin, 1971.

Reich, Charles. *The Greening of America*. Penguin, 1972.

Reiche, Reimut. *Sexuality and Class Struggle*. New Left Books, London, 1970.

Robinson, Paul. *The Freudian Left*. Harper and Row, 1969.

Roszak, Theodore. *The Making of a Counter Culture*. Faber, 1971.

Schechner, Richard. *Public Domain*. Bobbs-Merrill, 1969.

Schrag, Peter. *The Decline of the WASP*. Simon & Schuster, 1971.

Simmons, J. L. *Deviants*. Glendessary Press, 1969.

Slater, Philip. *The Pursuit of Loneliness*. Allen Lane, 1971.

Tiger, Lionel. *Men in Groups*. Panther, 1971.

Toffler, Alvin. *Future Shock*. Bodley Head, 1970.

Young, Jack. "The Zoo-keepers of Deviancy." *Anarchy 98*, London, April 1969.

Index

About the Author

DENNIS ALTMAN is the author of seven books including *The Homosexualization of America, AIDS in the Mind of America,* and the novel *The Comfort of Men.* He teaches in the politics department at La Trobe University, Melbourne, Australia.